Mark Twain
AND THE LIMITS OF POWER

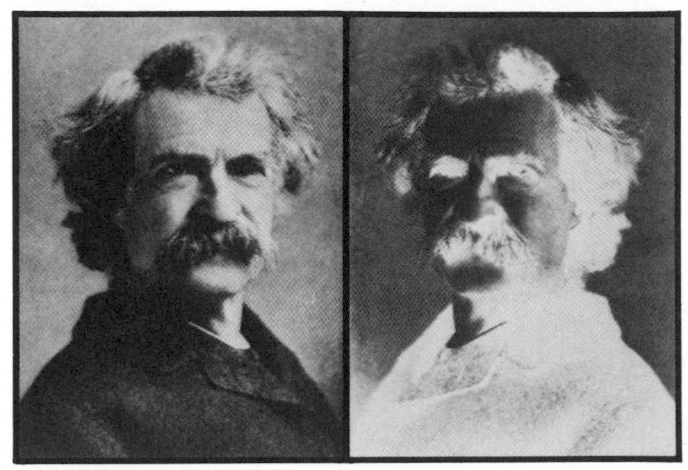

Mark Twain

AND THE LIMITS OF POWER

Emerson's God in Ruins

by James L. Johnson

THE UNIVERSITY OF TENNESSEE PRESS / KNOXVILLE

THIS BOOK IS DEDICATED TO

Mary and Amanda

FOR THEIR COURAGE IN UNCERTAIN TIMES

Clothbound editions of University of Tennessee Press books are printed on paper designed for an effective life of at least 300 years, and binding materials are chosen for strength and durability.

Library of Congress Cataloging in Publication Data

Johnson, James L. (James Lyn), 1945-
Mark Twain and the limits of power.
Bibliography: p.
Includes index.
1. Twain, Mark, 1835-1910—Philosophy. 2. Emerson, Ralph Waldo, 1803-1883—Influence—Twain. 3. Self in literature. I. Title.
PS1342.P5J6 818'.409 81-16052
ISBN 0-87049-342-6 AACR2

Contents

Preface

Critics are most familiar with that Mark Twain who ended his career in skepticism and bitterness and who described in his later work a full-blown determinism that emphasized man's subjection to training and environment. This book does not challenge that portrait, but it does attempt to qualify it by articulating that element in Twain's thought to which his reluctant determinism was a reaction. My purpose is to demonstrate that Twain's writings are profoundly reliant on the prospect of a free Self—a Self who, like Emerson's, is capable of both creating and controlling his human environment. To that end, I offer first a synopsis of Emerson's conception of an empowered Self, tracing its rise and decline, and defining some of the intellectual problems that accompanied that concept. This chapter is meant to serve as a frame of reference for the body of the book, in which I deal specifically with novels from Twain's early, middle, and late career. There I approach the works as reflections of Twain's multiple problems—intellectual, artistic, and to some extent emotional—in "saving" the free but continually threatened Self he envisioned but could never quite successfully dramatize.

In this respect the book is both a critical interpretation of some of Twain's major and minor pieces, and a short intellectual history: a record of the fate of a romantic idea passing from one mind to another, from one era to another.

This book could not have been written without the aid of more people than I can name here. First recognition must go to my wife, Mary, whose dedication to this project held fast when my own flagged, and whose constant encouragement, moral and material, has been most responsible for its ultimate fruition. I owe thanks to Professor James Cox of Dartmouth, who read the manuscript and encouraged its publication, and whose fine work on Mark Twain has helped me to clarify many of my own notions about that man and his work. Professor Paul Baender of the University of Iowa gave the manuscript a thorough scrutiny in both style and content, and provided excellent guidance in the removal of excesses and in the focusing of some of my arguments.

I wish to thank, too, those friends who explored with me, in many hours of late-night conversation, the ideas that form the core of this book. Their willingness to listen, to speculate, and to challenge aided me enormously both in finding the right questions to ask and in articulating answers. In particular I would like to mention Richard Dillman, who patiently listened to my endless talk and offered many valuable suggestions, and John Richter, whose acuity in matters both literary and personal eased my way on more occasions than he knows.

Finally, I owe my profound gratitude to two of my teachers. The first is Professor Martha Banta, now of the University of Washington. Some fifteen years ago, in the course of only one academic year, she first taught me how to read and then fired my fascination for things American. More recently she was kind enough to read this manuscript and to offer both her encouragement and her aid in the pursuit of its publication. She has thus touched my life in ways significant enough to defy even a full description, let alone adequate repayment.

The second is Professor Clark Griffith of the University of Oregon, from whom I learned the real excitement of speculation. In the initial formulation of the ideas here presented, he kept at bay both his own skepticism and that of others, and he encouraged me to suspend my own until I could finally articulate ideas and relationships which in the beginning I sensed only dimly. More than any other single factor, it was his incisive teaching that made the writing of this book not only possible, but enjoyable. Inevitably I must own, and gratefully I *do* own, that there is much of him in these pages.

Short References

Anderson	Quentin Anderson, *The Imperial Self* (New York: Knopf, 1971).
CWE	*The Complete Works of Ralph Waldo Emerson,* ed. Edward Waldo Emerson 12 vols. (Boston: Houghton Mifflin, 1903-4).
Fate of Humor	James Cox, *Mark Twain: The Fate of Humor* (Princeton: Princeton Univ. Press, 1966).
Gibson	*Mark Twain's Mysterious Stranger Manuscripts,* ed. William M. Gibson (Berkeley: Univ. of California Press, 1969).
God's Fool	Hamlin Hill, *Mark Twain: God's Fool* (New York: Harper, 1973).
HF	*Adventures of Huckleberry Finn (Tom Sawyer's Comrade)* (New York: Charles L. Webster and Co., 1885).
JA	*Personal Recollection of Joan of Arc* (New York: Harper, 1896).
JMN	*The Journals and Miscellaneous Notebooks of Ralph Waldo Emerson,* ed. William H. Gilman, Alfred R. Ferguson, George P. Clark, Merrel R. Davis, Merton M. Sealts, Harrison Hayford, Ralph H. Orth, J. E. Parsons, A. W. Plumstead, Linda Allardt, and Susan Sutton Smith, 14 vols. (Cambridge: Harvard Univ. Press, 1960–). In quoting from the *JMN* I have silently omitted the editors' textual apparatus used to indicate Emerson's

	cancellations, revisions, insertions, and the like. My version represents Emerson's final intent according to the editorial indications.
Kaplan	Justin Kaplan, *Mr. Clemens and Mark Twain: A Biography* (New York: Simon and Schuster, 1966).
Life	Norman O. Brown, *Life Against Death: The Psychoanalytical Meaning of History* (Middletown, Conn.: Wesleyan Univ. Press, 1959).
MT&HF	Walter Blair, *Mark Twain and Huck Finn* (Berkeley: Univ. of California Press, 1960).
MT's Hannibal	*Mark Twain's Hannibal, Huck and Tom,* ed. Walter Blair (Berkeley: Univ. of California Press, 1969).
"No. 44"	"No. 44, The Mysterious Stranger," in *Mark Twain's Mysterious Stranger Manuscripts,* ed. William M. Gibson (Berkeley: Univ. of California Press, 1969).
Notebook	*Mark Twain's Notebook,* ed. Albert Bigelow Paine (New York: Harper, 1935).
Whicher	Stephen E. Whicher, *Freedom and Fate: An Inner Life of Ralph Waldo Emerson* (Philadelphia: Univ. of Pennsylvania Press, 1953).
WMT	*The Works of Mark Twain,* ed. John C. Gerber, Franklin R. Rogers, Paul Baender, Terry Firkins, Bernard L. Stein, Edgar M. Branch, Robert H. Hirst (Berkeley: Univ. of California Press, 1972–).
Writings	*The Writings of Mark Twain,* Author's National Edition, 25 vols. (New York: Harper, 1907–18).
"YS"	"The Chronicle of Young Satan," in *Mark Twain's Mysterious Stranger Manuscripts,* ed. William M. Gibson (Berkeley: Univ. of California Press, 1969).

Mark Twain
AND THE LIMITS OF POWER

Introduction

The greater part of these pages is devoted to a study of Mark Twain's fascination—one might almost say obsession—with characters who possess, or wish to possess, an extraordinary ability to dominate the worlds in which they find themselves. It is my thesis that Twain retained throughout his career an emotional commitment to the nineteenth-century notion that man could dominate and even create his human environment. In his efforts to portray characters so gifted, however, he repeatedly found himself confronting moral and philosophical issues that called into question the benevolence, and eventually the sanity, of the characters he created and loved.

Some criticism has touched on Twain's power figures, beginning with Paul Baender's unpublished dissertation of 1956, entitled "Mark Twain's Transcendent Figure."[1] More recently, Judith Fetterly approaches the topic in her article, "Yankee Showman and Reformer: Mark Twain's Hank Morgan,"[2] as does Stanley Brodwin in his "Mark Twain's Masks of Satan: The Final Phase."[3] But while each of these has been valuable to the present study, none has delineated the scope or depth of Twain's concern with power. Hank Morgan's technological expertise and Young Satan's magical sway are both later, more explicit versions of a power with which Twain had long been fascinated. Baender's work is the only one of length which tries to place Twain's concern for power in a nineteenth-century context; he suggests

[1]Diss. Univ. of California (Berkeley), 1956.
[2]*TSLL* 14 (Winter 1973), 667–79.
[3]*AL* 45 (1973), 206–27.

that the source of Twain's interest lies in part in "the more vulgar literature of the period. . . . the heap of biographies and tales concerning western heroes."[4]

The influence on Twain of Southwestern regional literature was certainly great, and it is not surprising that Baender should have looked there for a plausible ancestry of Twain's fascination with power figures. These tales do show similarities between, say, a Western giant like Davy Crockett and a man of awesome capabilities like Hank Morgan. The exaggeration of human capacity is a stock-in-trade of many Southwestern tales, as Constance Rourke has shown us.[5] One might compare, for example, the tale of Davy Crockett saving the world by unfreezing the sun, and walking away with "a piece of sunrise in my pocket,"[6] with Twain's own feelings one day in Nevada. Enchanted by the perspective of Western space, Twain imagines himself swelling, growing larger, until

> you look disdainfully down upon the insignificant village of Carson, reposing like a cheap print away yonder at the foot of the big hills, and in that instant you are seized with a burning desire to stretch forth your hand, put the city in your pocket, and walk off with it.[7]

Yet there is another precedent in our literature for Twain's interest in power figures, and a secondary purpose in these pages is to suggest that Twain's work demonstrates the same sort of fascination for the Man-God as may be seen in the essays and journals of Ralph Waldo Emerson. In *A Connecticut Yankee,* for example, Hank Morgan narrowly misses being burned at the stake in the opening pages. He saves himself by raising his hand deliberately toward the sun, which darkens in an eclipse. It is the first of Hank's big "effects," and surely it is a spurious one. Yet Emerson wonders if such "effects" need be spurious at all:

[4]Baender, 36.

[5]*American Humor: A Study of the National Character* (New York: Harcourt, Brace, 1931), 36.

[6]"Crockett's Morning Hunt," in *The Comic Tradition in America,* ed. Kenneth S. Lynn (New York: Norton, 1958), 153–54.

[7]*The Pattern for Mark Twain's* Roughing It: *Letters from Nevada by Samuel and Orion Clemens, 1861–1862,* ed. Franklin R. Rogers (Berkeley: Univ. of California Press, 1961), 24.

> Perhaps after many sad doubting idle days, days of happy honest labor will at last come when a man shall have filled up all the hours from sun to sun with great and equal action, shall lose sight of this sharp individuality which contrasts now so oddly with nature, and ceasing to regard shall cease to feel his boundaries, but shall be interfused by nature & shall [so] interfuse nature that the sun shall rise by his will as much as his own hand or foot do now. (*JMN* VII 397)

Particularly in his earlier, more radical essays, Emerson established himself for succeeding generations as the American prophet of possibility. He perceived in man the ability to achieve the right "axis" of being, and thereby to assert his mastery over the world of time and circumstance. Repeatedly, he envisions man's transformation from a "bastard" hemmed in by a world that demands compromise, to a "Titan" to whom the world offers its services. I would suggest, then, that Twain's interest in power figures has its correspondences in the Northeastern cultural milieu as well as in the Southwestern folk imagination, in the more genteel currents of thought as well as in the regional vernacular.

My argument in part is that there exists a surprising correlation between Twain's power figures and the imperious Self sketched so persistently in Emerson's work. For both men, the strength of the empowered Self lies not so much in his ability to adjust to the world, as in his ability to make the world adjust to him. He does not manage *in* the world so much as he manages the world itself. He is able to dominate experience in an almost magical way—as though he had indeed "ceased to feel his boundaries" and were able to treat the world as an extension of himself.

Twain and Emerson were much preoccupied, in the course of their respective careers, with the same problem: that of realizing in practical terms the capabilities they believed man harbored within him. For Emerson the gap between the Self he envisioned and the implacable experience of the real world was one he never successfully bridged. Stephen Whicher's *Freedom and Fate: An Inner Life of Ralph Waldo Emerson* admirably traces the progressive disillusionment Emerson felt between his first call for man to "put Nature under foot" (*CWE* I 58) and "work down upon my world" (*JMN* V 332), and his later, more tame acquiescence to the world of practical limitations. Emerson never totally lost faith in the ideal Self he imagined; if he came to question, painfully, its realization, he always saw its grace—he saw it, that is, as the culmination of a benevolent moral order, a figure resplendent not only in its extraordinary capacities, but in the perfection of its moral apprehension. Such a figure was a natural end, for Emerson, of a world steeped in harmony.

Twain, too, was much given to seeing his power figures as benevolent. One need only consider Hank Morgan's persistent attempts to free sixth-century England from its blind cruelty and its stultifying superstitions. His is in many ways a benevolent sacrifice of self for the good of others, and he thus commands the sympathies and respect of both the reader and Twain himself. But Hank Morgan fails, and in his fall he demonstrates a capacity for destruction at least as great as his power for construction. And if the ending of *A Connecticut Yankee* must temper our respect for Hank with horror at his easy use of Gatling guns and electric fences, so too does it temper Twain's. In other words, while Twain seems to have shared with Emerson an initial faith in the realization of an ideal Self, and a faith in the benevolence of that Self, he could not maintain that faith as he explored the implications of such power in his novels.

The problem may be demonstrated in capsule form by a brief reference to Walt Whitman, whose speaker in "Song of Myself" embodies many of the characteristics of Emerson's ideal Self. In 1889, when Hank Morgan had already been consigned to his fate, Twain could write to Whitman in an ecstatic vein: "Wait thirty years. . . . You shall see . . . Man at almost his full stature at last!—and still growing. . . . Wait till you see that great figure appear."[8] We are familiar with the "great figure" as Whitman saw him: one grown to heroic proportions through an unabashed emphasis on the Self, through his assumptions, implicit and explicit, that the Self stands at the center of things, and will hold:

[8]Camden's Compliment to Walt Whitman, May 31, 1889, Notes, Addresses, Letters, Telegrams, ed. Horace Traubel, Philadelphia, 1889, 64–65; quoted in Baender, 65.

To me the converging objects of the universe
  perpetually flow,
All are written to me, and I must get what the
  writing means.
I know I am deathless,
I know this orbit of mine cannot be swept by a
  carpenter's compass,
I know I shall not pass like a child's carlecue
  cut with a burnt stick at night.[9]

Whitman's speaker holds our sympathies through the paradox that, though he lionizes the Self, there is yet room in his world for the rest of us:

I celebrate myself, and sing myself,
And what I assume you shall assume,
For every atom belonging to me as good belongs to you.[10]

The speaker's confidence and benevolence are characteristics that Twain found attractive in his own conception of an empowered Self. But as he wrote his novels, Twain discovered, to his consternation, that the larger and more masterful the Self became, the less benevolent he was likely to be. It is as though Twain's empowered Self were always inclined to reverse the personal pronouns in that last line, and thus turn the passage's tone from promise to threat:

I celebrate myself, and sing myself,
And what I assume you shall assume,
For every atom belonging to you as good belongs to me.

Progressively, the Self for Twain becomes more and more morally suspect as it is portrayed in action in the real world. What charges Twain's novels, however, is not simply the emotion of his discovery that man could not be better than he is; rather, Twain's later bitterness toward man seems directly proportional to the degree of emotional investment he originally had

[9]Walt Whitman, *Leaves of Grass,* ed. Sculley Bradley and Harold W. Blodgett (New York: New York Univ. Press, 1965), 47–48.
[10]Ibid., 28.

in the ideal Self. What was destroyed for Twain was more than a hope; it was a conviction, and the novels record the stages of its crumbling. One has the sense that Twain watches with something of disbelief as his conviction suffers its first serious cracks in *Tom Sawyer* and *Huckleberry Finn.* In *A Connecticut Yankee* the Self is tested again, and is found wanting. *Joan of Arc* may be seen as an effort to restore faith in the dream, while *The Mysterious Stranger* carries out the implications of power let loose in the world to its bitter conclusions.

My perception of correspondences between Twain and Emerson may at times seem to make of the two rather strange associates. We have become so acclimated to seeing Twain as an embittered determinist and Emerson as an optimistic sage that any linking of the two may seem spurious at the outset. Still, at least one critic has pursued the correspondences to a limited degree. Elwood Johnson, in an article entitled "Mark Twain's Dream Self in the Nightmare of History," sees *The Mysterious Stranger* as reflecting the same "double consciousness" regarding freedom and determination as plagues Emerson in his own dichotomous formulation of the Reason and the Understanding. *The Mysterious Stranger,* says Johnson, "serves as an example of the version of individualism that insists that the outer world is only an extension of the inner world: the individual creates the universe, God, and nature out of a dream center within himself."[11] This is the approach to Twain I intend to pursue here, and I argue that such solipsism is a fundamental ingredient in much of Twain's best work.

To this approach Hamlin Hill has offered a cautionary remark: "Such a reading would gain immensely if it were possible to show Clemens' knowledge of the philosophies of Emerson or Kant or Hegel."[12] Demonstration of such knowledge is not really possible—but neither is it necessary unless one insists on demonstrating direct influence. I am not arguing in these pages for any influence of Emerson on Twain. Rather, the correspondences I

[11]Elwood Johnson, "Mark Twain's Dream Self in the Nightmare of History," *Mark Twain Journal,* 15, No. 1 (Winter 1970), 12.

[12]Hamlin Hill, "Mark Twain," *American Literary Scholarship: An Annual/ 1970,* ed. J. Hilbert Robbins (Durham: Duke Univ. Press, 1972), 88.

point out are cultural ones, the result of two widely divergent sensibilities coming to terms with a shared nineteenth-century disposition to believe that extravagant ideals might cease to be mere mental constructs, and might become objectified in the real world. Emerson's effectiveness as essayist and lecturer grew out of his role as cultural preacher, as enunciator of aspirations already shared, however inarticulately, by his American audience. The call for independence from Europe, the cry for a proud self-reliance, and the faith that man and nature, the Me and the Not Me, shared in some special way a common heritage and a common fate—these ideas have come to be recognized as among the exponents of the nineteenth-century American imagination. And as Quentin Anderson puts it in *The Imperial Self,* Emerson's countrymen "wanted what he wanted; the freedom to imagine themselves possessed of a power literally realized by no man, and openly fantasied by most people only when they are infants: the power to dispose of the whole felt and imagined world as a woman arranges her skirt" (Anderson, 56). Mark Twain shared in that desire. He poured much of his creative energies into dramatizing such power at large in the world, and in the end he found himself in near despair over the implications he discovered in it.

I

The Wonderworker

Man is the wonderworker. He is seen among miracles.
—Emerson, "Divinity School Address"

I

Emerson's Coleridgean division of man's faculties into two, the Reason and the Understanding, enabled him to describe both what he saw man to be, and what he believed man could be. The disparity between the two conceptions was great, and Emerson devoted much of his intellectual energies, especially in his early career, toward exhorting his hearers to leave off the dull dwarfism of their common existence and to ascend to their rightful state—to become, that is, a race of Titans (*CWE* I 156). In those epiphanic moments in which Emerson felt a coexistence with nature and with universal law, he beheld in man "extravagant possibilities" (*JMN* VII 146), and for a time he believed those possibilities might be realized not just in the mind, as intellectual constructs, but in the world of circumstance, and there become practical expressions of heretofore unrealized energies.

The chief stumbling block to man's "ascension" was his distrust of his deepest self—his proclivity to live under the aegis of the Understanding alone. The Understanding, as Emerson explained it in *Nature,* is a prudential faculty, a necessary and beneficial portion of the intellect, but one which comprises only half of man's force. It deals with the "Not Me," all that is separate from the "Me," in practical ways:

> Every property of matter is a school for the understanding—its solidity or resistance, its inertia, its extension, its

> figure, its divisibility. The understanding adds, divides, combines, measures. . . . Our dealing with sensible objects is a constant exercise in the necessary lessons of difference, or likeness, of order. . . . What tedious training, day after day, year after year, never ending, to form the common sense. . . . (*CWE* I 36–37)

Man uses the Understanding to deal with the Not Me in mechanical ways; he learns of the world's qualities through data communicated to his mind through the senses. The relation of the Me and the Not Me is largely, thus far, as Locke formulated it in his *Essay on Human Understanding:* the mind is a passive receptor of impressions gathered mechanically through the senses. The province of the Understanding is "Space, time, society, labor, climate, food, locomotion, the animal, the mechanical forces . . ." (*CWE* I 36).

But Emerson qualifies the distinctiveness of the Me and the Not Me, the perceiver and the perceived, by speaking of nature as a "discipline." In his metaphor, nature becomes not simply a mass of external phenomena, but a teacher, whose purpose it is to instruct man in the workings of a larger scheme. The Not Me, after all, operates in "ministry" to man; it exists to fulfill man's needs. Through its physical processes, nature provides man the commodities he needs for his "temporary and mediate, not ultimate" existence (*CWE* I 12). In its beauty it provides satisfation for man's aesthetic sensibilities. In its orderliness it provides man with linguistic analogies so that he might better express his thoughts. In its cyclical self–sacrifice for man's benefit, it provides him with a moral example. "All parts necessarily work into each other's hands for the profit of man" (*CWE* I 13). "Nature is thoroughly mediate. It is made to serve. It receives the dominion of man as meekly as the ass on which the Saviour rode. It offers all its kingdoms to man as the raw material which he may mold into what is useful" (*CWE* I 40).

The assertion of nature's ministry to man is an important element in Emerson's philosophy, for it establishes the relation of man to the physical world around him as a homocentric one. Man becomes the center of things, and the purpose of nature is to serve that center. Further, nature becomes, to a degree, personified, animistic; it actively reaches out to man to teach and to discipline. Part of Emerson's purpose in *Nature* is to awaken in his auditors a sense of their own importance. By placing them on a center to which the grand designs of nature conspire, he hopes to ready them for his enunciation of an even greater place for them in God's scheme. Even here, on the level of the Understanding, man is invested with a kingly estate: "Every rational creature has all nature as his dowry and estate. It is his, if he will. He may divest himself of it; he may creep into a corner, and abdicate his kingdom, as most men do, but he is entitled to the world by his constitution" (*CWE* I 20).

But the apprehension of the world through the Understanding, even in such a manner as Emerson formulates it with man as the central receptor of its services, is still limited. The Understanding enables man to apprehend only a part of experience; it does not explain or account for other apprehensions Emerson considered to be existent in man's life—a "haunting awareness of transcendental forces peering through the cracks of the visible universe."[1] For there was that in the Not Me, Emerson felt, which answered to the intuitions of the Me, intuitions that rose from man's Reason. In addition to a world apprehended empirically, there was one felt emotionally, which was connected with, but not limited to, the objects apprehended by sense impressions.

Man's second faculty, the Reason, is for Emerson a higher faculty to which the Understanding—strict empiricist that it is—should be subservient. The Reason is the means by which man comes to doubt that "things are ultimates" (*CWE* I 49). Thus the empirical world of Locke is conceived as a surface world, through which man may, by the exercise of the Reason, peer into the cause of Nature, the mind of the Creator. Man "does not deny the sensuous fact: by no means; but he will not see that alone. He does not deny the presence of this table, this chair, and the walls of this room, but he looks at these things as the reverse side of the tapestry, as the *other end,* each being a sequel or completion of a spiritual fact which nearly concerns him" (*CWE* I 330–31).

Emerson begins *Nature* by calling for man to establish "an

[1]Philip Wheelright, "Poetry, Myth, and Reality," in *The Language of Poetry,* ed. Allan Tate (Princeton: Princeton Univ. Press, 1942), 10.

original relation to the universe" (*CWE* I 3), and it is through the exercise of the Reason that this relation is to be established. The spiritual truths which nature exists to embody are meant to liberate man from the limitations of empirical sight:

> The first effort of thought tends to relax this despotism of the senses which binds nature to us as though we were a part of it, and shows nature aloof, and, as it were, afloat. Until this higher agency intervened, the animal eye sees, with wonderful accuracy, sharp outlines and colored surfaces. When the eye of Reason opens, to outline and surface are at once added grace and expression. These proceed from imagination and affection, and abate somewhat the angular distinctness of objects. If the Reason be stimulated to more earnest vision, outlines and surfaces become transparent, and are no longer seen; causes and spirits are seen through them. The best moments of life are these delicious awakenings of the higher powers, and the reverential withdrawing of nature before its god. (*CWE* I 49–50)

The exercise of Reason, then, carries man from fact to spirit, from effect to cause. Through Reason he apprehends the source of things and discovers there not a stranger of whom he need be in awe, but a whole of which he is a part. He discovers that he himself participates in the workings of spirit—that in fact his highest Self is spirit:

> We learn that the highest is present to the soul of man; that the dread universal essence, which is not wisdom, or love, or beauty, or power, but all in one, and each entirely, is that for which all things exist, and that by which they are; that spirit creates; that behind nature, throughout nature, spirit is present; one and not compound it does not act upon us from without, that is, in space and time, but spiritually, or through ourselves: therefore, that spirit, that is, the Supreme Being, does not build up nature around us, but puts it forth through us, as the life of the tree puts forth new branches and leaves through the pores of the old. (*CWE* I 63–64)

If Locke's epistemology was limited to the passive reception of sense impressions,[2] Emerson's, through the German and English Romantics, expanded to an assertion of man's participation in the creation of what he perceived. The rapport between nature and man exists because they are part and parcel of each other. To apprehend the spirit behind the fact is to come home to oneself, and the solidities and resistances of empirical data—space, time, society, labor, and so forth—are phenomena which come into being as an expression of Spirit of which man himself partakes. What was important to Emerson was, as Charles Feidelson points out, "the habitual posture of the mind—beholding"[3]; and that posture was one in which the "axis of vision is . . . coincident with the axis of things" (*CWE* I 73). The effect of such beholding was the realization that the Not Me and the Me are not separate, but unified, and that the character of the Not Me is dependent upon one's axis of vision—dependent upon one's highest Self. To "behold" via the Reason was to unify the consciousness with all that had previously seemed external to it. The forms of nature answer to, and are reflections of, forms that are already preexistent in the mind of the beholder. "Once inhale the upper air," Emerson attests, "being admitted to behold the absolute nature of justice and truth, and we learn that man has access to the entire mind of the Creator, is himself the creator in the finite" (*CWE* I 64).

The bridging of the Lockean gap between the mind and nature was the basis for Emerson's hope for "extravagant possibilities." The difference between living in the Understanding and living in the Reason was the difference between slavery and mastery. The poet, for example, provides a glimpse of man's rightful state:

> He unfixes the land and the sea, makes them revolve around the axis of his primary thought, and disposes them anew. . . . The sensual man conforms thoughts to things; the poet conforms things to his thoughts. The one esteems nature as rooted and fast; the other, as fluid, and impresses his being thereon. . . . The Imagination may be defined to

[2]Sherman Paul, *Emerson's Angle of Vision* (Cambridge: Harvard Univ. Press, 1952), 20.

[3]Charles Feidelson, Jr., *Symbolism and American Literature* (Chicago: Univ. of Chicago Press, 1953), 128.

> be the use the Reason makes of the material world. (*CWE* I 51–52)

The latter pages of *Nature* press home the dual picture of man—the dwarf who exists, unnecessarily, under the exclusive aegis of the Understanding, and the Titan who may be, if he will, the creator in the finite:

> At present, man applies to nature but half his force. He works on the world by the understanding alone. He lives in it and masters it by penny-wisdom; and he that works most in it is but a half-man, and whilst his arms are strong and his digestion good, his mind is imbruted, and he is a selfish savage. His relation to nature, his power over it, is through the understanding, as by manure; the economic use of fire, wind, water, and the mariner's needle; steam, coal, and chemical agriculture; the repairs of the human body by the dentist and the surgeon. This is such a resumption of power as if a banished king should buy his territories inch by inch, instead of vaulting at once into his throne. Meantime, in the thick darkness, there are not wanting gleams of a better light,—occasional examples of the action of man upon nature with his entire force,—with reason as well as understanding. Such examples are, the traditions of miracles in the earliest antiquity of all nations; the history of Jesus Christ; the achievements of a principle, as in religious and political revolutions, and in the abolition of the slave-trade; the miracles of enthusiasm. . . . many obscure and contested facts, now arranged under the name of Animal Magnetism; prayer, eloquence; self-healing; and the wisdom of children. These are examples of Reason's momentary grasp of the scepter; the executions of a power which exists not in time or space, but an instantaneous instreaming causing power. (*CWE* I 72–73)

The "discovery" that matter is a manifestation of Spirit, and that man participates in Spirit, enables man to assume what Emerson calls "the erect position," and to follow literally the exhortation to "Build therefore your own world" (*CWE* I 76). Man no longer need be a "god in ruins" (*CWE* I 71), for in him lie the powers of the creator himself.

> Man is the dwarf of himself. Once he was permeated and dissolved by spirit. He filled nature with his overflowing currents. Out from him sprang the sun and moon. . . . The laws in his mind, the periods of his actions externized themselves into day and night, into the year and the seasons. (*CWE* I 71)

Man is thus not simply the center of the phenomenal world, whose workings bend in to serve his needs; he is also the source and origin of that world, which recognizes him as "its God." He stands, as it were, on a point in space, while the world radiates from him, created as a copy and portrait of his mind. The multiplicity which the Understandng sees is, finally, illusory, for the awakened Reason apprehends a unity which encompasses all things. The conjoining of fact, spirit, and consciousness collapses into One the knower and the known. "The immobility or bruteness of nature is the absence of spirit; to pure spirit it is fluid, it is volatile, it is obedient. . . . What we are, that only can we see" (*CWE* I 76).

II

As Stephen Whicher has noted, Emerson could be comfortable with a homocentric universe by virtue of a conviction that the soul of man "does not merely . . . contain a spark or drop or breath or voice of God; it *is* God" (Whicher, 21). The doctrine was a radical reversal of the traditional Christian belief in the incarnation of God into man. For Emerson, man was become God. In a stroke, Emerson dismissed the Fall as a permanent limitation of man's nature, and in doing so entered a "period of aroused expectations" (Whicher, 47) during which he felt that man's ascension to truly god-like status was imminent.

In "The American Scholar," "The Divinity School Address," and "Self–Reliance" his voice is that of a New England Gabriel come with a new Annunciation calculated to prod his lethargic hearers into a wakeful exercise of powers that had too long slumbered. And there is something in it of madness, after all. With his lecturer's eloquence and the power of words, he would have man assume omnipotence. Whicher sees in the Emerson of the late 1830s a man "a little beside himself with hope":

> If there is no bar or wall in the soul, where man, the effect, and God, the cause, begins, what hinders man from being a 'creator in the finite'? His intuitions speak to him of a Love, Freedom, Power which *is* now potentially at the bottom of his heart. Then why not realize it in every sense . . . ? (Whicher, 47)

"The American Scholar" suggests one sense in which man may realize his powers. The business of man, as Emerson imagined it, was to continue that creative expressiveness he had heretofore relegated to God. Every moment could be a new Genesis, conducted through a sort of rhythmic systole and diastole of the consciousness:

> The scholar of the first age received into him the world around; brooded thereon; gave it the new arrangement of his own mind, and uttered it again. It came into him life; it went out from him truth. It came into him short-lived actions; it went out from him immortal thoughts. It came into him business; it went out from him poetry. It was dead fact; now, it is quick thought. (*CWE* I 87)

And in this alchemical process of transmuting life into truth there is the sacredness of "the act of creation, the act of thought" (*CWE* I 88), and an "exhibition of the power of the self to image the world it has incorporated" (Anderson, 14). Yet the passage from "The American Scholar" is couched in abstracts and metaphor. The direction of Emerson's wish becomes even more explicit in "The Transcendentalist." Emerson's ideal Man

> takes his departure from his consciousness, and reckons the world an appearance. . . . His experience inclines him to behold the procession of facts you call the world, as flowing perpetually outward from an invisible, unsounded centre in himself . . . and necessitating him to regard all things as having a subjective and relative existence, relative to that aforesaid Unknown Centre of him. . . . All that you call the world is the shadow of that substance which you are, the perpetual Creation of the powers of thought. . . . You think me the child of my circumstances: I make my circumstances. (*CWE* I 332–34)

Increasingly, Emerson envisions the ideal Self as having the power to effect major changes in the world around him—not through the "penny-wisdom" of the Understanding, with its emphasis on external machinery, but through the wider, more magical power of the Reason. If the world proceeds outward from the Self, and images the Self, what hinders man from changing the world by realizing the highest within him? The conquest of delimiting circumstance is Emerson's goal; he envisions a state in which "Man . . . seems a young child, and his huge globe a toy" (*CWE* I 119). In his rightful state, when he "sees" correctly, Man will realize that the boundaries of seemingly unalterable circumstance can be unsettled by a brave trust in his deepest Self. "Our globe seen by God is a transparent law, not a mass of facts. The law dissolves the fact and holds it fluid. Our culture is the predominance of an idea which draws after it this train of cities and institutions. Let us rise into another idea; they will disappear" (*CWE* II 302).

In "Circles" Emerson presents the idea of Man's expansion or dilation as he overcomes circumstance. The Self perceives certain boundaries to its activity—a circumference which it takes to be a whole beyond which it cannot step. Yet the exercise of the Reason dissolves those boundaries, and the Reason's eye draws a yet wider circle. The Self expands to fill the newly created sphere. The process is capable of infinite repetition, the self assuming greater and greater size, greater and greater ability to subdue facts which once were thought to be unalterable.

> The life of man is a self-evolving circle, which, from a ring imperceptibly small, rushes on all sides outwards to new and larger circles, and that without end. The extent to which this generation of circles, wheel without wheel, will go, depends on the force or truth of the individual soul. For it is the inert effort of each thought, having formed itself into a circular wave of circumstance,—as for instance an empire, rules of an art, a local usage, a religious rite,—to heap itself on that ridge and to solidify and hem in the life. But if the soul is quick and strong it bursts over that boundary on all sides and expands another orbit on the great deep, which also runs up into a high wave, with attempt again to stop and to bind. But the heart refuses to

> be imprisoned; in its first and narrowest pulses it already tends outward with a vast force and to immense and innumerable expansions. (*CWE* II 304)

The systole and diastole thus continues: what is created by the Self is incorporated, the Self perceiving its oneness with it; a new circumference is drawn, with yet new facts created, to be dissolved and incorported in their turn. The Self creates and expands, creates and expands: "There is no outside, no inclosing walls, no circumference to us. . . . The Man . . . fills the sky" (*CWE* III 304). As Whitman puts it,

> From this hour I ordain myself loos'd of limits
> and imaginary lines,
> Going where I list, my own master total and
> absolute,
> Listening to others, considering well what they say,
> Pausing, searching, receiving, contemplating,
> Gently, but with undeniable will, divesting myself
> of the holds that would hold me.[4]

"The holds that would hold me" are manifold, and their conquest begins when Man cuts himself loose from dependence on any circumstance foreign to himself. "Self-Reliance" drives home Emerson's plea for Man to depend wholly on the "aboriginal Self" (*CWE* II 63) and to hold as oppressive all external authority that would seek to impose limits upon him. "He who knows that power is inborn, that he is weak because he has looked for good out of him and elsewhere, and, so perceiving, throws himself unhesitatingly on his thought, instantly rights himself, stands in the erect position, commands his limbs, works miracles . . ." (*CWE* II 89). Men thus become "not minors and invalids in a protected corner, not cowards fleeing before a revolution, but guides, redeemers, and benefactors, obeying the Almighty effort and advancing on Chaos and the Dark" (*CWE* II 47).

Stephen Whicher rightly calls attention to the discrepancy between Emerson's moralistic language and the revolutionary implications of his thought. Emerson could believe in the virtuousness of the course he urged because of his faith that Spirit itself

[4] *Leaves of Grass,* 151.

was virtuous, that the new state of being he envisioned was itself virtue personified. To write "Whim" on the lintels of the doorpost was to "rise as by specific levity . . . into the region of all the virtues" (*CWE* II 275). What to his contemporaries seemed "sheer summer madness"[5] was to Emerson a natural state of grace. Nevertheless, Emerson's ardor suggests a fascination for the power of the newly sighted individual. "'Overturn, Overturn, and overturn,' said our aged priest, 'until he whose right it is to reign, shall come into his kingdom'" (*JMN* IV 384). Emerson's moralistic language, Whicher notes, "sanctioned and masked" a "radical egoistic anarchism" (Whicher, 49). "The lesson he would drive home is man's entire independence. The aim of this strain in his thought is not virtue, but freedom and mastery. It is radically anarchic, overthrowing all the authority of the past, all compromise or cooperation with others, in the name of the Power present and agent in the soul" (Whicher, 56).

III

The first implication of Emerson's proposed radical independence is a dissolution of social bonds. "In Emerson," says Quentin Anderson, "society was not spurned; it was judged irrelevant to human purposes in the measure that it forced or encouraged each of us to assume a distinct role. Transcendentalism, which Emerson described as 'The Saturnalia or excess of Faith' in individual powers and individual sufficiency, simply attempted to supplant society" (Anderson, 5). The Emersonian Self is "a consciousness which denies that our sense of ourselves is based on a reciprocal or dramatic or dialectic awareness of one another" (Anderson, 5). A radical trust in the godhood of the Self by necessity sets the individual apart from the mass of men who live by the more comfortable expedients of societal regulation. Emerson's Man becomes himself to the degree that he separates himself, psychologically if not geographically, from society. "Society everywhere," says Emerson in "Self-Reliance," "is in conspiracy against the manhood of every one of its members" (*CWE* II 49).

[5]Francis Bowen, *The Christian Examiner,* 23 (November 1837), quoted in Perry Miller, *The Transcendentalists* (Cambridge: Harvard Univ. Press, 1950), 177.

For Emerson, then, identity comes not from imposed social roles, but from reliance on the intuitions of the Reason. In this sense Man is "self-begotten," a product of himself and not of any religious, social, or cultural heritage. "In the eye of the philosopher, the Individual has ceased to be regarded as a Part, and has come to be regarded as a Whole. He is the World."[6] Indeed, functioning as a conforming member of society tends to undercut Man's rightful dignity and force. "It is one of those fables which out of an unknown antiquity convey an unlooked for wisdom, that the gods, in the beginning, divided Man into men. . . . But unfortunately, this original unit, the fountain of Power, has been so distributed into multitudes . . . that it is spilled into drops, and cannot be gathered" (*CWE* I 82–83).

But Man in his rightful state need not be "distributed." Acting and thinking from his own godhood, he no longer need be defined as a "part" of the social fabric. Insofar as he is true to the godhood within him, the "huge world comes round."

Emerson is explicit about the opposition between communal values and self-reliance. He defines heroism as "an obedience to a secret impulse of an individual's character," and notes that it "works in contradiction to the voice of mankind and in contradiction, for a time, to the voice of the great and good" (*CWE* II 251). Man Thinking is by definition his own arbiter of right action and wrong, and he plies his oar with hardly a glance at the opinions—or the objections—of others. His is a

> self-trust which slights the restraints of prudence, in the plenitude of its energy and power to repair the harms it may suffer. The hero is a mind of such balance that no disturbances can shake his will. . . . There is somewhat not holy in it; it seems not to know that other souls are of one texture with it; it has pride; it is the extreme of individual nature. Nevertheless we must profoundly revere it. . . . Heroism feels and never reasons, and therefore is always right. (*CWE* II 250)

Two points should perhaps be made explicit here. The posi-

[6] *The Early Lectures of Ralph Waldo Emerson,* ed. Stephen E. Whicher, Robert E. Spiller, and Wallace E. Williams (Cambridge: Belknap Press of Harvard Univ. Press, 1964) II, 214.

tion of Emerson's hero is a strange one, both socially and morally. Emerson's hero defines himself without reference, either positive or negative, to society. That is, he does not derive a sense of self from his role within the social fabric—as, say, "farmer," "minister," or "teacher." Part of the thrust of "The American Scholar" is that such roles as arise from social division of labor are limiting and fail to incorporate the whole possibilities of man. But neither does the hero define himself through his rejection of social roles and values, as, for example, Theron Ware tries to do in Harold Frederic's *The Damnation of Theron Ware.* The self as "rebel" is still a self determined in relation to society. For Emerson, the hero is too self-sufficient even for this. The hero creates himself, as it were, from nothing.

The situation has its moral equivalents as well. To say that heroism works "in contradiction . . . to the voice of the great and good," to admit readily that there is "somewhat not holy" in heroism, is to play fast and loose with the standards by which society ordinarily judges the moral quality of an act. "For the hero that thing he does is the highest deed, and it is not open to the censure of philosophers and divines" (*CWE* II 251).

Emerson comes very close to giving the hero a sort of limitless moral credit. To hold him to mere social standards of good and evil seems pointless, for those standards are themselves established without reference to the All, to which the hero has immediate access, and which must naturally take precedence. It is a situation in which "the satanic and angelic are alike meaningless" (Anderson, 5). In his essay on Napoleon, Emerson found Napoleon's comment on criminality interesting enough to quote: "' They charge me,' he said, 'with the commission of great crimes; men of my stamp do not commit crimes. Nothing has been more simple than my elevation, 't is in vain to ascribe it to intrigue or crime . . . Of what use . . . would crimes be to me?' " (*CWE* IV 231).

What moral credit Emerson does extend to his hero is, of course, not unlimited. Napoleon, who seems best to exemplify the possibilities of man as he exercises his power, does not escape censure. But Emerson's urge to qualify indicates a contradiction between the theory he formulated and the fact as he found it. In this instance, the contradictory impulses of admiration and condemnation reveal a reluctance to push the implications of power to their natural conclusions. Napoleon, for all of his power, lacked a moral center. He tried to exercise power "without moral principle" (*CWE* IV 258), and Emerson professed to be not surprised that Napoleon's energy comes to nought in the end. For Emerson, power was grounded in the moral sentiment—its source was always in the perception of a benevolent truth: a truth benevolent to all men, not just to one. To find a man whose self-reliance had in fact made much of the huge world come round to him was to find an objective proof of his theoretical pudding. On the other hand, to find that power residing in a man who was "singularly destitute of generous sentiments" (*CWE* IV 253), a man who "cheated at cards" (*CWE* IV 255), and a man who, after all, was "not . . . a gentleman, at last" (*CWE* IV 256), was to find the clear fountain of power considerably muddied. What was Emerson to do with Napoleon? He does the only gracious thing, one supposes: with his eye on purity, Emerson measures Napoleon and finds him wanting. At the last, he denies him the name of hero. Napoleon is a "rogue," an "imposter," a "Scamp Jupiter" (*CWE* IV 256), but he is not a hero. Still, one has the sense that Emerson leaves Napoleon reluctantly. While the mean motives repelled him, the power attracted him. It was an opportunity, perhaps, to endorse a manifestation of what he proclaimed in theory, that heroism "works in contradiction, for a time, to the voice of the great and good." But if theoretical heroism might forfeit the sanctions of philosophers and divines, in practice it nevertheless should remain gentlemanly.

Whicher points out that Emerson's essay "Heroism" is the most radical formulation of his ideal, that it is his "clearest recognition of the unsanctified aspect of practical power" (Whicher, 66). The mastery, energy, and instinct for success are traits of the hero which "bear no obvious or necessary relation to virtue" (Whicher, 68). Although Emerson usually tempers his formulation by insisting that the hero becomes such only by acting from the moral sentiment, nevertheless the "Nietzschean Superman is already half-explicit in Emerson's hero" (Whicher, 69). If Emerson could, on the one hand, assert confidently that the Man was all, he found it difficult to recognize his own sentiment when it assumed flesh. He was too much the Victorian gentleman, too much the humanist, to accept Napoleon as one of his own.

With the radical separation of the Self from society, and with the amorality implicit in Emerson's hero, there is also the attendant rejection of the past as a source of binding authority. This rejection takes form in Emerson's denial that divine revelation ends with the Bible; and it spills over into his declaration of literary independence from the "courtly muses of Europe" in "The American Scholar" (*CWE* I 114). But as it affects his vision of Man Thinking it has other important strains, for it coincides with his idea of Man as the creator of himself. To proclaim that "An institution is the lengthened shadow of one man" (*CWE* II 61) is to see the individual as the originating point in a chain of causation—not as the culmination of past chains of cause and effect. Thus the individual is exempt from the assembled authority of tradition. Creator and created, he stands outside of time, and replaces the authority of the past with the authority of the Self.

Emerson's rejection of the past is at one with his emphasis on newness, youth, infancy. Indeed, Emerson's habit seems to be one of associating the strength of independence with the child, and the weakness of limitation with age. This motif appears early in *Nature,* when he describes his experience of oneness with the world: "In the woods, too, a man casts off his years, as a snake his slough, and at what period soever of life is always a child" (*CWE* I 9). In "Self-Reliance" his touchstone for right action is the same: "Infancy conforms to nobody; all conform to it." "The nonchalance of boys who are sure of a dinner, and would disdain as much as a lord to do or say aught to conciliate one, is the healthy attitude of human nature" (*CWE* II 48). His warnings of the dangers of consistency are in part a warning against the debilitating influences of time, since conformity to one's past actions and pronouncements prevents the continual renewal and creation of the Self. In his lectures Emerson hoped to "invite men drenched in time to recover themselves & come out of time, & taste their native immortal air" (*JMN* VII 271). And this association of time with sickness is made more explicit, and more moralistic, in "Circles":

> Why should we import rags and relics into the new hour? Nature abhors the old, and old age seems the only disease;

> all others run into this one. We call it by many names,—fever, intemperance, insanity, stupidity and crime; they are all forms of old age; they are rest, conservatism, appropriation, inertia; not newness, not the way onward. We grizzle every day. I see no need of it. Whilst we converse with what is above us, we do not grow old, but grow young. Infancy, youth, receptive, aspiring, with religious eye looking upward, counts itself nothing and abandons itself to the instruction flowing from all sides. But the man and woman of seventy assume to know all, they have outlived their hope, they renounce aspiration, accept the actual for the necessary and talk of the Holy Ghost; let them be lovers; let them behold truth; and their eyes are uplifted, their wrinkles smooth, they are perfumed again with hope and power. (*CWE* II 319)

It is not too much to say of Emerson's Titan that there should be only two tenses in his language, the present and the future. The past—his own and his culture's—has no holds on him. "I AM," Emerson proclaims to his journal, "& Time is below me" (*JMN* VII 231).

This subordination of time to the all-sufficient Self further weakens communal bonds. Emerson's call to reject the past and time itself as limiting factors for the individual is in effect a call to rejoice in orphanhood; it is a call to cut oneself off from the most ordinary of human circumstances:

> A genetic account of the aspects of the self, a sense of the various ways in which parents, landscapes, fairy tales, encounters with strangers, are or might be constitutive of our sense of the world, these things almost make a catalogue of what Emerson could not afford to know without binding himself to human circumstances in a way he found crippling. . . . It involves us fatally with generations and with the idea of time to try to reckon with the place of our immediate forbears. This is a question . . . of a sense of the self based on a sense of relationships with others, as opposed to an attempt to imagine it as self-begotten. (Anderson, 32–33)

In his program of Man become God, Emerson was interested in

promoting a means "not of identifying oneself with the fathers, but of catching up all their powers into the self, asserting that there need be no more generations, no more history, but simply the swelling diapason of the expanding self" (Anderson, 58).

If Emerson's schema for the awakened Self seems to us hopelessly idealistic, if his plan for the perfection of man seems blind to the very real limitations that the external world imposes on all of us, still his dream should not strike us as unfamiliar. Twentieth-century psychology, particularly in Freud, has made us fairly conversant with some of Emerson's ideas, though it has couched them in a rather different and more clinical language. Freud begins his *Civilization and Its Discontents* with a consideration of the "oceanic feeling"—a feeling which by its description seems to have much in common with Emerson's "Saturnalia of Faith." What Freud describes is "a feeling of indissoluble bond, of being one with the external world as a whole,"[7] and he relates it specifically to the experience of the infant, who "does not as yet distinguish his ego from the external world."[8] "We are perfectly willing to acknowledge that the 'oceanic' feeling exists in many people, and we are inclined to trace it back to an early phase of ego-feeling. . . . The 'oneness with the universe' . . . sounds like a first attempt at religious consolation, as though it were another way of disclaiming the danger which the ego recognizes as threatening it from the external world."[9]

Freud's characterization of infancy as a state in which the world is felt to be an extension of the self has strong affinities with Emerson's thought. Indeed, Freud's "pleasure principle" and "reality principle," stripped of their more technical accoutrements and explications, may be said to be imaged in the polar formulations encountered so frequently in Emerson: Reason and Understanding, Vision and Form, Titan and bastard, youth and old age. Stephen Whicher's study is titled with two of the poles, Freedom and Fate, and it traces the manner in which Emerson moved from pleasure principle (Freedom) to reality principle

[7]Sigmund Freud, *Civilization and Its Discontents,* trans. and ed. James Strachey (New York: Norton, 1962), 12.

[8]Ibid., 13–14.

[9]Ibid., 19.

(Fate), and sought, finally, to accommodate the second without denying the first.

Freud's theories seem to be generally helpful in clarifying the impulses and directions of Emerson's thinking. For example, in calling the infant ego primarily narcissistic, Freud notes that "the development of the ego consists in a departure from primal narcissism and results in a vigorous attempt to recover it."[10] Norman O. Brown, in *Life Against Death* (an essentially romantic study of human psychology and one which seeks to revise Freud's theories at key points) notes that "the aim of Eros is union with the objects outside the self," and that the union is effected through psychological "incorporation" of the external. Quoting Freud, Brown points out that "the infant develops a pure pleasure-ego instead of a reality ego, a pure pleasure ego which absorbs into identity with itself the sources of its pleasure. . . . Hence 'the ego feeling we are aware of now [as adults] is thus only a shrunken vestige of a far more extensive feeling—a feeling which embraced the universe and expressed an inseparable connection of the human ego with the external world.'" "The ultimate aim of the ego," Brown goes on, "is to reinstate what Freud calls 'limitless narcissism' and find itself once more at one with the whole world in love and pleasure" (*Life,* 45–46).

For most of us in the latter half of the twentieth century, nurtured as we have been on a more cynical and more frugal vision of human nature, it is difficult to understand how Emerson could have envisioned a recovery of "primal narcissism" that would evidence instincts of generosity and morality. It is difficult for us to understand, that is, why he should have been puzzled at the ungentlemanly behavior of Napoleon. But our own assumptions concerning the pejorative and anarchic implications of selfishness were not shared by Emerson; on the contrary, selfishness grounded in Unity was, by definition, generous. "Culture, the height of culture, highest behaviour consist in the identification of the Ego with the universe," says Emerson, "so that when a

[10]Sigmund Freud, *Collected Papers,* ed. J. Riviere and J. Strachey, 5 vols., International Psycho-Analytical Library, no. 7–10, 37 (New York: International Press, 1924–50), IV, 57; quoted in Norman O. Brown, *Life Against Death* (Middletown: Wesleyan Univ. Press, 1959), 46.

man says I think, I hope, I find,—he might properly say, the human race thinks, hopes, & finds,—he states a fact which commands the understandings & affections of all the company . . ." (*JMN* XI 203). Or in Whitman:

> I celebrate myself, and sing myself,
> And what I assume you shall assume,
> For every atom belonging to me as good belongs
> to you.[11]

and

> There was a child went forth every day,
> And the first object he look'd upon, that object
> he became,
> And that object became part of him . . .[12]

Nor would such selfishness exclude the religious instincts. Emerson apparently was not much taken with Spinoza; he found the rigorous mathematical demonstrations of philosophical proofs distasteful.[13] Still, Spinoza's highest virtue was the "intellectual love of God," a virtue which Bertrand Russell defines as the "understanding of everything as [being] a part of god."[14] Norman O. Brown indicates how Spinoza's philosophy is grounded largely in a Freudian narcissism:

> The ultimate aim of the Freudian Eros—to affirm union with the world in pleasure—is substantially the same as Spinoza's formula for the ultimate aim of human desire—the intellectual love of god. God, in Spinoza's system, is the totality of Nature. . . . for Spinoza, the energy of the individual is essentially directed at self-maintenance, self-activity, self-perfection . . . which is also self-enjoyment. . . . Thus for Spinoza, as for Freud, the self-perfection (narcissism) of the human individual is fulfilled in union with the world in pleasure. . . . His allegiance to the pleasure principle brings him to recognize the narcissistic, self-enjoying character of human desire, and hence to recognize that human perfection consists in an expansion of

[11]*Leaves of Grass,* 28.
[12]Ibid., 364.

the self until it enjoys the world as it enjoys itself. (*Life,* 46–47)

For Emerson and Spinoza, if not for Freud or for us, the recovery of "primal narcissism" was rooted in God. Such narcissism is, of course, not troubled by perceptions of the difference between Self and Other. Subject and object merge into One, so that love of Self *is* love of Other, and all love of Other is first narcissistic. Brown pushes the implications of the narcissistic quality of love a bit further, and points out that in the classical myth "Narcissus needs a pool, a mirror, in which to see himself. And, in the mysticism of Boehme, the psychogenesis of Creation is God's need for self-reflection . . . and for a mirror . . . in which to see himself" (*Life,* 50). "In Plato's *Symposium,* after Eros has satisfied its own want by coming to possess the essence of Beauty, it passes on to a further stage . . . which Plato calls 'giving birth in beauty'—as if the satisfied Eros must overflow, out of its own abundance, into creativity. And in Luther, the perfect Agape of God is . . . a love overflowing into creativity. These images suggest that the self-activity and self-enjoyment of the narcissistic Eros must consist in an overflow outward into the world" (*Life,* 49).

The overflowing exuberance of narcissism is thus godlike in its ability to create the world around it. Nietzsche's Zarathustra can say, "I love him whose soul is overfull so that he forgets himself and all things are in him"; and "His word pronounced *selfishness* blessed, the wholesome healthy selfishness that wells from a powerful soul—from a powerful soul to which belongs the high body . . . around which everything becomes a mirror—the supple, persuasive body, the dancer whose parable and epitome is the self-enjoying soul."[15] Emerson, scarcely less moderate, can long for the day when man's "victorious thought comes up with and reduces all things, until the world becomes at last only a realized will,—the double of the man" (*CWE* I 40).

[13]Ralph L. Rusk, *The Life of Ralph Waldo Emerson* (New York: Scribner's, 1949), 308.

[14]Bertrand Russell, *A History of Western Philosophy* (New York: Simon & Schuster, 1945), 576.

[15]*The Portable Nietzsche,* ed. Walter Kaufman (New York: Viking, 1954), 128, 302; quoted in *Life,* 51.

IV

The linking in Emerson's philosophy of benevolence, generosity, and morality with what amounts to a recovery of "primal narcissism" is consistent in theory. It was the rock of practice on which his philosophy foundered. The theoretical solipsism which offers the thesis that "other persons and things are bits, phases, or projections"[16] of a benevolent Me/God renders the notion of conflict between Self and Other impossible—a logical absurdity. Only in a world where Self and Other were *not* linked, where the words were in fact pronouns with experientially different referents, could conflict arise. In that world, a generous solipsism would dissolve from an exuberant and joyful creativity into a mean self-seeking.

Emerson's reverse picture of Napoleon, his condemnation of Napoleon, emphasizes the man's "absorbing egotism" (*CWE* IV 257), his "powers of intellect without conscience" (*CWE* IV 257), his being "singularly destitute of generous sentiments" (*CWE* IV 253). What Emerson avoided was the statement of the obvious: that the world is so constituted as to make Self and Other experientially distinct, and that practical assumptions of power in such a world become, by definition, ungenerous, even dangerous, and far more liable to be destructive than creative. If in theory the Titan Napoleon commands the imaginations of the multitude, so that they see their better selves reflected in the energy of the hero, still there had to come a time for the cry "*Assez de Bonaparte*" (*CWE* IV 258).

What Emerson could not bring himself to admit in his reflections on Napoleon was that it was not the *man* who failed; it was the world. And after all, the conditions which caused the French to lose heart in Napoleon—the continuation of the struggle, the elusiveness of completion—may be read as something very similar to the campaigns of growth and dilation Emerson would have his own hearers embark upon: ". . . when men saw that after every victory was another war; after the destruction of armies, more conscriptions; and they who had toiled so desperately were never nearer to their reward—they could not spend what they

[16] C. D. Rollins, "Solipsism," *Encyclopedia of Philosophy* (New York: Macmillan, 1967).

had earned, nor repose on their down-beds, nor strut in their chateaux—they deserted him" (*CWE* IV 257).

Emerson labored to be what Matthiessen called him, "the practical American idealist,"[17] and the phrase in its form and content encapsulates the problem that came to haunt him. The practical world, to which Emerson remained committed, forever seemed to be nay-saying the idealism to which he was equally committed. The question for Emerson in the late 1830s and into the 1840s was how to reconcile the infinite possibilities he perceived for the individual with a practical world which pronounced "Finite!" with such conviction.

"I complain in my own experience," Emerson confides to his journal, "of the feeble influence of thought on life, a ray as pale & ineffectual as that of the sun in our cold & bleak spring. They seem to lie—the actual life, & the intellectual intervals, in parallel lines & never meet. . . . it takes a great deal of elevation of thought to produce a very little elevation of life" (*JMN* V 489). The next month Emerson comes close, perhaps, to a truth: "Why do we seek this lurking beauty in skies, in poems, in drawings? Ah because there we are safe, there we neither sicken nor die. I think we fly to Beauty as an asylum from the terrors of finite nature" (*JMN* VII 9).

But Emerson was not ready—would never be ready—to deny the reality of the infinitude of Man. Limitations—the past, the progression of time, the fastness of the physical world, age—these tempted his faith, but remained for him illusions, to be denied as insuperable impediments. "I seem to be a god dreaming, & when shall I awake & dissipate these fumes & phantoms?" (*JMN* VII 128).

More than twenty years later, in 1860, he was still asserting that the "fumes and phantoms" *would* dissipate, that "for an instant the air clears and the cloud lifts a little," leaving Man Thinking to see "the gods still sitting around him on their thrones—they alone with him alone" (*CWE* VI 325). But by that time the rigor and energy of his hope had diminished considerably. If in the 1830s experience had seemed to him deep and full of promise, in the 1840s and 1850s it began to seem more

[17]F. O. Matthiessen, *American Renaissance* (New York: Oxford Univ. Press, 1941), 27.

shallow, less fruitful. In the face of his denial, the world still continued to assert itself *as Other,* until finally he had to come to terms with it *as Other,* without losing faith in man's potential to master it. In "Experience" Emerson's tone changes from the exuberant, challenging oratory of the earlier essays to a more subdued and even somber inflection. "Where do we find ourselves?" he asks at the beginning, and then goes on to enumerate a bleak world of man dominated by temperament, by time, by surface, by chaos (*CWE* III 45). Certainly Emerson enunciates faith in the essay—but it is a faith in which the Titan individual has begun to be lost.

For one thing, the extremity is tempered. The emphasis is not so much on subduing the world as it is on living with the world. "Human life is made up of the two elements, power and form, and the proportion must be invariably kept if we would have it sweet and sound. Each of these elements in excess makes a mischief as hurtful as its defect" (*CWE* III 65). There is in life, he says, an ebb and flow, a sliding scale on which man rides, now approaching the First Cause, now the limitations of flesh. "I know that the world I converse with in the city and in the farms, is not the world *I think.* I observe the difference, and shall observe it. One day I shall know the value and law of this discrepance. But I have not found that much was gained by manipular attempts to realize the world of thought. . . . I say this . . . in reply to the inquiry, Why not realize your world?" (*CWE* III 84–85).

The Emerson who once chided Man with the notion that he was like a "banished king" trying to "buy his territories inch by inch, instead of vaulting at once into his throne," now becomes a more temperate Emerson, who counsels, "Patience and patience, we shall win at the last" (*CWE* III 85). The essay "Experience" ends on a note curiously tired, in which the faith is asserted clearly, but in which the conviction seems drained off as the prophet of possibility gropes for words and finds only a weak sentiment to start his oratorical rise: "Never mind the ridicule, never mind the defeat; up again, old heart!—it seems to say,—there is victory yet for all justice; and the true romance which the world exists to realize will be the transformation of genius into practical power" (*CWE* III 85–86).

The direction is slightly different. It is not the individual who exists to realize the transformation, but the world. Whicher points out that in the clash between experience and vision, Emerson salvaged his faith by hitching it to a rising star—the idea of evolution:

> Originally he could reconcile present limitation with potential divinity because he considered the first temporary; the future would bring the reconciliation. With time this expectation evaporated, and he was left with the unmitigated contradiction of fact and faith. This dilemma the notion of evolution alleviated. It restored to him the vision of a future reconciliation of his two worlds—now nothing so personal or immediate as his first hopes, but still a *pou sto* for his faith. (Whicher, 143)

If the individual cannot at once vault into his throne, still in the sweep of geologic time Nature works toward ideal ends. Man lies in the lap of a "sublime and friendly Destiny" (*CWE* I 371), a beneficent but "terrible communist" which reserves "all profits to the community, without dividend to individuals" (*CWE* I 373). If the individual is powerless, still the end of Nature is Man, as he will one day be. "I Am" was modified to "I Grow" (Whicher, 143), and in that modification Emerson was able to view with some equanimity the "yawning gulf . . . between the demand and supply of power" (*CWE* IV 183). In his later years Emerson settles more firmly into what Whicher calls "acquiescence"—an acceptance of the individual's limitations in a world where the fulfillment of the energy and promise of youth seemed so elusive, and where no man, himself included, quite measured up to the first and fine idea.

V

The first and fine idea, however, was emotionally charged, and it is *that* idea which constitutes Emerson's legacy. As Karl Keller puts it,

> . . . the Emerson myth that survived . . . is not the one of decline from freedom to fate which Stephen Whicher iden-

> tified but the heroically proportioned idealism. . . . The canonized Emerson is the one who attempted to provoke to self-love through exaggeration, hyperbole, and alarm. . . . Emerson criticism has by and large been timid about admitting . . . that on his own unique mythic level Emerson meant something close to an aggressive anarchism that is monstrously narcissistic and plainly subversive of communal ties. It is the unkindest cut that whereas in much of the critical writings about him, Emerson has been canonized as the ideal democrat, some of the best minds of his own time knew him for dangerous.[18]

In a critical response to Emerson's *Nature,* Francis Bowen wrote in the January 1837 issue of the *Christian Examiner* a passage which predicted the dilemma of Emerson and of those who, like Mark Twain, would embrace his dream. The reader of *Nature,* said Bowen,

> feels as in a disturbed dream, in which shows of surpassing beauty are around him, and he is conversant with disembodied spirits, yet all the time he is embarrassed by an uneasy sort of consciousness, that the whole combination of phenomena is fantastic and unreal. . . . They [the transcendentalists] are among men, but not of men. . . .we may at least request them to beware lest they strip truth of its relation to Humanity, and deprive it of its usefulness. Granted that we are imprisoned in matter, why beat against the bars in a fruitless attempt to escape, when a little labor might convert the prison to a palace, or at least render the confinement more endurable. The frame of mind which longs after the forbidden fruit of knowledge in subjects placed beyond the reach of human faculties, as it is surely indicative of a noble temperament, may also, under peculiar circumstances, conduce to the happiness of the individual. But if too much indulged, there is danger lest it waste its energies in mystic and unprofitable dreams, and

[18]Karl Keller, "Emerson and the Anti-Imperialist Self," in *Ralph Waldo Emerson: New Appraisals,* ed. Leonard Nick Neufeldt (Hartford: Transcendental Books, 1973), 90.

> despondency result from frequent failure, till at last, disappointment darkens into despair. . . .[19]

If Emerson managed to escape despair, he did so only by sacrificing his belief in the immediate transformation of bastard into Titan—he did so, that is, at the expense of his dream. But for others the "disturbed dream" survived, complete with its monstrous narcissism, its aggressive anarchism, and its emotional attraction. Mark Twain's imagination was charged with it at least as early as 1861, when in his *Gate City* correspondence he images a giant scooping up Carson City and dropping it casually in his pocket:

> I said we were situated on a flat, sandy desert. True. And surrounded on all sides by such prodigious mountains that when you stand at a distance from Carson and gaze at them awhile,—until, by mentally measuring them, and comparing them with things of smaller size, you begin to feel their vastness expanding your soul like a balloon, and ultimately find yourself growing, and swelling, and spreading into a colossus, and I say when this point is reached, you look disdainfully down upon the insignificant village of Carson, reposing like a cheap print away yonder at the foot of the big hills, and in that instant you are seized with a burning desire to stretch forth your hand, put the city in your pocket, and walk off with it.[20]

If one's first response to the passage is to see it in a response to "the sublime," still the attitude revealed in words like "disdainfully," and "insignificant village," and "cheap print" cuts across the grain of the usual piety associated with the sublime. The emphasis here is not on the insignificance of man in the face of a great Creator. And if feelings of admiration, reverence, and

[19]Miller, 174–76.

[20]Rogers, 24. See also Edward Wagenknecht, *Mark Twain: The Man and His Work* (Norman: Univ. of Oklahoma Press, 1961), 20. Wagenknecht also cites this passage in support of his argument that "In the face of the grander aspects of nature, Mark Twain was always inclined to be impressed by the pettiness and insignificance of man and his fevered, hectic doings." He thus attaches a significance to this passage quite opposed to my own.

respect are related (if inferior) effects of the sublime,[21] surely those submissive emotions are expunged in the grandiose feelings of superiority this narrator betrays. The passage is a playful piece, of course, but there are elements in it, too, that suggest such a giant to be capable of an appalling indifference to others. It is a suggestion with many echoes throughout Twain's work, and one which comes to a particularly dark fruition years later in *The Mysterious Stranger.*

By 1869 the power figure was firmly established in Twain's mind, and in three passages in *Innocents Abroad* he reveals an interest in and an attraction toward the figure that is strikingly similar to Emerson's own. In chapter thirty-seven, Twain records his experience in meeting Czar Alexander, the "Autocrat of all the Russias":

> A strange, new sensation is a rare thing in this humdrum life, and I had it here. There was nothing stale or worn out about the thoughts and feelings the situation and the circumstances created. It seemed strange—stranger than I can tell—to think that the central figure in the cluster of men and women, chatting here under the trees like the most ordinary individual in the land, was a man who could open his lips and ships would fly through the waves, locomotives would speed over the plains, couriers would hurry from village to village, a hundred telegraphs would flash the word to the four corners of an empire that stretches its vast proportions over a seventh part of the habitable globe, and a countless multitude of men would spring to do his bidding. I had a sort of vague desire to examine his hands and see if they were of flesh and blood, like other men's. Here was a man who could do this wonderful thing, and yet if I chose I could knock him down. The case was plain, but it seemed preposterous nevertheless—as preposterous as trying to knock down a mountain or wipe out a continent. If this man sprained his ankle, a million miles of telegraph would carry the news over the mountains—valleys—uninhabited deserts—under the trackless sea—and

[21]Samuel H. Monk, "The Sublime: Burke's *Inquiry,*" in *Romanticism and Consciousness,* ed. Harold Bloom (New York: Norton, 1970), 33.

> ten thousand newspapers would prate of it; if he were grievously ill, all the nations would know it before the sun rose again; if he dropped lifeless where he stood, his fall might shake the thrones of half a world! (*Writings* II 109–10)

Van Wyck Brooks in *The Ordeal of Mark Twain* notes that for Twain "Actual kings were . . . nothing less than an obsession: kings, empresses, princes, archduchesses—what a part they play in his biography! He is always dragging them in, into his stories, into his letters, writing about his dinners with them, and his calls upon them."[22] Here, the enthusiasm and hyperbole of the passage evidence a genuine fascination for the Czar's ability to "do this wonderful thing." The excitement arises from the strange juxtaposition of the mundane and the marvelous—in the fantastic idea that a man of so common an exterior could, like God in Genesis, speak, and with the Word change the world. It is as if Twain had taken a lesson from Emerson's words in "Self-Reliance":

> The world has been instructed by its kings, who have so magnetized the eyes of nations. It has been taught by this colossal symbol the mutual reverence that is due from man to man. The joyful loyalty with which men have everywhere suffered the king, the noble, or the great proprietor to walk among them by a law of his own, make his own scale of men and things and reverse theirs, pay for benefits not with money but with honor, and represent the law in his person, was the hieroglyphic by which they obscurely signified the consciousness of their own right and comeliness, the right of every man. (*CWE* II 63)

The second and third passages from *Innocents Abroad* have to do, appropriately, with Napoleon:

> Napoleon III, Emperor of France! Surrounded by shouting thousands, by military pomp, by the splendors of his capital city, and companioned by kings and princes—this is the man who was sneered at and reviled and called

[22]Van Wyck Brooks, *The Ordeal of Mark Twain* (New York: Dutton, 1920), 19.

> Bastard—yet who was dreaming of a crown and an empire all the while; who was driven into exile—but carried his dreams with him; who associated with the common herd in America and ran foot races for a wager—but still sat upon a throne in fancy. . . . found himself a prisoner, the butt of small wits, a mark for the pitiless ridicule of all the world—yet went on dreaming of coronations and splendid pageants as before; who lay a forgotten captive in the dungeons of Ham—and still schemed and planned and pondered over future glory and future power; President of France at last! a *coup d'etat,* and surrounded by applauding armies, welcomed by the thunders of cannon, he mounts a throne and waves before an astounded world the scepter of a mighty empire! Who talks of the marvels of fiction? Who speaks of the wonders of romance? Who prates of the tame achievements of Aladdin and the Magii of Arabia? (*Writings* I 120–21)

The usual pattern for the "Mark Twain" narrator of *Innocents Abroad* is to find a deflating reality subsequent to such bursts of enthusiasm, so that the reader may enjoy the continual and repeated exposure of the narrator's gullibility. But no such deflation occurs in regard to the exuberance expressed *vis à vis* Napoleon. The emphasis in this passage on Napoleon's dogged retention of the dream suggests that Twain is excited by the prospect that a dream seems to have found its tangible dress in reality. This excitement he will try later to recapture in *The Adventures of Tom Sawyer.* The repeated comparisons with fiction and romance and the wondrous tales of Aladdin echo Emerson's own conviction that the world exists to realize romance. The passage is in its attitude toward Napoleon similar to the first pages of Emerson's own ruminations on the earlier French emperor. And if Emerson at last came round to his reservations about him, so too does Twain. A few pages later in *Innocents Abroad* Twain tempers his exuberance: "I cannot feel friendly toward my quondam fellow American Napoleon III, especially at this time, when in fancy I see his credulous victim, Maximillian, lying stark and stiff in Mexico, and his maniac widow watching eagerly from her French asylum for the form that will never come—but I do admire his nerve, his calm self-reliance, his shrewd good sense" (*Writings* I 155).

The passages from *Innocents Abroad* on Napoleon III are almost mirror reflections of Emerson's own dilemma in regard to Napoleon I: an exuberant admiration of power, coupled uneasily with a halting dismay at the cruelty such power produced. It was a dilemma which would continue to plague Twain for the rest of his career. Like Emerson, Twain was never quite willing to abandon the idea that man could exercise his energies in such a way as to become a Titan. Like Emerson, he was reluctant to believe that a person who succeeded in becoming a Titan would perforce pursue his solipsistic self-love at the expense of others. Like Emerson, he had difficulty in clearly imagining such a figure at large in a world where the "bars of matter" seemed so unbending (and it was just such a world he was increasingly committed to portraying in his work).[23] But unlike Emerson, Twain could not avoid facing, if only gradually, the impossibility of the whole business. And Bowen's warning to Emerson's contemporaries might well have been written for Twain himself, that "despondency [may] result from frequent failure, till at last, disappointment darkens into despair."

[23]The comic strategy of exposing the foolishness of a gullible narrator's romantic dreams necessitates a conflict between the world as the narrator perceives it and the world as it (supposedly) really exists. James Cox explores this strategy in detail in *The Fate of Humor.* Implicit in my argument is the assertion that Twain retained an emotional commitment to the very sort of romantic unrealities his comic strategy led him to ridicule.

II

The Adventures of Tom Sawyer

The soul is not twin-born but the only begotten, and though revealing itself as a child in time, child in appearance, is of a fatal and universal power, admitting no co-life.

—Emerson, "Experience"

I

Sometime in 1897, while he was in Switzerland, Twain rummaged his memory for details of his boyhood home. His jottings, to which he gave the title "Villagers of 1840-3," record details of the lives of Hannibal residents, and Walter Blair's research has verified most of the biographical information Twain set down. While Twain changed some of the villagers' names, and while some of the events are to a greater or lesser degree invented, Blair cites the fragment as evidence of Twain's "enduring power of recall" (*MT's Hannibal,* 24).[1] The curious thing about the fragment, however, is not so much Twain's accuracy, but the contradiction it evidences between the details he remembered and the generalizations he came to—or felt impelled to include— about Hannibal and its populace.

The fragment in its manuscript form covers some thirty-four pages (a dozen in its published form), and in that space are recorded nearly twenty instances of prostitution and illicit sex, unnatural deaths (including murder and suspected murder),

[1]Bernard DeVoto also briefly discusses the "Villagers" fragment in *Mark Twain at Work,* 15–16, as does Albert Stone in *The Innocent Eye: Childhood in Mark Twain's Imagination* (New Haven: Yale Univ. Press, 1961), 74, both in relation to Twain's prudishness.

brutal assaults, and grotesque cases of physical affliction and mental derangement. Of the Ratcliffe family, for example, Twain notes that one son

> had to be locked into a small house in corner of the yard—and chained. Fed through a hole. Would not wear clothes, winter or summer. Could not have a fire. Religious mania. Believed his left hand had committed a mortal sin and must be sacrificed. Got hold of a hatchet, nobody knows how, and chopped it off. Escaped and chased his mother all over the house with a carving knife. (*MT's Hannibal,* 37–38)

Of Sam Bowen, one of Twain's childhood friends, this entry:

> Pilot. Slept with the rich baker's daughter, telling the adoptive parents they were married. The baker died and left all his wealth to "Mr. and Mrs. S. Bowen." They rushed off to a Carondolet magistrate, got married, and bribed him to antedate the marriage. Heirs from Germany proved the fraud and took the wealth. Sam no account and a pauper. Neglected his wife; she took up with another man. Sam a drinker. Dropped pretty low. Died of yellow fever and whiskey. . . . (*MT's Hannibal,* 32)

The Blankenship daughters were charged with prostitution; a "Hanged Nigger" confessed to the rape and murder of a girl of thirteen, and to the rape of "many . . . white married women who kept it quiet partly from fear of him and partly to escape the scandal"; Ed and Dick Hyde were "tough and dissipated. Ed. held his uncle down while Dick tried to kill him with a pistol which refused fire" (*MT's Hannibal,* 31, 369).

And so on. The details accumulate to portray a village with more than its share of depravity, dissipation, and brutality. But in the midst of these reminiscences, Twain could describe quite another village, one in which purity and prudence were watchwords:

> *Chastity:* There was the utmost liberty among young people—but no young girl was ever insulted, or seduced, or even scandalously gossiped about. Such things were not

> even dreamed of in that society, much less spoken of and referred to as possibilities.
>
> Two or three times, in the lapse of years, married women were whispered about, but never an unmarried one. (*MT's Hannibal,* 35)

And, apparently ignoring his own entry on Sam Bowen, Twain contrasts the crassness of the nineties with the more spiritual Hannibal of his youth, where among the young folk

> To get rich was no one's ambition—it was not in any young person's thoughts. The heroes of these young people—even the pirates—were moved by lofty impulses: they waded in blood . . . to rescue the helpless, not to make money; they spent their blood and made their self-sacrifices for "Honor's" sake, not to capture a giant fortune; they married for love, not for money or position. It was an intensely sentimental age, but it took no sordid form. (*MT's Hannibal,* 35)

"Villagers of 1840-3" was not written for publication. While the bulk of it reflects fact, it is still a combination of accurate memories and working notes for possible stories (*MT's Hannibal,* 26). There was no need for consistency in what Twain set down, but neither was there any need to distort the picture of Hannibal (referred to in the piece as "St P") into something that never was. Exactly why he did so is probably not ascertainable, but the wild contrast bespeaks a conflict in Twain that appears in most of his major works: a commitment to portraying both a gentle and innocently idyllic world that is patently subjective and imagined, and a world of grotesque harshness that, if not more "real," is at least reflective of a very different order of experience, one much more consonant with actuality. It is this conflict that Richard Chase has in mind when he describes Twain's fictional province as "not the novel proper, but the borderland between novel and romance."[2] It is a conflict between experience as we would wish it to be, and experience as we wish it were not, and Twain was never very successful at drawing a clear distinction

[2]Richard Chase, *The American Novel and Its Tradition* (Garden City, N.Y.: Doubleday, 1957), 156.

between the two—not in his fiction, and to some degree, not in his own thinking. When he took pen in hand, Twain was often given to portraying both worlds. Like a metal rod suspended between two magnets, his imagination swayed now in one direction, now in the other. In somewhat the same way as Emerson with his "parallel lines that never meet," he was plagued with the problem of doing justice to both.

In trying to keep the two orders of experience properly balanced, Twain associated them with two stages of life. In the "Villagers" fragment, one notices that while the brutalities are ascribed to adults, the idyllic generalizations pertain to children. There are only two passing references in the fragment that ascribe unsavory activities to the children of Hannibal. In one, Twain's childhood sweetheart, Laura Hawkins, "fell out of her chair and Jenny [Brady] made that vicious remark." (The remark itself is not recorded.) In another, one Roberta Jones "scared old Miss - - - - - into the insane asylum with a skull and a doughface" (*MT's Hannibal,* 30, 32). If the "vicious remark" was intentional, the scare trick was performed in fun, and its tragic results were not anticipated. Roberta Jones precipitated tragedy, but she is not held morally accountable.

In the light of the later "Villagers" fragment it is somewhat surprising to see Twain calling Hannibal "this tranquil refuge of my childhood" in *Life on the Mississippi* (*Writings* IX 429). But clearly he was much given to seeing childhood as a "refuge" from the darker problems he associated with adulthood, and in some moods he could very nearly convince himself, or part of himself, that the idyllic world of childhood he imagined was more "real" than—and certainly preferable to—the adult world he actually inhabited. In his account of visiting Hannibal in *Life on the Mississippi,* he tells of climbing Holliday's Hill to get a "comprehensive view" of the village. With the village spread below him, he sees "the town as it was, not as it is": "The things about me and before me made me feel like a boy again—convinced me that I was a boy again, and that I had simply been dreaming an unusually long dream . . ." (*Writings* IX 428-29). The wistful entry into a Hannibal Arcadia is described in metaphors of life and death, freedom and captivity: "I stepped ashore with the feeling of one returned out of a dead-and-gone generation. I had a sort of realizing sense of what the Bastille prisoners must have felt when they used to come out and look upon Paris after years of captivity" (*Writings* IX 428).

The association of childhood with freedom, innocence, and life, and of adulthood with imprisonment, corruption, and death, were to become implicit considerations in Twain's thinking and works. In his mind adulthood carried unacceptable burdens and limitations. The adult was both a victim of and usually a spokesman for a society whose standards were hypocritical and whose workings were base, destructive, and cruel. Most of Twain's satiric bent was to be devoted to exposing the falsity and brutality of a society operated by adults.

The child, however, lived for Twain in what Kenneth Lynn describes as a "magic circle,"[3] a charmed world in which adult hypocrisy and cruelty were largely foreign elements. The child, to Twain's mind, was untainted by base motives of personal gain at the expense of others; he acted spontaneously rather than by craft or guile; he was by nature benevolent; and—a point in which Twain look a special delight—his imagination was incredibly fertile, active, and unfettered. As yet unassimilated into a structured community, the child had no fixed social identity. He was free to adopt any "self" he cared to imagine.

This last characteristic of the child might have remained for Twain no more than a fanciful delight with which to adorn stories for boys and girls. In *The Adventures of Tom Sawyer,* in fact, the narrator's tone is often that of a condescending but indulgent adult chuckling over the extravagant imaginings of a little boy.[4] But it became for Twain, even in *Tom Sawyer,* something more important. It touched on that notion that some part of Twain was willing to take more seriously—the notion that the imagination might be potent enough to clothe itself in reality, that dreams, as with Napoleon, might one day sire a very tangible throne. The charmed circle of the child's world, then, accrued another dimension: the child was not only free and naturally benevolent and

[3]Kenneth Lynn, *Mark Twain and Southwestern Humor* (Westport, Conn.: Greenwood Press, 1960), 187.

[4]James Cox makes a similar point in *The Fate of Humor,* 136, when he says that Tom's play is a "drama [in] which the juvenile reader can believe and the adult reader can indulge with a mixture of nostalgia and gentle irony."

innocent; he was also able to touch the real world with his innocent imagination, and to transform it from something resistant and base to something pliable and enjoyable. Unlike the adult, who had to accommodate himself to a world fixed in its outlines and circumstances, it was the child's privilege to arrange the world to satisfy himself.

The distinction Twain made between the worlds of children and adults might well remind one of Emerson's assertion that "old age seems the only disease. . . . fever, intemperance, insanity, stupidity and crime; they are all forms of old age" (*CWE* II 319). Twain could go ashore at Hannibal and be "convinced . . . that I was a boy again." For a moment it was an escape from time, a Lazarus-like rise from the dead, and he could half believe in that moment that the pressures and disillusionments of his own adulthood could fall away, or at least be reduced from the status of "reality" to that of "dream."

Twain was a complicated man, of course, and any description of his thinking is likely to fall prey to oversimplification. Yet it is necessary to make this claim, at least: so great was his dissatisfaction with the real world that he found it almost *necessary* to give credence to the charmed world of children. This is not to say that he was incapable of distinguishing the real from the imagined. In 1876 he could write to Will Bowen, his best boyhood friend and brother of Sam Bowen, telling him to stop dwelling on the sentimental never-never land of childhood, and denying that the past held anything "worth pickling for present or future use."[5] Nevertheless, both his fiction and his biography testify to a commitment to the charmed circle which was more emotional than logical, and which was largely removed from the clearer sight of a more common, if more prosaic, sense.

He remained fascinated throughout his career with children as subjects for his work, and toward the end of his life, his emotional commitment to them rose to the surface of his actual life. In 1908 he organized a coterie of young admirers, all of them girls, into an "Aquarium Club." The members he referred to as his "angel fish":

[5]Quoted by Dixon Wecter in "Mark Twain," in *The Literary History of the United States,* ed. Robert E. Spiller, et al., 3 vols., 4th rev. ed. (New York: Macmillan, 1953), 929.

> Clemens transcribed their names into his notebook—Dorothy Butes, Dorothy Quick, Dorothy Harvey, Dorothy Sturgin, Hellen Martin, Helen Allen, Irene Gerken, Margaret Blackmer, Louise Paine, Frances Nunnally, Jean Spurr, and Marjorie Breckenridge—careful to note the girls' ages, eleven and a half to seventeen years, averaging thirteen years. They visited him in a steady stream throughout 1908, but less frequently than his letters implored them to.
>
> . . . Of all the letters Clemens is now known to have written in 1908, ninety-four were to Members of the Aquarium—almost half the total correspondence. Almost always they were long, chatty, childlike letters, frequently composed over a number of days. All pleaded for visits. . . . It seems inescapably true that Clemens was immersing himself in a milieu of small girls who were preferable to the adults who surrounded him. . . . he was diverting himself with contrived nostalgia. . . . (*God's Fool,* 195–96)

And to one Gertrude Natkin he wrote, "Don't get any older—I can't have it. Stay always just as you are—youth is the golden time" (*God's Fool,* 127). "It was apparently a more real demand than it might seem," says Hamlin Hill, "for when Gertrude turned sixteen in early April, Twain was strangely unhappy":

> So you are 16 today, you dear little rascal! Oh come, this won't do—you musn't move along so fast, at this rate you will soon be a young lady and next you will be getting married. . . .
>
> *Sixteen!* Ah what has become of my little girl? I am almost afraid to send a blot [a kiss], but I venture it. Bless your heart, it comes within an ace of being improper! Now, back you go to 14!—then there's no impropriety. (*God's Fool,* 127)

The aging Twain's devotion to his "angel fish" obviously carries darker and sadder implications, but for the present it is enough to note that his attachment to the child world he imagined was to be long lasting, and that it was more than just material for his craft.

Twain's emotional commitment to the charmed circle of

childhood is important. If the adult world was not worth believing in, surely the charmed world was worthy of allegiance. His belief in it was in a way a kind of stopgap to despair; it was a much happier, much kinder, much more satisfactory world. Nevertheless, his devotion to it was destined to become adulterated as he began to paint it in words. For if he was committed to the innocent world of children, he was also, as a novelist, committed to the truth of what it was to be a human being. And as he wrote, he was to discover two problems that tended to undercut his faith in the charmed circle. The first was the fact that, in real life, children inevitably grow up. The same Sam Bowen who once cavorted on Holliday's Hill eventually slept with the rich baker's daughter, perpetrated fraud, and died of yellow fever and whiskey. Experience seemed to lead in one direction: not out of the Bastille and back to Hannibal, but the other way about, from Hannibal to the Bastille, from freedom to limitation, from potential to disability.

This was a portion of experience that Twain could not accept gracefully, and he had real difficulty portraying it in his fiction. "We grizzle every day," Emerson says in "Circles"; "I see no need of it." For Twain "need" did not seem to be the question; it was sad enough that it happened. Though he told Howells that he wanted to write a story in which a boy would be carried to adulthood,[6] he could never successfully accomplish it. When it came to the point, something in his deepest imagination rebelled.

The second problem that confronted Twain was more serious, and it, too, was first confronted by Emerson. For Emerson, the empowered Self was by definition benevolent; he acted for the good of mankind. Lesser men, those not yet awakened, saw in the Titan their own potential and better selves. But with Napoleon, something was wrong—a lack of grace at the core. As Whicher says, "There was a high-level conflict between insight and holiness; they ought to be unanimous, but experience did not find them so" (Whicher, 135). The Titan at large in the world proved to be something quite different, and much less honorable, than

[6]Frederick Anderson, William M. Gibson, Henry Nash Smith, eds., *Selected Mark Twain-Howells Letters, 1872–1910* (Cambridge: Belknap Press of Harvard Univ. Press, 1967), 49.

Emerson had theorized. So too with Twain. It was all very well for him to contemplate the purity of the empowered child in generalizations. But writing novels required that the generalizations be filled out with details, that the hero become engaged with others, that he respond to the world as well as provoke responses in others. Above all, the hero had to act in a world that the reader could recognize as one roughly equivalent to his own. As Twain placed his empowered figure in such a world, he began to see something troublesome: a mean and destructive egoism that was not at all consonant with what he thought he remembered about children.

Kenneth Lynn sees Twain's early travel books as showing "a lonely American backtrailing in time toward that magic circle" of Hannibal and the child world. "In *The Adventures of Tom Sawyer,* the long voyage is over; Twain's persona is now a boy in Paradise."[7] The world of *Tom Sawyer* is in many ways a Paradise, but only because Twain went to considerable lengths to keep it so, by exorcising from it anything that smacked too strongly of a real world. As for the long voyage to Paradise, with *Tom Sawyer* it had really just begun.

II

The Adventures of Tom Sawyer is not an initiation story, though several critics have argued that it is—that Tom progresses from boyhood pranks to adult responsibility, from a rebellion against St. Petersburg society to an acceptance of it.[8] Walter Blair suggests that "as the story progresses, wholly boylike actions become more infrequent while adult actions increase," although "no such simple and melodramatic device as a complete reformation is employed." He cites as "adult actions" Tom's decision to take Becky's punishment at the hands of the schoolmaster, his

[7]Lynn, 187.

[8]See, in addition to those here quoted, Albert Stone, *The Innocent Eye,* 79; William C. Spengemann, *Mark Twain and the Backwoods Angel* (n.p.: Kent State Univ. Press, 1966), 45; Henry Nash Smith, *The Development of a Writer,* 82; and Louis D. Rubin, Jr., "Mark Twain: *The Adventure of Tom Sawyer,*" in Hennig Cohen, ed., *Landmarks of American Writing* (New York: Basic Books, 1969), 165.

testimony for Muff Potter, his concern for Aunt Polly's distress over his presumed death, and his insistence at the end of the novel that Huck become "respectable."[9]

A similar and somewhat stronger argument is Hamlin Hill's, which stresses a manuscript note by Twain that shows an intention to take Tom from boyhood to early manhood, and then through "the Battle of Life in many lands." Tom, according to the note, was to return to St. Petersburg in middle age and "meet grown babies & toothless old drivelers who were the grandees of his boyhood. The Adored Unknown a [illegible] faded old maid and full of rasping, puritanical vinegar piety." Hill notes that Twain eventually decided not to have Tom leave St. Petersburg, but that he deliberately arranged and regrouped "critical situations toward the end of the book where maturer judgment and courage were vital," and he argues that this regrouping reveals Twain's "deliberate intention of showing Tom's maturation."[10]

A distinction must be made, however, between Twain's "deliberate intentions" and his actual practice. Twain wrote the book in fits and starts, shaping episodes and scenes as he recollected experience from his own boyhood, and drawing on various of his previous writings. He interrupted the book in September 1874, saying he had "pumped myself dry," and did not return to it until the early months of 1875 (*MT&HF,* 50-70, *passim*). During the interruption he worked on some *Old Times in the Mississippi* sketches for publication in the *Atlantic.* Twain's characteristic method of writing was to improvise and allow a story to shape itself. Initial intentions were never very binding on him; he was by and large incapable of tight plotting.

This accounts in part for Blair's qualification that "no such simple and melodramatic device as a complete reformation is employed" to show Tom's maturation. While Blair's phrase implies that Twain was a conscious and deliberate craftsman, meticulously evading a complete initiation to avoid simplicities, the truth of the matter is that the attempt to make Tom move toward maturity was largely an afterthought. The book was

[9]Walter Blair, "On the Structure of *Tom Sawyer,*" *Modern Philology* 37 (1939), 75–88.

[10]Hamlin Hill, "The Composition and the Structure of *Tom Sawyer,*" *AL* 32 (1961), 391.

molded, after its episodes were substantially complete, in order to fit an idea foreign to the spirit of the tale. If Twain initially wanted a book showing a boy moving to adulthood, what he wrote was something else, and the later attempt to make the book conform to an earlier idea only served to confuse things.

The disparity between intention and practice contributed to Twain's uncertainty over the novel's intended audience. In July of 1875 he told Howells it was "*not* a boy's book, at all. It will be only read by adults. It is only written for adults." But by the following November, he was ready to take Howells' own view of the matter, and to issue the novel as "a book for boys, pure and simple. . . . It is surely the correct idea."[11] Finally, in the Preface to the novel, written in 1876, he tries to have it both ways: "Although my book is intended mainly for the entertainment of boys and girls, I hope it will not be shunned by men and women on that account, for part of my plan has been to try to pleasantly remind adults of what they once were themselves."

The source of Twain's confusion lies in his dual commitment to idyl and to truth. The spirit of the novel is what DeVoto has termed it: the novel is "a pastoral poem, an idyll of America." In it "time curves back on itself and boyhood is something more than realism, it is a distillation, a generalization, a myth."[12] The world of St. Petersburg exists in a haze, a gratifying mist through which harsh details are almost systematically filtered out: "Saturday morning was come, and all the summer world was bright and fresh, and brimming with life. There was a song in every heart; and if the heart was young the music issued at the lips. There was a cheer in every face and a spring in every step" (*WMT* IV 46). Such passages occur with enough frequency in the book, especially in the earlier sections, to color the reader's reaction to the whole. They set a mood of softness and innocence that is never wholly gainsaid.[13]

[11]*Selected Mark Twain-Howells Letters, 1872-1910,* 48, 62.

[12]Bernard DeVoto, *Mark Twain at Work* (Cambridge: Harvard Univ. Press, 1942), 19.

[13]James Cox in *The Fate of Humor,* 133, notes that such writing has the effect of "screening out the impact of unpleasurable impulses." Judith Fetterly also notes that "the tone of the novel is essentially genial" in her article, "The Sanctioned Rebel," *Studies in the Novel* 3 (1971), 302.

Simply put, St. Petersburg is not a world in which children are easily turned into adults, for such a change requires that the child meet a real world and adjust himself, painfully but with more or less success, to its undesirable circumstances. Much of the idyllic quality of St. Petersburg is attributable to the fact that Twain has excluded from the novel a world in which experience produces consequential changes in character. Tom's world is one in which "adventure" replaces "experience"; his encounters with the alcoholic Muff Potter, the grave-robbing Dr. Robinson, the vengeful Injun Joe—encounters which should ordinarily produce some difference in his perception of the world—leave his character essentially untouched.[14] The extent to which Twain was committed to excluding such changes may be surmised by recalling that, in the *Old Times* sketch published in January 1875, the cub pilot learns that successful steamboating requires tremendous effort. The lesson comes at the expense of his childish illusions:

> Here was something fresh—this thing of getting up in the middle of the night to go to work. It was a detail in piloting that had never occurred to me at all. I knew that boats ran all night, but somehow I had never happened to reflect that somebody had to get up out of a warm bed to run them. I began to fear that piloting was not quite so romantic as I had imagined it was; there was something very real and worklike about this new phase of it. (*Writings* IX 47)

For the cub, an irrevocable change of character takes place, and by the time he finishes his apprenticeship and masters his profession,

> I had made a valuable acquisition. But I had lost something, too. I had lost something which could never be

[14]Virginia Wexman argues that the "dark world of violence" is subsumed in a comic pattern because "dark" events are preceded by similar "play" events. Thus, for example, the murder of Dr. Robinson is softened for the reader by the preceding Robin Hood game, in which Tom "murders" Joe Harper. Her citation of similarities between these two scenes lends weight to my own argument at the end of this chapter regarding the relationship between Tom and Injun Joe. See Virginia Wexman, "The Role of Structure in *Tom Sawyer* and *Huckleberry Finn*," *American Literary Realism* 6 (Winter 1973), 1–11.

> restored while I lived. All the grace, the beauty, the poetry, had gone out of the majestic river. . . . a day came when I began to cease from noting the glories and the charms which the moon and the sun and the twilight wrought upon the river's face; another day came when I ceased altogether to note them. Then, if that sunset scene had been repeated, I should have looked upon it without rapture. . . . Since those days, I have pitied doctors from my heart. What does the lovely flush in a beauty's cheek mean to a doctor but a "break" that ripples above some deadly disease? Are not all her visible charms sown thick with what are to him the signs and symbols of hidden decay? Does he ever see her beauty at all, or doesn't he simply view her professionally, and comment upon her unwholesome condition all to himself? (*Writings* IX 78, 80)

Twain's emphasis on the cub's growth to a sad maturity could hardly be more explicit. What was for the cub to be a kind of static existence in which piloting would be a perpetual source of pleasure and play, becomes instead a profession burdened with responsibility and work, and the change produces inevitable shifts in his personality. By contrast, Tom Sawyer is spared such dreary contacts with reality, such glimpses of the death's head beyond youth. Twain allows him to escape the drudgery of white-washing Aunt Polly's fence, and to increase his wealth into the bargain. "If he had been a great and wise philosopher, like the writer of this book," Twain comments, "he would now have comprehended that Work consists of whatever a body is *obliged* to do and that Play consists of whatever a body is not obliged to do." There is very little in the novel that Tom is finally obliged to do, or to become. "Tom said to himself that it was not such a hollow world, after all" (*WMT* IV 50).

Just as Tom escapes the real world of work, of change through experience, so too do the rest of the villagers. The trial of Muff Potter is not so much a serious undertaking to determine a man's guilt or innocence, but an "event" which serves to entertain the community and break the tedium of its life. The real world is distorted by the populace, as Muff, who "hain't ever done anything to hurt anybody," is transformed by them into some creature of melodrama, "the bloodiest-looking villain in this country" (*WMT* IV 168). Cheated of a fine hanging when Muff goes free, the town is to some degree reimbursed by later having Injun Joe's grave to visit—again as entertainment: ". . . they brought their children, and all sorts of provisions, and confessed that they had had almost as satisfactory a time at the funeral as they could have had at the hanging" (*WMT* IV 221). Even the grief of the villagers at the presumed deaths of Huck, Tom, and Joe Harper has a quality of unreality about it. It is a grief as much indulged in as truly felt, and the quality of self-indulgence prevents the reader from taking it too seriously.[15]

Judith Fetterly has argued convincingly that the adults of the village are in many ways as childish as the young people. Citing their proclivity to "show off" for each other at the Sunday School gathering in chapter three, she notes that if the adults "are in any way different from the children, the difference does not make them more positive than the children but more negative. The children admit, after all, that they are showing off to gain attention but the adults have to pretend they are doing something else. The children are honest; the adults are hypocrites." She comes to the core of the initiation question when she concludes: ". . . it hardly makes sense to assume they [the adults] provide the yardstick which charts a growth from something negative to something positive."[16]

In *Tom Sawyer* Twain consistently by-passes the real world of work, of growing up. The novel was written in the spirit of nostalgia; it springs primarily from that part of Twain that sentimentalized and idealized childhood. It became to some extent an exercise in wish-fulfillment, the creation of a world he wanted rather than a world that was. Freud describes the sort of attitude that seems to have been operative here. It is an attitude that

> regards reality as the sole enemy and as the source of all suffering, with which it is impossible to live, so that one must break off all relations with it if one is to be in any way happy. The hermit turns his back on the world and will

[15]Both Cox and Fetterly make similar observations in *The Fate of Humor* (139) and "The Sanctioned Rebel" (298).

[16]Fetterly, "The Sanctioned Rebel," 300–1.

> have no truck with it. But one can do more than that; one can try to recreate the world, to build up in its stead another world in which its most unbearable features are eliminated and replaced by others that are in conformity with one's own wishes.[17]

Twain shares with his hero this desire to create a world more amenable to one's own desires; author and character are reflections, to a degree, of each other. Tom, for example, has an almost compulsive desire to be the center of attention—all eyes must focus on him if he is to be satisfied. The only portion of the Sunday sermon that holds any interest for him is the minister's

> grand and moving picture of the assembling together of the world's hosts at the millennium when the lion and the lamb should lie down together and a little child should lead them. But the pathos, the lesson, the moral of the great spectacle were lost upon the boy; he only thought of the conspicuousness of the principal character before the on-looking nations, his face lit with the thought, and he said to himself that he wished he could be that child, if it was a tame lion. (*WMT* IV 68)

Twain, famous for his attention-getting antics, is in this respect Tom's alter-ego. He had, as Howells remarked, "the love of strong effect, which he was apt to indulge through life."[18] His ostentatious seal-skin coat, the white suit of his later years, and his parade down Dover Street in London wearing a "three-piece costume of one bathrobe and two slippers" (*God's Fool,* 175)—all of it was calculated to attract the eyes of the crowd.

The other characteristic of Tom that points back to his creator is his ability to "re-create the world, to build up in its stead another world" with features more consonant with his own wishes.[19] Just as Twain creates an idyllic world in his novel, a

[17]*Civilization and Its Discontents,* 28.

[18]William Dean Howells, *My Mark Twain: Reminiscences and Criticisms,* ed. Marilyn Austin Baldwin (Baton Rouge: Louisiana State Univ. Press, 1967), 6.

[19]Louis Rubin postulates that Tom would become a novelist were he to grow up, and one "capable of writing *Tom Sawyer.*" See his "Mark Twain: *The Adventures of Tom Sawyer*" in *Landmarks of American Writing,* 169.

world in which a harsh and limiting reality is softened and avoided, so too does Tom create *his* own world, one much more satisfying to his own desires. If there is a difference between Tom and Twain here, it lies in the fact that Twain could create such a world only in *Tom Sawyer,* in words on a page; Tom, however, manages to do the job in deed, at least in St. Petersburg.

Judith Fetterly has pointed out that St. Petersburg's arch enemy is "the boredom which lies at its heart,"[20] and that it is Tom's role in the novel to relieve that boredom with his gifted flair for the dramatic. The dullness and monotony of the church and school, St. Petersburg's representative institutions, drive Tom into a more exciting and adventurous world, that of his own imagination. Away from the classroom, Tom can be a military general, a Robin Hood, a Black Avenger—anything but a bored pupil reciting for a bored schoolmaster. In the early parts of the novel, the narrative tone is often condescending toward Tom's imaginative flights. His self-pitying visions of his own death in chapter three, for example, suffer rudely when a maidservant inadvertently douses him with cold water. Similarly, the stilted dialogue between Tom and Joe Harper as they play at Robin Hood in chapter eight is occasion for a mild burlesque of the romantic novel and the patronization of a child's play.

But in the context of the novel as a whole, these imaginative fancies take on more seriousness, for nearly everything that Tom imagines comes eventually to pass, not as "pretend" games, but as part of the world to which others must react. His fantasies overflow, as it were, from his mind, and spill into the world, there to take on flesh. The "pretend" world of Tom's mind and the real world of activity begin to blend; the distinctions between the real and the conjured begin to break down. Emerson's parallel lines begin to meet.

In chapter six, to take a minor but significant example, Tom searches for some ailment that will deliver him from the trials of attending school. He decides to pretend that his toe is "mortified." As he moves into his act, he "fancied that he began to feel pain in the toe." And soon, with a concerned and frightened Sid and Aunt Polly at his bedside, "Tom was suffering in reality now,

[20]Fetterly, "The Sanctioned Rebel," 293.

so handsomely was his imagination working, and so his groans had gathered quite a genuine tone." Eventually Aunt Polly dismisses the ailment, and "The groans ceased and the pain vanished" (*WMT* IV 72–73).

The episode is a minor one, another example of the endearing antics of the lovable Bad Boy. But the suggestion that Tom's imagination can produce real pain points toward more central episodes, wherein Tom's fantasies issue in real occurrences. The list is fairly extensive. In chapter three Tom imagines himself to be the general of a great army; in chapter thirty-five Judge Thatcher announces his intention "to look to it that Tom should be admitted to the national military academy," for he "hoped to see Tom . . . a great soldier some day" (*WMT* IV 233).

In chapters three and eight Tom indulges in fantasies of his own death and of the mourning that event would occasion. The fantasy is realized in chapters fifteen and seventeen, when Tom is allowed to listen to Aunt Polly's remorse over his presumed drowning, and then to attend his own funeral. Tom's treasure hunt with Huck in chapter twenty-five begins as make-believe typical of child's amusement, but it too becomes real in chapter twenty-six when Injun Joe discovers, with Tom's own tools and in the very place Tom had suggested looking, a buried box of gold.

What Tom wants, Tom gets. His Robin Hood impersonations take on the authenticity of fact, for like Robin Hood Tom is an "outlaw" (the Bad Boy of convention), but beloved nevertheless by the people. He dreams of robber gangs and murderous adventures, and Injun Joe appears, complete with a bloodied knife and at least one murder to his credit. Like the little child leading the hosts, Tom leads St. Petersburg from its stultifying monotony into one theatrical dramatization after another, and all of it real. And those who follow after him—the people of St. Petersburg who form parades in his honor and who themselves set out looking for buried treasure—are grateful to him. Perhaps it is pretentious to equate the scamp Tom with something so grand and so dignified as Emerson's Titan, but the parallels between the two hold with some consistency. In Tom, the self and the world do not stand opposed; the world offers no opposition to the realization of romance. Tom's capacious ego, his desire to be the focus of attention, and his desire to build a world more suitable to his imagination, are continually gratified. His fantasies issue in an objective reality to which others must attend, and they attend to it joyfully. "Infancy conforms to nobody," Emerson had put it; "all conform to it" (*CWE* II 48). "When a man says I think, I hope, I find,—he might properly say, the human race thinks, hopes, & finds,—he states a fact which commands the understandings and affections of all the company" (*JMN* XI 203). The boredom which characterizes the adult world of St. Petersburg is the "sole enemy and the source of all suffering, with which it is impossible to live." And Tom's answer to it is to do as Emerson urged; he treats the huge globe as his toy and "conforms things to his thoughts" (*CWE* I 52). Dissatisfied with the world as he finds it, he builds his own world, makes his own circumstances, and watches, without a flicker of surprise, as the world "becomes at last only a realized will" (*CWE* I 40), a reflection of his own consciousness.

The absence of a world of work becomes indicative of Twain's desire to remove those factors in the novel that might teach Tom his limits—that might bring him to a serious recognition that the world is not an extension of himself, but exists outside and without reference to his own ego. In chapter four, for example, Tom trades his boy's wealth for Bible tickets, thus fraudulently gathering entitlement to a Bible prize and, more importantly, the praise of others. When the prize is awarded, he is elevated "to a place with the Judge and the other elect. . . . it lifted the new hero up to the judicial one's altitude, and the school had two marvels to gaze upon in place of one" (*WMT* IV 63). The glory is short-lived, however, as Tom is called upon to display publicly the knowledge he never acquired.

The scene is thus set for Tom to suffer a very painful, because very public, humiliation. The lesson he is about to learn is that playing the impostor for the sake of undeserved acclaim may have unpleasant consequences. And while we may assume that Tom suffers public embarrassment from his exposure, Twain chooses to close the scene before Tom loses the reader's approval. The broader lesson for Tom is that the world may not always succumb easily to one's wishes. The problem has to do with the effects of play in a world that will not willingly conform itself to the game.

We can properly assume that Tom's public embarrassment might produce something akin to the cub's experience when he learned that piloting was not always comfortable. We might expect, that is, that Tom would begin to learn the art of accommodation, the art of work, and that he would adapt himself to circumstances that were unpleasant but unavoidable. But it is precisely here that Twain draws the "curtain of charity" (*WMT* IV 65) to leave those effects undramatized and unexplored.

A similar situation marks the murder episode, in which Tom comes close to a threatening world, but then is saved from its serious implications. In the graveyard Tom and Huck watch aghast as Injun Joe drives his knife into Dr. Robinson's breast. The boys flee, "speechless with horror" (*WMT* IV 98), until they reach the old tannery. But here the seriousness of what they have witnessed is undercut by the playfulness Twain imposes on their taking of the oath of silence. Huck suggests that "there orter be writing 'bout a big thing like this. And blood," and "Tom's whole being applauded this idea. It was deep, and dark, and awful; the hour, the circumstances, the surroundings, were in keeping with it" (*WMT* IV 99).

We can appreciate Tom's response because he is a boy, but on the other hand Twain distances the grim reality from the reader by focusing attention on the romantic and boyish qualities of the response. There is the tongue-clamping laboriousness of the handwriting, there is Huck's gullible admiration of Tom's "facility in writing, and the sublimity of his language"; and there is the humor of the slightly garbled syntax of the oath itself: "Huck Finn and Tom Sawyer swears they will keep mum about this and they wish they may Drop down dead in their tracks if they ever tell and Rot" (*WMT* IV 100). Such distancing cannot help but spill over to include Tom as well. In spite of the proclaimed fear and terror, Tom has merely become involved in an adventure.

One incentive, Freud remarks, "to the recognition of an 'outside,' an external world, is provided by the frequent, manifold and unavoidable sensations of pain and unpleasure the removal and avoidance of which is enjoined by the pleasure principle, in the exercise of its unrestricted domination. A tendency arises to separate from the ego everything that can become a source of such unpleasure. . . ."[21] Twain goes some distance to keep from Tom any such incentive. He protects Tom from any experience that might seriously impair his "unrestricted domination": boredom, humiliation, the serious threat of death, lasting or serious disappointment, growing up—the "Battle of Life" in general. Both Tom and Twain play hooky from reality.

So successful is Tom's domination of the world that he becomes the culture hero of St. Petersburg: not merely the chief exemplar of community values, but a figure able to decree what values and activities are most acceptable. Thus by the end of the novel St. Petersburg and its environs are invaded by "men—pretty grave, unromantic men, too, some of them"—looking for buried treasure (*WMT* IV 232). The boy's play has become adult activity; "the reason of many of the citizens tottered under the strain of the unhealthy excitement," Twain says of it (*WMT* IV 232). And

> Wherever Tom and Huck appeared they were courted, admired, stared at. The boys were not able to remember that their remarks had possessed weight before; but now their sayings were treasured and repeated; everything they did seemed somehow to be regarded as remarkable; they had evidently lost the power of doing and saying commonplace things; moreover, their past history was raked up and discovered to bear marks of conspicuous originality. The village paper published biographical sketches of the boys. (*WMT* IV 232)

This is more than a case of a boy having been assimilated into society; it is a case of his having moved beyond the conventional norms, and of the society struggling to catch up. In the index for the first edition, the final chapter bears the title "A New Order of Things," and while Twain probably did not write the title, it is nevertheless appropriate; the new order is one created and guarded by Tom.

By the end of the novel Huck has been transformed from homeless waif to adopted child, and he lives with the Widow

[21]*Civilization and Its Discontents,* 14.

Douglas. But unable to adjust to the restraints of collars and shoes, he disturbs the new order by disappearing. Tom discovers Huck among the empty hogsheads at the wharf, and urges him to return to the Widow. Blair has argued that Tom in this scene shows an acceptance of the adult values he once disparaged. But if Tom searches out Huck in order to return him to the respectable fold, there is also more than a touch of self-gratification in his motives. The new order of things is Tom's, and he is reluctant to see it violated. Huck makes a rather moving and convincing speech concerning the trespasses the Widow has made upon his nature. "Don't talk about it, Tom," he says. "I've tried it, and it don't work. . . . It ain't for me. . . ." And Tom's placating remark that "everybody does that way" is met with Huck's stubborn assertion of his own identity: "Tom, it don't make no difference. I ain't everybody, and I can't *stand* it" (*WMT* IV 233-34). But Tom is not to be moved. Using simultaneously the carrot of adventure and the stick of threatened exclusion, Tom maneuvers Huck into conformity with his own ideas of what should be:

> "A robber is more high-toned than what a pirate is—as a general thing. In most countries they're awful high up the nobility—dukes and such."
>
> "Now, Tom, hain't you always ben friendly to me? You wouldn't shet me out, would you Tom? You wouldn't do that, now, *would* you, Tom?
>
> "Huck, I wouldn't want to, and I *don't* want to—but what would people say? Why, they'd say, 'Mph! Tom Sawyer's Gang! pretty low characters in it!' They'd mean you, Huck. You wouldn't like that, and I wouldn't." (*WMT* IV 235)

Huck submits to Tom's vision—just as everyone and everything else in St. Petersburg has submitted. For Huck, Tom's dream may include some unpleasant things, but it's the only dream in town. And the answer to Huck's question is that Tom certainly *would* "do that" if it came to it. "Child in time, child in appearance," Tom is "of a fatal and universal power," and he does indeed admit no co-life.

III

In *Tom Sawyer* Twain created a character who, as James Cox has said, objectified "the possibilities of the pleasure principle" (*Fate of Humor,* 146). He provided the character with a world which would bend to his will—a world whose facts, in Emerson's phrase, seemed "flowing perpetually outward from an invisible, unsounded centre in himself" (*CWE* I 334), and so would offer no resistance, no "reality principle," to a steadily expanding ego. At times Twain found it necessary to be evasive, to withdraw the threat of a circumstance too real for Tom to dominate effectively; but in the main the relationship between Tom and his world is one in which Self and Other are very nearly merged.

Tom comes very close to being a dramatization of Freud's "primal narcissism," a character who expresses "an inseparable connection of the ego with the external world" (*Life,* 45). Further, his identity, his sense of self, does not rise so much from a social role imposed upon him by the community; rather, like Emerson's Titan, he creates himself from the resources of his own mind and ego, becoming Robin Hood not just in fancy but in fact; a wept- and mourned-over boy not just in fancy but in fact; a hero to and leader of the multitudes, not just in fancy but in fact. He can cast off with impunity the cultural heritage of his elders—their church and school, their hypocritical pretense and their boredom; his own imagination and self-enjoying energy are enough. In the extremity of his individualism, the huge world comes round to him, and on his terms.

In all of this Twain was giving way to that part of him that saw childhood as a sort of perfect world, a prelapsarian charmed circle untouched by the problems of an adult world. In writing the novel, he was stepping into an imagined past of extraordinary freedom and extraordinary power; he was, as Lynn has said, "backtrailing in time" to a Hannibal that "stood out of time altogether, insulated from the taint and the tragedy of history."[22] To the degree that Twain, in the process of writing, could be "convinced . . . that I was a boy again" and that in his own adulthood he "had simply been dreaming an unusually long dream," Tom the Good Bad Boy was a projection of his own

[22]Lynn, 187.

personality, the embodiment of his own wishes for himself. Tom Sawyer could create his own world and life from his mind; Mark Twain could dictate an autobiography described as "a testament and a testimonial, an egocentric attempt to find in his own life an alternative to the real world in which he lived" (*God's Fool,* 136-37).

To a degree, both Tom and his creator show affinities with the sort of hero Georg Lukács, in his *Theory of the Novel,* describes for the novel of abstract idealism. The soul of the hero, says Lukács, is such that the hero, "with the most authentic and unshakeable faith, concludes that the idea, because it *should* be, necessarily *must* be." If and when "reality does not satisfy this *a priori* demand," the hero "thinks that reality is bewitched by evil demons and that the spell can be broken and reality redeemed either by finding a magic password or by courageously fighting the evil forces."[23] Lukács describes an action in which the hero's quest to realize his ideal in the real world is doomed to failure, and in this regard his description is not accurate for *Tom Sawyer.* But he does note that the soul of the hero is

> at rest in the transcendent existence it has achieved on the far side of all problems; no doubts, no search, no despair can arise within it. . . . nothing can shake it in its inner certitude, because it is incapable of experiencing anything. The complete absence of an inwardly experienced problematic transforms such a soul into pure activity. Because it is at rest within its essential existence, every one of its impulses becomes an action aimed at the outside. The life of such a person with such a soul becomes an uninterrupted series of adventures which he himself has chosen. He throws himself into them because life means nothing more to him than the successful passing of tests. His unquestioning, concentrated interiority forces him to translate that interiority—which he considers to be the average, everyday nature of the real world—into actions; in respect of this aspect of his soul he is incapable of any contemplation; he

[23]George Lukács, *The Theory of the Novel,* trans. Anna Bostock (Cambridge: MIT Press, 1971), 97.

lacks any inclination or possibility of inward-turned activity. He has to be an adventurer.

. . . .

> The unique quality of these novels, their dreamlike beauty and magic grace, consists in the fact that all the seeking which is in them is, after all, only a semblance of seeking. Every errant step of their heroes is guided and made safe by an unfathomable, metaformal grace. . . . The novels are in substance vast fairytales, for in them transcendence is not captured, made immanent and absorbed in the object-creating, transcendental form. . . . the shadow of transcendence fills the cracks of earthly life and turns the matter of life . . . into a substance that is . . . woven out of shadows.[24]

Tom Sawyer ignores the realities Twain later described in the "Villagers" fragment; it is in some ways Twain's "magic password" with which he would redeem reality. He is himself an image of Tom, who scoffs at any attempt to rid the world of warts without using ritual spells and chants (*WMT* IV 75). He is also the grace that guides and makes safe "every errant step" of his hero and in so doing turns the "matter of life . . . into a substance that is . . . woven out of shadows." But it is only Tom, and not Twain, who is "at rest . . . on the far side of all problems." Twain's attraction to and affection for Tom and his world notwithstanding, still it *was* necessary to "save" Tom on occasion from a reality that was too threatening, and the fact reveals Twain's essential dissatisfaction with the fairy-tale world he had provided his hero. Life in St. Petersburg offered no real challenge, no real test for Tom's ability to dominate experience. Things were too easy, and the power Tom wielded over the world—as attractive as it might be—was unconvincing.

There were other problems too for Twain. Tom was conceived as a character invested with all the essential innocence of an unfallen Adam. The pranks he perpetrated and the fibs he told

[24] Ibid., 99, 102.

were never meant to be seen as marks of moral stain. He was not "bad," after all, "only misch*ee*vous. . . . he was the best-hearted boy that ever was" (*WMT* IV 128). He was at bottom benevolent and humane. But as Tom continued to dream, and as the world continued to be shaped in conformity to his dreams, negative undercurrents began to ripple in a counter-direction.[25] The continual expansion of Tom's ego required that other selves be assimilated to his own—that his desires become theirs. By making the villagers hail Tom in his every victory, by making them as essentially childlike as Tom, Twain was able to satisfy this demand somewhat. But Tom showed signs of a selfishness that was destructive too; he was in some ways willing to allow others to suffer in order that his own fantasies might be fulfilled.

The scene in which Tom overhears Aunt Polly's expressions of grief at his presumed death illustrates the choice that Twain came to in regard to Tom's moral character—and his reluctance to face that choice squarely. Tom returns from Jackson's Island to reconnoiter the village, eavesdrops on Aunt Polly and Mrs. Harper, and learns that his funeral is to be held the following Sunday. At this point, Twain has placed Tom in a dilemma: Tom must decide between generously easing Aunt Polly's distress, or callously ignoring her pain for his own aggrandizement. For Twain, the choice is much the same. Were he to allow Tom to comfort Aunt Polly—and deny Tom the triumph of attending his own funeral—he would be confirming Tom's benevolence and humanity. To have Tom keep his status a secret, on the other hand, would be to allow Tom his triumph at the expense of his kindness.

Hamlin Hill discusses this scene in some detail in reference to Twain's decision to keep Tom in St. Petersburg rather than let him depart for "the Battle of Life in many Lands." He argues that the bark scroll Tom had prepared for Aunt Polly was originally

[25]Thomas Blues, in his *Mark Twain and the Community* (Lexington: Univ. of Kentucky Press, 1970), follows an argument similar to my own when he describes (5) "Tom's notion of a dominant relation to the adult community and . . . Mark Twain's method of protecting him from the consequences of its realization." James Cox and Judith Fetterly also remark the more negative qualities of Tom Sawyer. See *The Fate of Humor,* 147, and "The Sanctioned Rebel," 303.

intended to inform her of his departure, and that Twain "sprinkled the page with signs of his indecision":

> Deliberating what course to take, he wrote at the top margin, "Sid is to find and steal the scroll," and "He is to show the scroll in proof of his intent." In the left margin, he wrote two further lines and cancelled them. Across the page itself he wrote, "No, he leaves the bark there, & Sid gets it." Then he suggested, "He forgets to leave the bark." This was the point at which he had "pumped himself dry" and found that "at page 400 of my manuscript the story made a sudden and determined halt and refused to proceed another step."

Hill argues that "If the note was merely to contain the message, 'We ain't dead—we are only off playing pirates,' the author's ruminations over what would happen to it are completely out of proportion." If the bark were to announce Tom's departure, on the other hand, it would serve as preparation for his later return to the village.[26]

Yet Twain's ruminations about the scroll may not be out of proportion when one considers that the use Tom was to make of it might threaten the innocence to which Twain was so much committed. If Tom's dream were to come true, it was going to be at the expense of his kindly aunt. If it was *not* going to come true, Tom's triumph would be undercut. Twain might indeed have avoided the problem by allowing Sid to find and keep the scroll—but Sid, as Model Boy, would have no convincing motive for keeping its content secret. He would be far more likely to expose Tom's whereabouts and so ruin the funeral.

Twain eventually, and perhaps predictably, tried having it both ways. As Aunt Polly sleeps, Tom looks on:

> His heart was full of pity for her. He took out his sycamore scroll and placed it by the candle. But something occurred to him, and he lingered, considering. His face lighted with a happy solution of his thought; he put the bark hastily in his pocket. Then he bent over and kissed the faded lips, and

[26]Hill, "The Composition and Structure of *Tom Sawyer*," 387–88.

> straightway made his stealthy exit, latching the door behind him. (*WMT* IV 129-30)

Tom's decision is in keeping with the character who manipulates the world to conform to his own wishes, but it is out of character for the innocence and benevolence Twain is anxious for him to retain. As though troubled by Tom's willingness to prolong Aunt Polly's grief, Twain returns to the problem later. Aunt Polly chastizes Tom with the observation that "it is a pity you could be so hard-hearted as to let *me* suffer so. . . . you could have come over and give me a hint some way that you warn't *dead,* but only run off" (*WMT* IV 142). To this Tom weaves the tale of his "dream," and recounts as a dream vision all that occurred as he had watched Aunt Polly, Sid, Mary, and Mrs. Harper discussing the deaths of the boys. Sid is skeptical, but Aunt Polly is quite willing to believe that "The sperrit was upon you! You was a-prophecying—that's what you was doing. . . . There must a been an angel there," she concludes; "There *was* an angel there, somewheres!" (*WMT* IV 144).

The only angel, of course, was Tom himself, and Twain is still trying to believe that in Tom there *is* "an angel there, somewheres." When Tom describes that portion of his "dream" in which he kissed the sleeping Aunt Polly, Sid casts aspersions on the likelihood of such a thing happening. But Aunt Polly is sharp with him: "Shut up, Sid! A body does just the same in a dream as he'd do if he was awake." And Aunt Polly goes off "to call on Mrs. Harper and vanquish her realism with Tom's marvelous dream" (*WMT* IV 145).

The passages bristle with ironies that seem to be nearly out of control. The reference to Tom as an angel rings with ambivalence; Twain has portrayed him as benevolent, but his actions smack of selfishness. The dream was not really a dream—yet in the course of the novel dreams *have* vanquished reality, and Tom is proof that dream selves and waking selves are often very close kin. The angel Tom hovers on the brink of being the devil Tom—a situation that precedes by thirty years the Satan who is not really *the* Satan, but only his nephew, and who is innocent enough to avoid any moral stain from behavior that should bring a dreadful reckoning. And the imminent confusion of real world and dream world anticipates a theme that was to preoccupy Twain in his later life, in stories like "The Great Dark" and the long manuscript, "Which Was the Dream?"

A few years after the completion of *Tom Sawyer* Twain confronted the problem of selfishness in a speech to the Monday Evening Club. Selfishness, he said, may be of two kinds, "brutal and divine. . . . he who sacrifices others to himself exemplifies the first, whereas he who sacrifices himself for others personifies the second—the divine contenting of his soul by serving the happiness of his fellow man."[27] But in his fiction such homilies were never so straightforward. For Tom, in sacrificing others to himself, tends to content the souls of others as well.[28] This could be the case so long as Self and Other were, as Emerson assumed, part and parcel of each other, so that the hero could show his contemporaries their own potentials. But as soon as Other was objectified in a person with separate needs and desires, it had to be either adjusted to, or trampled. Heroism could not admit the first, and benevolence could not withstand the second. Twain tries to ride a fine line between the two, unwilling either to sacrifice Tom's power, or to admit his willingness to inflict pain and suffering on others.

The dilemma appears again, more pointedly, in the cave episode. Here Twain seems to have recognized the problem he faced with the power figure. McDougal's cave is a "vast labyrinth of crooked aisles that ran into each other and out again and led nowhere":

> It was said that one might wander days and nights together through its intricate tangle of rifts and chasms, and never find the end of the cave; and that he might go down, and down, and still down, into the earth, and it was just

[27]Albert Bigelow Paine, *Mark Twain: A Biography* (New York: Harper, 1912), II, 744.

[28]Blues notes that the community "willingly capitulates to his selfish desires" (*Mark Twain and the Community,* 9); Cox sees the village as having been made "not simply . . . to play the dupe but made to like the role" (*The Fate of Humor*, 138); Judith Fetterly argues that the village wants the "excitement and release" that Tom provides in his pursuit of pleasure ("The Sanctioned Rebel," 301).

> the same—labyrinth underneath labyrinth, and no end to any of them. (*WMT* IV 196)

At the upper levels of the cave there is romping and play and laughter; Tom feels "the ambition to be a discoverer" (*WMT* IV 209), and so he moves to a yet lower level, where there are beauty and wonders: ". . . a bewitching spring, whose basin was encrusted with a frost work of glittering crystals; it was in the midst of a cavern whose walls were supported by many fantastic pillars . . ." (*WMT* IV 209–10). Still lower, however, there are darkness and threat, and the echoes that come from Tom's calls for help do not reflect the innocent boy of a pastoral idyl. Rather, his voice returns to him "a ripple of mocking laughter"; it "sounded so hideously that he tried it no more" (*WMT* IV 211, 214). The three days and nights of harrowing the underworld climax when Tom at last sees "a human hand, holding a candle." He "lifted up a glorious shout, and instantly that hand was followed by the body it belonged to—Injun Joe's!" (*WMT* IV 215).

In the depths of the cave, beneath the laughter and sparkle of Tom's surface, Twain glimpsed another part of Tom's character (and perhaps of his own): a "half-breed" capable of atrocity and murder, an outlaw shorn of humanity, no longer beloved, and willing to trample on whoever gets in his way. It is no coincidence, then, that Injun Joe enters the novel as, in effect, the product and reflection of Tom himself, the coinage of his own imagination.[29] Tom has always been given to dreams of robbery and murder, of kidnapping and revenge, and always he saw himself as leader of the pack. It is not surprising, either, that in the last chapter he could ignore Huck's plaintive insistence that "I ain't everybody," and maneuver him back into confinements he had so lately escaped.

Tom's face-to-face meeting with Injun Joe is only tentative. Injun Joe immediately flees, for which Tom is "vastly gratified" (*WMT* IV 215), and a direct collision—or merging—of angel

[29]Leslie Fiedler notes that "the outlaw figure represents a grotesque travesty of the boy himself, his innocence distorted into an image of guilt." See his *Love and Death in the American Novel,* rev. ed. (New York: Dell, 1966), 281.

and devil is averted. Twain chooses to do again what he has done before—save Tom from any real unpleasantness, and save at the same time his own vision of an empowered, benevolent child. Tom escapes from the cave, and again gathers to himself the homage of the multitude. As for Injun Joe, Twain does with him what he must: he locks him away, seals him off from Tom and from St. Petersburg with a curtain sheathed this time not in charity, but in iron. For Tom to remain both powerful and benevolent, Injun Joe must be hidden away, exorcised, expunged. Tom, of course, will be resurrected in other novels, given other names, and given the best of good intentions. But nearly always, like some Siamese twin joined to him by a ligature at the waist, Injun Joe will rise with him—the haunting antithesis of beauty and grace, no longer so easily cast aside.

For the present, though, the cave still holds *two* possibilities for Twain. At its depth there lies not just Injun Joe, but also the buried treasure. With Injun Joe safely put to death, Tom returns to the cave, again descending, to take possession. Tom "proposed to explore. He stooped and passed under; the narrow way descended gradually. He followed its winding course, first to the right, then to the left, Huck at his heels. Tom turned a short curve, by and by, and exclaimed—'My goodness, Huck, looky here!' It was the treasure box, sure enough" (*WMT* IV 226).

Sure enough. The treasure is what *should* be there. It is, as Cox says, Tom's "reward . . . for his capacity to have dreamed it into reality with his make-believe imagination" (*Fate of Humor,* 147). Such power should rightly end in golden possibility; far better that than to end in an Injun Joe. And the gold goes, significantly, to "the best-hearted boy that ever was," not to the murderous half-breed. For the moment, Twain can gloss over the fact that it *was* Injun Joe who came into possession of it first. Hamlin Hill, in his biography of Twain, has said that Twain, like Jay Gatsby, managed to come out all right in the end (*God's Fool,* xxviii). The same may be said for Tom Sawyer. But it was, as Huck might say, "a tight spot," and Twain knew it.

III

Adventures of Huckleberry Finn

I remember an answer which when quite young I was prompted to make to a valued adviser who was wont to importune me with the dear old doctrines of the church. On my saying, "What have I to do with the sacredness of traditions, if I live wholly from within?" my friend suggested,—"But these impulses may be from below, not from above. I replied, "They do not seem to me to be such; but if I am the Devil's child, I will live then from the Devil." No *law can be sacred to me but that of my nature. Good and bad are but names very readily transferable to that or this; the only right is what is after my constitution; the only wrong what is against it.*

—Emerson, "Self-Reliance"

I HAD shut the door to. Then I turned around, and there he was. I used to be scared of him all the time, he tanned me so much. I reckoned I was scared now, too; but in a minute I see I was mistaken. That is, after the first jolt, as you may say, when my breath sort of hitched—he being so unexpected; but right after, I see I warn't scared of him worth bothering about.

—*Huckleberry Finn,* Chapter V: "Huck's Father"

I

"Now I was feeling pretty comfortable all down one side," says Huck in the latter pages of *Huckleberry Finn,* "and pretty uncomfortable all up the other" (*HF,* 283). The description might well be taken to apply to Twain himself when he completed *The Adventures of Tom Sawyer.* For that book clearly left him in a mixed mood, and his quandary over what to make of his hero Tom was one which followed him for the rest of his career. In 1890, in an interview with Kipling, he intimated one plan for a continuation of the Tom Sawyer story: "I had a notion of writing the sequel to *Tom Sawyer* in two ways. In one I would make him rise to great honor and go to Congress, and in the other I should hang him."[1]

In fact Twain did do something of the sort. In the ten years between completing the draft of *Tom Sawyer* and the publication of *Huckleberry Finn,* while he worked sporadically and with difficulty on what has become his most respected novel, Twain penned several other works in which he returned to the duplicitous character of the empowered Self. Late in 1877 he published "The Facts Concerning the Recent Carnival of Crime in Connecticut," in which the narrator (obviously one "Mark Twain"), exasperated at the guilt inflicted upon him by his conscience, murders the offender and sets out on a guiltless and light-hearted career of mayhem. The offense of Conscience is not so much that he antagonizes Mark for being unkind to others, but rather that he is equally antagonistic when Mark is kind and benevolent:

> . . . I had fed a tramp, and fed him freely, supposing it to be a virtuous act. Straight off you said, "O, false citizen, to have fed a tramp" and I suffered as usual. I gave a tramp work; you object to it,—*after* the contract was made, of course; you never speak up beforehand. Next, I refused a tramp work; you objected to *that*. Next, I proposed to kill a tramp; you kept me awake all night, oozing remorse at every pore. Sure I was going to be right *this* time, I sent the tramp away with my benediction; and I wish you may live as long as I do, if you didn't make me smart all night because I didn't kill him. Is there *any* way of satisfying that malignant invention which is called a conscience? (*Writings* XX 316)

The torments of Conscience arise not as a result of Mark's sinful nature, but because of his having to relate to others—for his

[1]*New York Herald,* August 17, 1890. Quoted in William C. Spengemann, *Mark Twain and the Backwoods Angel* (n.p.: Kent State Univ. Press, 1960), 42.

assumption that others are entities for the sake of which he must alter and shape his own responses. Thus, if there is no way to satisfy the conscience, there is a way of cancelling its power: by cultivating a total indifference to other people.

The one person whom Mark "loved and honored most in all of the world" is his Aunt Mary. It is Aunt Mary's distinction that she alone could make Mark repent of his smoking. But "A happy day came at last, when even Aunt Mary's words could no longer move me. . . . the moment she opened the subject I at once became calmly, peacefully, contentedly indifferent—absolutely adamantinely indifferent" (*Writings* XX 302–3). And Conscience is aware of this danger to its powers, for he asserts that such callousness diminishes his abilities: "Take smoking for instance. I played that card a little too long, and I lost. When people plead with you at this late day to quit that vice, that old callous place seems to enlarge and cover me all over like a shirt of mail. It exerts a mysterious, smothering effect . . ." (*Writings* XX 319).

By the end of the tale the narrator has killed his conscience and has become "a free man." "I settled all my outstanding scores," he says, "and began the world anew" (*Writings* XX 325). And at that moment of his release, Aunt Mary's plea to him to "be saved" has its own pinch of irony: salvation in her terms is caring for others; salvation in Mark's terms is indifference—a sort of peaceful area beyond the bothersome encumbrances of all human relationships. Here others become merely obstacles to be surmounted or used in the pursuit of happiness and self-gratification: "I burned a dwelling that interrupted my view. I swindled a widow and some orphans out of their last cow, which is a very good one, though not a thoroughbred, I believe" (*Writings* XX 325). Mark becomes "dead to sorrow, dead to suffering, dead to remorse"; his "life-conflict is done," and a moral and emotional demise renders an exultant rebirth in which the fetters of human relationships are broken, and in which the Self finds its own fulfillment in a world begun anew. And one characteristic of the new world is that it is dream-like, "freighted . . . with tranquil satisfaction" (*Writings* XX 303).

"Carnival of Crime" has its thematic affinities with *Tom Sawyer:* the "Mark Twain" narrator, a professional writer, is a creator of new worlds, a version of the dreamer-boy Tom. Aunt Mary watches the appalling transformation of her nephew into a monstrous self-seeker, just as, to a lesser degree, Aunt Polly saw for a moment in Tom a boy who would not ease her grief at a crucial moment. There is a suggestion even here of Twain's mixed attitude toward it all. The narrator's ebullience is contagious; his new-found freedom has an energy that the reader must admit is attractive—perhaps because Mark's crimes seem exempt from recrimination, either by Conscience or by legalities. So comfortable is he with his new world that he can advertise the corpses of his victims for sale to the medical colleges. The narrator has in a sense succeeded in removing himself from the real world of consequences, either internal or external. His is a dream-like world of indifference.

Yet at the same time the new world is more than a little tinged with hysterics. "Your reason is deserting you!" Aunt Mary warns: "There is madness in your eye!" (*Writings* XX 324). Freedom and insanity seem interlocked. One recalls the narrator of Poe's "Berenice," who awakens from a "confused and exciting dream" to find that in its course he had compulsively extracted his wife's teeth.[2] But this "Mark Twain" speaks to us, as it were, from the dream itself, surrounded in his cellar by the corpses of passing tramps, gleefully toting up his sales and getting set for "the spring trade" (*Writings* XX 325).

If "Carnival of Crime" reflects a *Tom Sawyer* sequel in which the protagonist is made a candidate for hanging, *The Prince and the Pauper* is one in which Tom Canty is made a candidate for great honor. Tom is a poverty-ridden inhabitant of Offal Court in sixteenth-century London who falls under the influence of one Father Andrew, lately expelled from the royal court, and who listens to

> good Father Andrew's charming old tales and legends about giants and fairies, dwarfs and genii, and enchanted castles, and gorgeous kings and princes. His head grew to be full of these wonderful things, and many a night as he lay in the dark . . . he unleashed his imagination and soon

[2]*The Portable Poe,* ed. Philip Van Doren Stern (New York: Viking, 1966), 216.

> forgot his aches and pains in delicious picturings to himself of the charmed life of a petted prince in a regal palace. (*WMT* VI 51–52)

Tom's dreaming first has the effect of intensifying "the sordidness of his surroundings a thousand fold" (*WMT* VI 56), but eventually, through a case of mistaken identity, Tom Canty comes to occupy in reality the throne of Edward Tudor, Prince of Wales. The dream has once again found its expression in the real world, and experience bows before the innocent child.

Most of the novel is given over to Edward's plight as an unrecognized king faring poorly among the cruelties of English society. But Tom's experience as king shows his growing enjoyment of power: "'Truly it is like what I used to feel when I read the old priest's tales, and did imagine mine own self a prince, giving law and command to all, saying, "Do this, do that," whilst none durst offer let or hindrance to my will'" (*WMT* VI 171–72). Tom Canty (the name suggests the phrase "Can't he," with its ambiguous qualities of both query and insistent affirmation) has his brushes with a growing and destructive pride, and for a time he seems to move in the direction of the narrator in "Carnival of Crime," and to be capable of removing any who would oppose him. ". . . upon occasion, being offended, he could turn upon an earl, or even a duke, and give him a look that would make him tremble" (*WMT* VI 296). But Twain never allows Tom to move decisively in that direction. For the salient part of the boy's nature is compassion and benevolence, and even when he fears that the appearance of his mother and sisters might expose him and renew his beggardom, he suffers guilt that his thoughts should be so selfish.

When at last his mother does appear, out of an adoring crowd that cheers his way to coronation, he almost involuntarily denies her: "I do not know you, woman!" But immediately the splendors of his position pass away from him:

> as she turned for a last glimpse of him, whilst the crowd was swallowing her from his sight, she seemed so wounded, so broken-hearted, that a shame fell upon him which consumed his pride to ashes and withered his stolen royalty. His grandeurs were stricken valueless, they seemed to fall away from him like rotten rags. (*WMT* VI 305)

Here the power and the dream become secondary to the more important consideration of human relationships, and Twain moves thematically in a direction opposite to that of "Carnival of Crime." Significantly, the next chapter sees the arrival of the rightful king and details Tom's efforts to get out of his dream—to convince the court that he is not royalty. The confused identities are sorted out, and Tom is cited by Edward for his having "governed the realm with right royal gentleness and mercy" (*WMT* VI 332). Tom, of course, does not fall back to his former poverty. He is made the King's Ward, and he is given distinctive dress and placed in charge of Christ's Hospital, so that they who dwell there may "have their minds and hearts fed, as well as their baser parts" (*WMT* VI 332). If Tom does not himself become king, still he is of royal parts, and he obtains the equivalent of a seat in Congress, or better:

> Tom Canty lived to be a very old man, a handsome, white-haired old fellow, of grave and benignant aspect. As long as he lasted he was honored; and he was also reverenced, for his striking and peculiar costume kept the people reminded that "in his time he had been royal"; so, wherever he appeared the crowd fell apart, making way for him, and whispering, one to another, "Doff thy hat, it is the King's Ward!"—and so they saluted, and got his kindly smile in return—and they valued it, too, for his was an honorable history. (*WMT* VI 334–35)

There is also in *The Prince and the Pauper* an attendant theme of dream and madness. Edward, to all outward appearance a pauper, is thought to be mad when he claims to be a king. And Tom, at the beginning of the novel, may well be mad in fact as his dreams of royalty become obsessive; later he is thought to be insane when he denies that he is king. At the meeting of the two boys in the climactic chapter, the assemblage "stared in a bewildered way at one another and at the chief figures in this scene, like persons who wondered whether they were awake in their senses, or asleep and dreaming" (*WMT* VI 313). The waking world and the dream world, the world of rationality and the world of insanity, begin to touch and lose their distinctiveness. The novel ends happily, with the confusion at last sorted out by means of a riddle solved; but insofar as Tom's fantasies become actual, and insofar as he remains at the end a part of the royal entourage, who is to say where the dream ends and the actual begins? And who is to say that he is not, after all, benevolently insane?

"Carnival of Crime" and *The Prince and the Pauper* both give evidence of Twain's continuing concern with the problems he glimpsed in *The Adventures of Tom Sawyer,* and both are to a degree works in which the two sides of Tom Sawyer—his good heart and his troubling callousness—are explored further. The confusion of dream and reality that began to surface in *Tom Sawyer* is tentatively extended to encompass a new and more ominous vocabulary, for the words "mad" and "madness" and "insane" begin to sprinkle Twain's pages. More troubling yet, the "Mark Twain" of "Carnival of Crime" and the two boys of *The Prince and the Pauper* make it clear that there is yet another idea bound up with the others, that of freedom and captivity. For Tom Canty, royal prerogatives at first weigh heavily, but become gradually less and less confining as he realizes the extent to which others will conform themselves to his will. And "Mark Twain," comfortably established with the grisly inventory in his cellar, rejoices at having become, finally, "a free man" (*Writings* XX 325).

Probably in the late 1870s, but before 1882, Twain wrote another short piece entitled "The Holy Children." Set in a small frontier village, the story concerns three girls, "Hope and Mary, sisters, the one aged ten, the other eleven—and Cecilia, their stepsister, aged a little over ten." The girls

> were pale and fragile creatures; their bodily health was exceedingly poor, but their spiritual health was perfect. . . . They had early taken as their motto that Biblical verse which says that faith like to a mustard seed will enable its possessor to remove mountains. The end and object of their ceaseless supplications was to acquire that puissant faith. . . . they were satisfied a time would come when they themselves would be perfect and thus be able to bring down blessings from heaven at call.[3]

The children do "acquire that puissant faith," but only after their

[3]John S. Tuckey, ed., *Mark Twain's Fables of Man* (Berkeley: Univ. of California Press, 1972), 71.

blasphemous father, "who detested religion in all its forms, and was a hardened man and singularly profane," dies after eight days of illness. The death of the father acts as a kind of release, for upon his passing the children "grew in grace and power with marvelous celerity."[4] Henceforth, they become the agents through whom special providences are granted to individual villagers. Being kind and compassionate, the children never refuse a villager's request for intercession with the Lord, and their prayers are always granted.

A series of miracles follows: the village being afflicted with drought, Hope prays for rain and thus precipitates a deluge that threatens to flood the countryside until she is persuaded to pray for a cessation; the girls pray for cold weather to ease a fevered widow, and the snow that follows cures the widow but destroys the crops. "The children changed the weather many times, every day, to benefit various persons, and these changes were very trying to the general public, and caused much sickness and death. . . ."[5] The children are eventually requested to stop tinkering with the weather, and they turn their powers to curing the sick. But those they cure live to commit robbery and murder, and so the general dissatisfaction grows. Raising the dead results in law suits filed by potential heirs, and legal fines and penury for those resurrected. Parting a river to aid a procession destroys villages and farms upstream. At last, when the village brute is retrieved from near death and is made "good for thirty years more," the village holds an "indignation meeting" and passes several resolutions, including these:

> *Resolved,* That the promise "Ask and ye shall receive" shall henceforth be accepted as sound in theory, and true; but it shall stop there; whosoever ventures to actually follow the admonition shall suffer death. . . .
>
> . . . .
>
> *Resolved,* That whosoever shall utter his belief in special providences in answer to prayer, shall be adjudged insane and shall be confined.

[4]Ibid., 71.
[5]Ibid., 73.

> *Resolved,* That since no man can improve the Creator's plans by procuring their alteration, there shall be but one form of prayer allowed in this village henceforth, and that form shall begin and end with the words, "*Lord, Thy will, not mine, be done*;" and whosoever shall add or take from this prayer, shall perish at the stake.[6]

As Tuckey observes, the story is a satire on "the conventional Christian view of the benefits conferred upon humanity by special providence."[7] But taken together with "Carnival of Crime" and *The Prince and the Pauper* it is also an investigation of empowered children at large in a world where the authorial protection of *Tom Sawyer* is not exercised. Power in a world of romance is alluring; but power in a real world is quite another matter. The children are "the constant though innocent cause of trouble,"[8] and their compassion for others results, ironically, in disaster for the community. Blessedness is mingled here with calamity and death, until finally the denouement reaches apocalyptic proportions:

> . . . at last the children made the sun and moon stand still ten or twelve hours once, to accommodate a sheriff's posse who were trying to exterminate a troublesome band of tramps. The result was frightful. The tides of the ocean being released from the moon's control, burst in one mighty assault upon the shores of all the continents and islands of the globe and swept millions of human beings to instant death. The children, being warned by friends, fled to the woods, but they were hunted down, one after the other, by the maddened populace, and shot.[9]

The villagers, of course, are culpable for not looking beyond their own individual interests, but the children suffer from the same tunnel vision: an incapacity to see that what benefits one does not benefit others. It is a variation of the problem of Self and Other that troubled Twain in *Tom Sawyer.*

[6]Ibid., 76–77.
[7]Ibid., 69.
[8]Ibid., 75.
[9]Ibid., 77.

Unpursued in the piece is the intriguing suggestion that the children's father acts as a kind of block to the realization of puissant faith. The block may be attributed in this instance to the father's blasphemy, a sort of counter-force to religious inspiration (and madness). But one recalls that Tom Sawyer was himself an orphan, and that the relationship between Tom Canty and his father is severed twice in *The Prince and the Pauper:* first by the father changing his name to "Hobbs," and then by Twain's dismissal of him from the novel altogether. Even the "Mark Twain" of "Carnival of Crime" had as a boyhood idol not his father, but Aunt Mary (*Writings* XX 302). Quentin Anderson, in his description of the Emersonian Self, explicitly identifies that Self as one who excludes reference to the father and to the past the father represents. "Secular incarnation," Anderson says, "may be construed as the act not of identifying with the fathers, but of catching up all their powers into the self, asserting that there need be no more generations, no more history, but simply the swelling diapason of the expanding self. It was this inclusive fantasy," he continues, "from which Emerson fell back in later years, but he never found anything satisfactory to take its place . . ." (Anderson, 58).

The removal or denial of the father may well be a psychological *sine qua non* for Twain as well, in the push to move his children satisfactorily beyond the contraints of a circumscribed world. The creation or realization of the dream self, a self unfettered by the fleshly limitations that accompany the reality principle, requires the destruction of that representative who embodies all of those limitations: the past, tradition, time, aging, even mortality itself. But the question, increasingly, is whether such a move is possible in the real world, and whether those who make it are benevolent or malicious, compassionate or barbaric, waking or dreaming, sane or mad.

The question, too, is to what degree Twain's fictional explorations of the problem reflect an exploration of his own divided psyche. The marks that identify Twain with his characters appear and reappear: the odd juxtaposition of real memory and idealized dreaming in the "Villagers" fragment; the Hannibal passages in *Life on the Mississippi* that seem to lock Twain to the Tom Sawyer he creates ("The things about me and before me . . . convinced me that I was a boy again, and that I had simply been dreaming an unusually long dream."); the similarities of Tom and the dreamer and Twain the romancer of his own childhood; the fictional "Mark Twain" madman of "Carnival of Crime." Also, one recalls that that particular "Mark Twain's" primary victims were tramps, and that (another?) Mark Twain casts himself in just such a guise in the suggestive title of his next book, *A Tramp Abroad* (1880); and that the posse in "The Holy Children" are out to "exterminate" a "troublesome band of tramps" while the children themselves are exterminated. Good Boy, Bad Boy; feed a tramp, kill a tramp. It is hard not to entertain notions of whether Twain is at some level flirting with psychic beatification on the one hand and psychic suicide on the other—expressions of a man tangled in an infinite self-love and an infinite self-contempt. The Twain who later dressed himself in a spectacular suit of white, the color of purity, also included two illustrations in *Life on the Mississippi* to which his wife objected:

> One showed the author being cremated, with an urn initialed "M. T." standing in the foreground to receive the ashes. The other showed a corpse in graveclothes, chopfallen and with staring eyes. (Kaplan, 249).

In January 1897 Twain made a long entry in his notebook, a discussion of Jekyll and Hyde dualities, of dream selves and waking selves. In the middle of it, this:

> Now, as I take it, my other self, my dream self, is merely my ordinary body and mind freed from clogging flesh and become a spiritualized body and mind and with the ordinary powers of both enlarged in all particulars a little, and in some particulars prodigiously. (*Notebook,* 350)

The holy children are "exceedingly poor" in bodily health, but their spiritual health is perfect—released perhaps from the clogging flesh of a blasphemous father. And the Mark Twain of "Carnival of Crime" moves from a world of clogging human relationships into one of indifference in which the weeks of Aunt Mary's visit "melted away as pleasantly as a dream, they were so freighted, for me, with tranquil satisfaction" (*Writings* XX 303). In *A Tramp Abroad* Mark Twain and Harris move across the continent with the carefree irresponsibility of boys on a lark, taking at one point a raft trip down the Neckar. The motion of the raft lulls Twain into a kind of sleep, transforming existence to "a dream, a charm, a deep and tranquil ecstasy" (*Writings* III 107).

Between the completion of *Tom Sawyer* and the completion of *Huckleberry Finn* Twain was casting about in very troubled waters. His faith in childhood, in a world of innocence and benevolence, was being eroded by a current of doubt; his faith in the realization and benefits of power in the real world was being similarly undermined. But by and large he was sticking with his youngsters; if romance could be realized in the real world, it was the child who could accomplish it. And in the children he created he was exploring perhaps not just the fictional characters and their possibilities, but his own character and its propensities as well. He was already well into his most troublesome novel by the early eighties, and the boy he created there would shortly speak up to once again describe his mood:

> I had my mind on the children all the time; I wanted to get them out to one side, and pump them a little, and find out who I was. (*HF,* 281).

II

In *The Adventures of Tom Sawyer* Twain created a protagonist who could treat the world as if it were an extension of himself, and one whose solipsism was, in its major manifestations, unerringly successful. Tom could create both himself and his world—could make his own circumstances—and like Napoleon reap the rewards of riches and fame. But for Twain there was a cost. The solipsistic power was maintained only by a sort of *auctor ex machina* technique, a tacit, perhaps half-conscious recognition on Twain's part that any impingement of a world too real had to be kept to a minimum. And even with that, the interaction between the protagonist and other characters tended to precipitate a threat to Twain's fundamental assumption about the child: that his was a heart basically good, kind, and humane. Both circumstances tended to run counter to what Twain wanted to do with his novels—that is, write in a vein more realistic than romancelike, and show a benevolent hero who could still overcome the limitations of a real world.

Twain began *Adventures of Huckleberry Finn* in the summer of 1876, even as he was concluding his revisions of *Tom Sawyer.* The year before, he had announced to Howells his plans to "take a boy of twelve & run him on through life (in the first person) but not Tom Sawyer—he would not be a good character for it."[10] Huck Finn was a natural choice for the new venture. In *Tom Sawyer* Huck had already been shown to be a boy on whom the harsher experiences of life impinged considerably. He was not a natural leader, like Tom; nor was he given to expecting much more out of life than a run of hard luck. His imagination was less fanciful, his resources for dreaming less extensive, and his fear of the world more developed. He was practical, down-to-earth, and twelve—all qualities which would enable Twain to plausibly "run him on through life" without the extravagance of too much romance or the softening of too much idyl. If *Tom Sawyer* was a book in which experience became only adventure, *Huckleberry Finn* was to be one in which adventure became experience, and one in which the exigencies of life were to be met rather than avoided.

These considerations all seem implicit in the first paragraph of the tale, in which Huck notes that "Mr. Mark Twain" was guilty of "some stretchers" in *Tom Sawyer,* but that he, Huck, was going to give us the facts this time, without any tall-tale embellishments (*HF,* 2). Twain's voice comes through clearly: this will be a world of work, not of play; there will be fewer authorial interventions to protect the hero.

But in all of this Twain was not quite abandoning the dream of the empowered Self. He was still taken with the idea that making one's own circumstances was possible, that one need not be limited by the past or by the culture into which he had been born, that the limitations of outward circumstance could be overcome by a brave trust in the deepest longings of the self, and that the result could be heroic and honorable. The resistance of a harsher world would only add a finer brilliance to the ultimate victory.

The shift from the *Tom Sawyer* idyl to a more realistic world in

[10]*Selected Mark Twain-Howells Letters, 1872–1910,* 49.

Huckleberry Finn is shown in the first chapters. There the practical qualities of Huck's personality are emphasized, and his realistic attitude is contrasted with Tom's indulgence in fantasy.[11] When Tom's robber gang turns out to be sham, and when a promised caravan of Arabs, camels, and elephants proves to be only a Sunday-school picnic, Huck resigns from the gang, as do the other members. Tom, of course, has a ready explanation for the discrepancies that so trouble the rest:

> I didn't see no di'monds, and I told Tom Sawyer so. He said there was loads of them there, anyway; and he said there were A-rabs there, too, and elephants and things. I said, why couldn't we see them, then? He said if I warn't so ignorant, but had read a book called "Don Quixote," I would know without asking. He said it was all done by enchantment . . . we had enemies which he called magicians, and they had turned the whole thing into an infant Sunday school, just out of spite. (*HF,* 32)

Huck puts Tom's explanation to the test. Following Tom's remarks on magic lamps and genii, he secures a tin lamp and iron ring, and "rubbed and rubbed till I sweat like an Injun. . . . but it warn't no use, none of the genies come. So then I judged that all that stuff was only just one of Tom Sawyer's lies. I reckoned he believed in the A-rabs and the elephants, but as for me I think different" (*HF,* 33).[12]

Tom's childish dream is satirized in the passage—just as other childish dreams of a traditional pearly-gated heaven are satirized in the first chapters. But it is important to note that it is not the act of dreaming that comes under Twain's attack, but only the quality of the dream. (Indeed, Twain's working notes for later episodes included ideas of Huck and Tom romping through the

[11]William R. Manierre discusses in detail Huck's practicality in the first four chapters of the novel, and contrasts it with Tom's fantasy life. See his "Huck Finn, Empiricist Member of Society," *MFS* 14 (Spring 1968), 57–66.

[12]Perhaps the elephant idea found its fruition in "The Stolen White Elephant," a farcical detective story which Twain claimed was "left out of *A Tramp Abroad,* because it was feared that some of the particulars had been exaggerated. . . ." See *Writings XX,* 215–41.

countryside on a circus elephant. Had such an episode been included, the syndrome of dream-come-true would have been much like that in *Tom Sawyer*.) Tom becomes the object of satire because his dreams are too childish for the sort of mimetic quality this book is meant to carry. The novel was to take a boy into life, not into idyl and burlesque. Tom's belief in the elephants is just outrageous enough to place him in a rather unfavorable light. His attachment to camels and elephants is petty stuff; there is no contest for the reader's sympathy between Tom and this other boy, whose self-awareness and introspection seem limited only by his youth, and whose broodings bend so easily to much more serious, and much more probable, intimations of mortality:

> The stars was shining, and the leaves rustled in the woods ever so mournful; and I heard an owl, away off, who-whooing about somebody that was dead, and a whippowill and a dog crying about somebody that was going to die; and the wind was trying to whisper something to me and I couldn't make out what it was. . . . (*HF*, 20)

It is a passage that could never be produced, or thought, by Tom, for whom no death is real, his own least of all.

The more realistic, more "adult" quality of the novel is also shown in terms of Huck's initial predicament. He had last been seen at the end of *Tom Sawyer,* maneuvered out of his hogshead and back into the Widow's dining room, "combed to thunder," shod, and made fit for the collective life. "I ain't everybody," he had said then, "and I can't *stand* it." By and large, however, his protests held no real force, either for him or for the reader. Had *Huckleberry Finn* never been written, the fate of Huck in the previous book might never have been questioned. He did not enjoy being suited up, but what boy does? And what alternative, besides a low-life of poverty and thievery, could there have been? But *Huckleberry Finn* does show an alternative, and in its light Huck's fate at the Widow's hands becomes more significant. In *Tom Sawyer* Huck's restrictive life is the stuff of comedy; his exasperations are humorous, and the reader does not readily sense in them anything particularly insidious or destructive. But in *Huckleberry Finn* the restraints become sinister, for the "sivilizing" of Huck threatens to choke off an enviable state of grace and freedom that can exist only outside of social structures. James Cox is correct to say that that state of grace is bound up inextricably with Huck's desire to be "comfortable" (*Fate of Humor,* 178), for surely it is the combination of comfort and freedom that makes readers envy Huck as they do. The most seductive portion of Huck's nature is defined for us in his baggy pants and open collar.

So even early in the novel, when Huck tells us he is "getting sort of used to the widow's ways" (*HF,* 34), we worry not only that his enviable freedom might be curtailed, but that he himself might not recognize what he is losing. Through these pages, of course, we are aware that Huck still has an impulse toward freedom. His agreement to join Tom's gang, after all, was an attempt to live in the freedom of a boy's fantasy—and Huck was willing to submit to the Widow's restraints to gain that freedom. With Pap's arrival, Huck again submits to one restraint in order to declare another sort of independence: ". . . the old man . . . went for me, too, for not stopping school. He catched me a couple of times and thrashed me, but I went to school just the same, and dodged him or out-run him most of the time. I didn't want to go to school much, before, but I reckoned I'd go now to spite Pap" (*HF,* 45).

Huck's impulse toward real freedom seems checked at every side. He cannot enjoy the freedom of fantasy, for he is growing out of childhood, and so lacks the imaginative ability to substitute childish fantasy for reality and believe in it. He cannot loose himself from the claims of his father; the only freedom he can find in this respect is defiance, which in turn requires submission to other social conformities. No one is quite willing to do what Huck wants most: leave him alone. The final and most sinister of restrictions on Huck is his days-long confinement in Pap's cabin, where the combination of imprisonment and physical assault leads him finally to counterfeit his murder.

In all of Huck's stratagems, what we as readers most hope for is his success in getting away from the restraints imposed upon him by society—by the parental authorities of both the Widow and Pap. Those restrictions seem destined to make of Huck what he is not, or should not become: a respectably hypocritical townsman, or an irresponsible and brutal alcoholic. So as we read the novel we become a sort of silent chorus, urging Huck to cover his tracks well as he carefully plants the signs of his murder, and hurrying him on to that canoe and that river before Pap's return. Unlike the Widow or Pap, we, along with Twain, would give Huck what no one else seems willing to give him: a chance to become himself, a chance to put away the past and to create an identity without reference to the limitations of society or culture. With the best of intentions, we help him cut his throat, and then through the next twenty-four chapters we watch with self-satisfaction the consequences of that homicide. Our confidence in him is boundless.

Huck's "suicide" is in effect, for himself, for Twain, and for the reader, a celebration of orphanhood; it amounts to a vernacular dramatization of Emerson's call for men to loose all ties and to trust in the aboriginal Self. In taking to the river and Jackson's Island, Huck disclaims all social ties and launches himself into a psychological wilderness, where the essential Self may blossom and become the final moral arbiter of experience. Both Twain and the reader can accept the challenge because it is clear that Huck's innermost Self is gentle, and that the flowering of that Self will make him a saint among sinners.

Yet for all of the differences established in the first chapters between Huck and Tom, Huck's motives are remarkably similar to his friend's. For Tom, primer-school picnics must be transformed into exotic caravans, and hogdrovers and women in carts must be rich prey for daring highwaymen. Reality, that is, must become something more consonant with the imagination, lest life become too tedious. For Huck, social relationships must be cut short or avoided, lest life become too "uncomfortable," and not measure up to his own standards of freedom and pleasure. If Tom's goal is to live in a dream world of robber bands and pirates, Huck's goal is to live in a dream world of easy living, where "Other" will not impinge itself upon him with collars and rules that are foreign to his own self-enjoying soul.

There is something spiritual about Huck's quest too—a quality that led T. S. Eliot to speak of "the River God," and to identify Huck with "the spirit of the River." "Huck has not imagination," says Eliot, ". . . he has, instead, vision."[13] Lionel Trilling speaks in a similar vein. "*Huckleberry Finn* is a great book," he says, "because it is about a god—about, that is, a power which seems to have a mind and will of its own, and which to men of moral imagination appears to embody a great moral idea."[14] Both critics recognize something divine about Huck. His "vision" is that of a saint, one in which the narcissism of the child engages itself harmoniously with gentleness and love. Huck's instinctive search for comfort somehow touches on the prelapsarian, as though it were a casual conversation with God. In a cleaner and apparently less ironic vein, Huck's denial of Pap parallels the death of the blasphemous father in "The Holy Children"; it promises to release him from the limitations of flesh and introduce him to a world of more possibilities than the one he has left behind.

But such a move, it should be emphasized, is not one toward adulthood. Breaking ties with Pap—with the past and with time—is not a *rite de passage* that prepares Huck for a burgeoning adulthood. Rather, it is a step away from an impinging adulthood and back into childhood, back into "the old ways" which Huck admits he likes best (*HF,* 34), where the world is expected to offer itself for the child's enjoyment, and where enjoyment of the world amounts to enjoyment of the self. One of the most subtle ironies of the novel has to do with Huck's separating himself from others; for in moving away from society and companionship Huck attempts to relieve an anxiety that has its basis in feelings of separation and individuality, the hallmarks of adulthood and the reality principle. In perpetrating his own suicide, Huck seeks to recover a "primal narcissism" that would erase the distance between Self and Other, but the only practical way of accomplishing that goal is to effect a physical separation between himself and all those who demand that he change.

Norman O. Brown describes the situation when he speaks of birth as separation from the mother and the first experience of

[13]T. S. Eliot, "An Introduction to *The Adventures of Huckleberry Finn*" (New York: Chanticleer Press, 1950), rpt. in *Adventures of Huckleberry Finn,* ed. Sculley Bradley, et al. (New York: Norton, 1962), 321.

[14]Lionel Trilling, *The Liberal Imagination,* Anchor Books (Garden City, N.Y.: Doubleday, 1953), 103.

individuality—which is also the first experience of "death." "Anxiety," he says, "is a response to experiences of separateness, individuality, and death. . . . One effect of the incapacity to accept separation, individuality, and death [the shrinking ego] is to erotize death—to activate a morbid wish to die, a wish to regress to the prenatal state before life (and separation) began . . ." (*Life,* 115).

In *Tom Sawyer,* Tom's erotizing of death is clearly a wish to "regress"—to maintain his position as a child. In *Huckleberry Finn,* Huck is plagued with the same wish. "I felt so lonesome I most wished I was dead," he tells us in the first chapter (*HF,* 20), and it is a refrain that recurs often enough to characterize his personality. Huck's desire throughout the novel is to remove himself from society, from an environment which continually asserts itself as Other and so reinforces his feelings of separateness and individuality. At age twelve or thirteen, Huck is torn between the demands of time and nature, which age him physically and psychologically, and his own deepest demands, which pull him back toward a more comfortable childhood, where time and nature are not insuperable.

Huck's wish for "death" is charged with the ambivalence of both promise and threat. His "suicide" places him outside the confinements of the adult world, in an environment in which he might live "easy and comfortable" without the impingements of a real world. There he is free to create himself—to become whoever and whatever he wishes to be. There are no apparent boundaries, and his search for an identity, which occupies him throughout the book, is an attempt at becoming self-begotten. "I ain't everybody," Huck has said, and both Twain and the reader hope it is so.

Throughout the book Huck assumes and then discards identities. He is at various times Sarah Williams, George Alexander, George Peters, George Jackson, and a nameless member of a pox-stricken family. In one sense, Huck's freedom has indeed given him the power to create himself, and even his past. His assumption of identities is an expression of the Emersonian Self; it exhibits the assimilation of father-like powers of generation. It is what Anderson calls "the swelling diapason of the expanding self" (p. 58). But in another sense, the continual change of identities suggests a darker possibility—the inability to establish a sense of self without reference to the past. Huck's choice is one of becoming like everybody else, adopting a role which is convincing to others and acceptable to others, or to forego a social identity altogether. Increasingly, the first alternative is necessary for survival, and the second is acceptable only under the extraordinary conditions which come to exist, if only briefly, on the raft.

In the terms the novel itself establishes, self-creation would be an extraordinary exercise of solipsistic power, in which the usual limitations of reality—a natural growth into adulthood and adjustment to its confinements—might be overcome. But a retreat to a social identity would be a surrender into adulthood, and a "death" of the sort Huck (and Twain, in spite of his original intentions) would rather avoid.

Yet even as early as chapter seven, Twain must have been troubled at some half-conscious level by the darker implications that might accompany a radical freedom from the reality principle. He had glimpsed in Tom Sawyer the dangers of subduing the world to the demands of the imagination; he had seen that it could result in a destructive selfishness. Huck's compassion and benevolence were to be safeguards against such a disaster; the world he was to create was to be harmonious. Still, out of Pap's fit of delirium tremens, a violent nightmare that bypasses the logic and predictability of rational thought, comes a hint of other, more gloomy hazards. Pap calls his son the "Angel of Death," and the phrase, in its yolking of the holy and the sinister, echoes the same sort of ambivalence that Twain glimpsed in Tom Sawyer, and that he explored in "The Holy Children." Pap's nightmare suggests that Huck might bring, in the wake of his dreams of freedom, something less than saintly, and that the angel might at last prove more diabolic than holy. In Pap's hallucination Huck is clearly a threat that must be eliminated:

> He chased me round and round the place, with a claspknife, calling me the Angel of Death and saying he would kill me and then I couldn't come for him no more. I begged, and told him I was only Huck, but he laughed *such* a screechy laugh, and roared and cussed, and kept on chasing me up. Once when I turned short and dodged under his arm he

> made a grab and got me by the jacket between my shoulders, and I thought I was gone; but I slid out of the jacket quick as lightning, and saved myself. Pretty soon he was all tired out, and dropped down with his back against the door, and said he would rest a minute and then kill me. He put his knife under him, and said he would sleep and get strong, and then he would see who was who. (*HF,* 52)

Pap, with his greed and his racism, should be regarded here and elsewhere in the novel not simply as a figure who embodies the ragged edges of a corrupt social structure, but as one in whom resides the authority of reality itself. The struggle between Huck and his father is meant to determine who will prevail: the world, which demands of its sons accommodation to the Not Me, or Huck, with his desire to escape from those limitations. Pap's speech suggests, quite rightly, that Huck is *not* "only Huck," for, as in "The Holy Children," the child's freedom and power cannot be realized without the implicit destruction of the blasphemous and fallen father that gave him birth: the reality principle, the Not Me, that stands in his way, always ready to impose limitation and confinement. The direction of Huck's quest thus implies more than a moralist's challenge to a racist and hypocritical society; it implies more, even, than extreme social anarchy. It implies a fundamental assault on the structure of reality. For all of its sanctity and lyrical beauty, the quest is a radical abrogation of all that human beings take to be the givens of existence; and the successful conclusion of such a quest, if such a thing is imaginable, can only be, from the father's point of view, annihilation. Little wonder, then, that Pap sees in Huck a threat, and that he most wants to "sleep and get strong," and so discover "who was who."

Some six months earlier, Twain had written "Carnival of Crime," wherein "Mark Twain" had murdered a similar master, Conscience, and then blithely dispatched the tramps that called at his door. Here, fearful that his child might "come for him," Pap echoes the tramp theme in his hallucination of the dead coming to take him:

> Tramp—tramp—tramp; that's the dead; tramp—tramp—tramp; they're coming after me; but I won't go—Oh,

> they're here! don't touch me—don't! hands off—they're cold; let go—Oh, let a poor devil alone! (*HF,* 52)

The dovetailing of thematic suggestions renders the whole conflict between Pap and Huck extraordinarily complex. What does Huck become in the novel but a tramp abroad on the great river, "borrowing" what he needs as he drifts toward the Gulf: food, clothing, names, moralities? Perhaps the radical freedom Huck seeks will generate not the warmth of a saint's love, but the cold hands of a tramp come to destroy his father. And where does the tramp arrive (not once, but twice), but at "Mark Twain's" door—the Grangerfords' and the Phelps', both fictional counterparts of the Quarles' farm that Twain remembered from his own boyhood?[15] And finally, what should "Mark Twain" do with the tramp when he comes knocking? Feed him? Or kill him? "By and by," Huck tells us,

> I . . . got down the gun. I slipped the ramrod down it to make sure it was loaded, and then I laid it across the turnip barrel, pointing towards pap, and set down behind it to wait for him to stir. And how slow and still the time did drag along. (*HF,* 52)

III

Although Huck's brush with Pap in chapter six hints at the possibility of undesirable consequences of his break from the world, Twain does not yet see those consequences as inevitable. He remains, for the greater part of the novel, committed to the notion that Huck's quest is that of a saint. As though to reinforce that commitment, Twain later, in chapter seventeen, alludes to Bunyan's *Pilgrim's Progress,* one of the books "piled up perfectly exact" on the Grangerfords' parlor table. The broad similarities between Huck's situation and Christian's are apparent. Like Huck's, Christian's story is "about a man that left his family it didn't say why," and though Huck cannot be said to understand all that he reads there, his fascination for the tale is thematically

[15]Lynn, 223, 243.

appropriate: "I read considerable in it, now and then. The statements was tough, but interesting" (*HF,* 137).

The hero Christian, we recall, discovering that he has been living in the worldly City of Destruction, is determined to flee—determined to grasp "Life, life, eternal life." In his decision to set out for the Celestial City, he is encouraged by Evangelist, who tells him a hard but saving truth:

> . . . the King of Glory hath told thee, that he that will save his life shall lose it; and *he that comes after him, and hates not his father and mother, and wife, and children, and brethren, and sisters; yea, and his own life also, he cannot be my disciple.*[16]

The harsh requirement that Christian separate himself from human ties in order to reach salvation is echoed in Emerson's "Self-Reliance": "The doctrine of hatred must be preached, as the counteraction to the doctrine of love, when that pules and whines. I shun father and mother and wife and brother when my genius calls" (*CWE* II 51).

If Christian derives his initial impulse to move toward the Celestial City from a book, Huck derives his from the impulses of his deepest self—from his constitution, his "genius." But the Celestial City he seeks is not that of Bunyan's traditional heaven, but that of perpetual childhood, where growing up into accommodation is unnecessary. Christian struggles under the burden of inherited sin, Adam's original fall from grace, and Huck's own enormous burden is a condition somberly described by Emerson in "Experience": "It is very unhappy, but too late to be helped, the discovery we have made that we exist. That discovery is called the Fall of Man" (*CWE* III 75). Twain's commitment to his hero reflects his faith that it is *not* "too late to be helped," and that the Celestial City of childhood, a salvation every bit as blessed as Christian's, might be achieved in the here and now.

Nevertheless, the inherent conflict in such a break with the world, the conflict between good boy and bad boy, cannot be easily avoided. When Huck plants the "evidence" of his murder in chapter seven, there is beneath the calm and repertorial tone a vocabulary of violence:

[16]John Bunyan, *The Pilgrim's Progress,* ed. Robert Sharrock (Baltimore: Penguin Books, 1965), 41, 54.

> I took the axe and smashed in the door—I beat it and hacked it considerable, a-doing it. I fetched the pig in and took him back nearly to the table and hacked into his throat with the ax, and laid him down on the ground to bleed. (*HF*, 57)

Huck's is a desperate attack on the elements of the Not Me that would confine him, and on the worldly self associated with those elements. The passage is perhaps as close as we come in the novel to glimpsing Huck's frustration with a condition which most take for granted. It suggests, too, that the escape from and denial of the world might as easily issue in ferocity as in sainthood. In the midst of his task, he thinks of Tom: "I did wish Tom Sawyer was there, I knowed he would take an interest in this kind of business. . . . Nobody could spread himself like Tom in such a thing as that" (*HF*, 57).

Huck's "murder" of Pap and of himself pushes him through the Wicker Gate to an isolated spit of land in the middle of the river. Jackson's Island rests, significantly, somewhere between a slave state and a free, its geography an emblem of Huck's own condition. For Jackson's Island is not a state of total satisfaction for Huck. It provides him, as Martha Banta points out, with a place "completely *away from other people*," a "society-less place that is his alone, all alone," and it thus seems ideal for Huck.[17] There is no need here for him to accommodate himself to the demands of others—no need to interrupt his own comfort with the nagging claims of social responsibility. There is even a touch of pride in Huck as he settles in, for his possession of the island gives him a sense of mastery, perhaps for the first time: ". . . I went exploring around down through the island. I was boss of it; it all belonged to me, so to say, and I wanted to know all about it" (*HF*, 64). But Huck does not seem quite willing—or quite able—to accept the solitude his move has brought him, and in fact the sense of loneliness that nags him through the novel is the first of the snares that tempt him back into the world. "It got sort of lonesome," Huck records (*HF*, 64), and he turns to counting stars and listening to the river's current to wash out the uneasy feeling.

[17]Martha Banta, "Escape and Entry in *Huckleberry Finn*," *MFS* 14 (Spring 1968), 85.

In *The Rise of the Novel* some of Ian Watt's discussion of *Robinson Crusoe* might well apply to Huck's situation. "On the island," says Watt,

> Crusoe . . . enjoys the absolute freedom from social restrictions for which Rousseau yearned—there are no family ties or civil authorities to interfere with his individual autonomy. . . . Crusoe toys with the fancy that he is an absolute monarch; and one of his visitors even wonders if he is a god.
>
> . . . .
>
> Crusoe realises all these ideal freedoms, and in doing so he is undoubtedly a distinctively modern culture hero. Aristotle, for example, who thought that the man "who is unable to live in society, or who has no need because he is sufficient for himself, must either be a beast or a god," would surely find Crusoe a very strange hero. Perhaps with reason; for it is surely true that the ideal freedoms he achieves are both quite impracticable in the real world and in so far as they can be applied, disastrous for human happiness.

Crusoe, Watt reminds us, "has an exceptional prowess; he can manage quite on his own. And he has an excess: his inordinate egocentricity condemns him to isolation wherever he is."[18]

Huck's desire for companionship contends with his desire to be alone, and in his reaction to finding Jackson's Island inhabited, the fear of intrusion is uppermost, for the presence of Other will inevitably tend to cut short his freedoms. ". . . if I see a stump, I took it for a man; if I trod on a stick and broke it, it made me feel like a person had cut one of my breaths in two and I only got half, and the shorter half, too" (*HF,* 65).

Yet when Huck discovers that the intruder is Jim, Miss Watson's slave, his reaction is not one of disappointment, but of joy. "I was ever so glad to see Jim. I warn't lonesome, now" (*HF,* 67). The easing of loneliness is not the only reason Huck feels joy at Jim's presence, for with Jim, Huck gets a bonus. Jim, after all,

[18]Ian Watt, *The Rise of the Novel* (Berkeley: Univ. of California Press, 1957), 86–87.

is black, and a slave. He not only fills Huck's need for company, but he does so without raising the spectre of an Other for whom Huck must modify his own pleasures. Jim's status as slave insures that he will impose no troubling restrictions on Huck, no rules and regulations; for what is the slave but an extension of the white man's self—a tool that exists "at the pleasure" of his white master? By definition, the will and desires of the slave—his reality—need not be recognized.

The days that follow on Jackson's Island are idyllic for Huck. Untouched by an adult world of work, Huck revels in a child's world of play. The height of play occurs when Huck turns his attention to his first practical joke. Having once earlier refused to play a trick on Jim for fear of incurring Miss Watson's displeasure, Huck now makes up for the lost opportunity by planting a dead rattlesnake at the foot of Jim's pallet. The game becomes serious, however, when the snake's mate strikes, leaving Jim deathly ill. Pap's whiskey is the only available antidote, and for a time Jim's delirium echoes, though without detail, Pap's own bout with the jug.

Huck's play brings in its wake not the applause of a willing dupe, as usually happened with Tom Sawyer, but the real affliction of a victim. The practical joke exemplifies Huck's attitude toward Jim in the first part of the novel. Jim has not yet become for Huck more than an extension of himself—a dark face whose role is merely to fill in the interstices of loneliness in Huck's dream. The incident is a disturbing one, for it parallels the sort of callousness that attended Tom Sawyer's proclivity to use others for his own compulsive play. And if Tom never experienced the brunt of responsibility for his antics, neither does Huck in this case, for both Huck and his victim relegate the whole matter to "bad luck." Twain does not seem willing to pursue the matter of Huck's accountability, any more than he did Tom's. The fault does not lie with Huck, but with the stars—evil spirits and dark forces beyond control.

At stake in the episode for Twain is the matter of Huck as a Good Boy. Twain has once again found his protagonist to be showing evidence of a callousness that does not fit the theoretical ideal of the innocent child. Earlier in the novel, Huck could look over St. Petersburg at night and see "three or four lights twinkling, where there was sick folks, may be" (*HF,* 24). But those qualities of sensitivity and compassion here clash with the joke he has played on Jim, and if Huck is to retain the sympathies of the reader, and of Twain himself, he must be made to confirm what is best in him. There must be no more jokes.

It is Huck's humanity that is one of his most winning characteristics; it is what makes him deserving of freedom, and it is what makes the anarchism inherent in that freedom worth risking. If to become self-sufficient is to be either a beast or a god, it is Huck's gentleness and love that assure us he will be closer to the second than to the first. The confirmation of that kindness and humanity is his eventual recognition of Jim as a human being. The problem for Twain is that the confirmation of Huck's humanity is the very thing that inhibits the self-sufficiency he so wants Huck to achieve.

The crucial moment of Huck's recognition of Jim as human is, of course, the celebrated section in chapter fifteen in which Huck apologizes to a "nigger." The event rises from another practical joke, as though Twain, troubled by the implications of the first joke, seeks to rework the incident and make sure it turns out differently. This time Twain does not allow either Jim or Huck to evade its implications by throwing the blame on the forces of bad luck. The whole event seems calculated to dramatize Huck's benevolence and his break with a corrupt adult society.

Huck and Jim become separated from each other in a fog which shrouds the river, and Huck's attempt to catch the raft proves futile. When at last the fog lifts and Huck finds the raft again, "Jim was setting there with his head down between his knees, asleep, with his right arm hanging over the steering oar. The other oar was smashed off, and the raft was littered up with leaves and branches and dirt. So she'd had a rough time" (*HF,* 119).[19] Huck then plays his trick, convincing Jim that the fog, the separation, and the "rough time" were only events in a dream. And Jim's confused response is to question his own reality: "Well, looky here, boss, dey's sumf'n wrong, dey is. Is I *me*, or who *is* I? Is I heah, or whah *is* I? Now dat's what I wants to know?" (*HF,* 119). Huck treats reality as play, and the result is to

[19]It is significant that Huck's words, "she'd had a rough time," clearly refer to the raft, and not to Jim.

deny Jim a self of his own. For a moment, Jim feels as Huck has conceived of him: a subservient extension of himself, and lost in Huck's capacious ego.[20]

But Huck twists the knife a turn too far. Having convinced Jim the episode was a dream, he then flaunts its actuality, and thus derides Jim's submissiveness. There follows the famous dressing-down:

> When I got all wore out wid work, en wid de callin' for you, en went to sleep, my heart wuz mos' broke bekase you wuz los', en I didn' k'yer no mo' what become er me en de raf'. En when I wake up en fine you back agin', all safe en soun', de tears come en I could a got down on my knees en kiss' yo' foot I's so thankful. En all you wuz thinkin 'bout wuz how you could make a fool uv ole Jim wid a lie. Dat truck dah is *trash*; en trash is what people is dat puts dirt on de head er dey fren's en makes 'em ashamed.

"It made me feel so mean I could almost kissed *his* foot to get him to take it back," Huck records. "It was fifteen minutes before I could work myself up to go and humble myself to a nigger—but I done it, and I warn't ever sorry for it afterwards, neither. I didn't do him no more mean tricks, and I wouldn't done that one if I'd a knowed it would make him feel that way" (*HF,* 121).

The scene secures the benevolence in Huck that has made us, as readers, sympathize with the extravagance of his quest. We can rest assured that Huck is not merely the shallow product of a slave society, and that he is capable of moving beyond the moral corruption of white supremacy through an act of compassion and sympathy. Chadwick Hansen, in his article "The Character of Jim and the Ending of *Huckleberry Finn,*" argues that for Huck, Jim is the "white man's burden," that "by his constant presence, and his constant decency, and his constant humanity he forces Huck to do something more than drift with the river. He forces Huck to come to grips with that part of himself that belongs to

[20]Neil Schmitz, in "The Paradox of Liberation in *Huckleberry Finn,*" notes that "Jim exists somewhere beyond the pale of Huck's perception." Schmitz in some points anticipates my argument regarding the relationship between Huck and Jim. See *TSLL* 13 (Spring 1971), 131 and *passim.*

society. . . . forces him to decide to go to hell rather than betray his fellow human being."[21] In his assessment of Jim's role Hansen is correct, but the implications of Jim's presence seem to be more ambiguous than Hansen would allow. Huck's recognition of Jim as Other entangles him in commitment and responsibility, both of which contradict his intuitive desire to remain a child.

The apology has pushed Huck back through the Wicker Gate into the City of Destruction—out of the child's world of play and into the adult's world of work and responsibility. For all the admiration that Huck earns from the reader, and from Twain himself, his freedom is no longer absolute. Henceforth, Huck must modify his own actions, even deny his own needs, to accommodate the presence of someone separate from himself. The humbling of himself to Jim has made Huck "larger" in our eyes, for it has increased his humanity. But it has had another effect as well: it has set limits around him, cut his breath in half just as surely as if the Widow or Miss Watson had again fitted him out in collars and ties.

On the one hand, Twain has done what he intended: first, he has confirmed the benevolence of his child protagonist, a benevolence that had been threatened previously. Second, he has brought Huck face to face with real life by depriving him of the protection from consequence and change that had characterized *Tom Sawyer.* (There were enormous gains in this, for Huck acquires a depth of character that Tom never achieved.)[22] But on the other hand, he has undercut one of the most attractive possibilities the novel has thus far offered: the hope of an unbounded freedom in a life of ease and comfort. Ideally, "real life" and unbounded freedom should not be mutually exclusive, but in practice the two threatened to cancel each other out. As much as Emerson, Twain was proving himself to be the "practical American idealist," and the contradictions inherent in the label were making themselves felt in the novel.

[21]Chadwick Hansen, "The Character of Jim and the Ending of *Huckleberry Finn*," *Massachusetts Review* 5 (Autumn 1963), 58.

[22]Henry Nash Smith suggests that the increasing depth of Huck's character might have taken Twain by surprise. See *The Development of a Writer,* 119.

As in *Tom Sawyer,* Twain's original intentions were colliding with his deepest imagination. For as much as he wanted to take Huck and "run him on through life," he wanted even more to save Huck from the limitations and dangers of living. (Hence the implicitly contradictory structural components of the novel, in which Huck repeatedly escapes from the world, only to be sent on a recurring picaresque journey through its worst manifestations.) Twain wanted the boy to meet real life, but he was unwilling to have the boy change. What he wanted was a Robin Molineaux who could return home again, aware of but untouched by the corrupt city; experienced, but somehow still innocent; responsible, but still free; an adult, but still holding fast to all the prerogatives of the child. What he wanted, finally, was to show Huck achieving a version of Bunyan's "Life, life, eternal life"—a Celestial Playground of ease and comfort—without stopping his ears to the cries of his black brother. He wanted Huck in heaven; he just didn't want him there alone, and he didn't want him to forget others on his way.

Of course what Twain wanted for Huck was difficult, probably impossible, to show. The recognition of Jim as Other confirmed the innocence and benevolence of the boy, but that act, while it promised to separate him from a corrupt society, simply placed him in another society, with its own attendant obligations. And this society, made up of himself and Jim, was no more free, really, than the first.

Twain must have sensed as much. He goes a step further in confronting Huck with the world of responsibility, by giving him his first real battle of conscience. Realizing for the first time that Jim is almost free and that he must bear the responsibility for it, Huck is tempted to stop Jim's flight. To his credit, he does not respond automatically to the slaver's code. Between what he knows to be "right" and the performance of the deed falls his benevolence. He simply does not want to hurt anybody—not Miss Watson, and not Jim; but whatever he does he must hurt one of them. The trial is the result of his taking the world seriously, of recognizing both Miss Watson and Jim as separate from himself, as people with legitimate needs of their own. The world crowds him:

> That was where it pinched. Conscience says to me, "What had poor Miss Watson done to you, that you could see her nigger go off right under your eyes and never say one single word? What did that poor old woman do to you, that you could treat her so mean?" (*HF*, 123)

As much as Huck's inherited conscience plagues him in this scene, and threatens to haul him back into a corrupt society, the even greater snare for Huck is one we do not wish to recognize: his benevolence and compassion for others. That benevolence is the cause of his shrinking ego, the quality that pushes him to deny his own freedom and his own autonomous self. It is what leads him to recognize others as separate entities, and threatens to transform him from free child to enslaved adult. The direction Huck had taken was more radical, perhaps, than even Twain had anticipated. The easy life of play required nothing less than the severing of *all* human relationships, whether founded on social teachings or on spontaneous kindness, and in the struggle for freedom, Jim was as much of an encumbrance as Miss Watson. Freedom, as wide a world as it might be, left no room for compassion.

Huck could not be made to give Jim up. Such an act would be unforgivable. But neither could he be made to commit himself to helping Jim win his freedom. Neil Schmitz, noting that for Huck "freedom" means a place outside of society, and that for Jim it means "a secure and honorable place in society," argues that for Huck "Jim's freedom means the termination of his own; the abandonment of the raft and the river for concrete realities in Illinois."[23] This is true, and insightful as far as it goes. But Huck's quest for freedom has already been dealt a serious blow, even before the battle of conscience, in the moment Huck refused to play any more jokes on Jim. And if Twain pushes Huck closer to the real world by giving him his battle of conscience, he also hesitates at that point, reluctant to push Huck through the decision to the imprisonment on the other side—to make him an adult, that is, and slave either to society or to Jim.

Huck saves Jim largely by default, by a failure to act decisively. When the slave hunters question him about the man on

[23]Schmitz, 133–34.

the raft, Huck "didn't answer up prompt. I tried to, but the words wouldn't come. I tried, for a second or two, to brace up and out with it, but I warn't man enough . . ." (*HF,* 125). He tells them instead that he is a member of a pox-ridden family, and perhaps none of the lies he tells in the book contains so much truth. The failure to act in effect commits him to Jim, a situation we are accustomed to applaud—indeed, have no choice but to applaud—but one about which Twain was ambivalent.

It is perhaps no coincidence that a few pages after Huck's recognition of Jim as Other, the pair conclude that they may have passed Cairo in the fog. Cairo, though we learn it rather late, had been the jumping-off point for freedom, and missing it coincides with Huck's humbling apology to Jim and with his imprisonment in what amounts to a growing commitment to another. It coincides, too, with Jim's feverish work at bundling up the supplies when he thinks Cairo is still ahead: ". . . he worked all day fixing things in bundles," says Huck, "and getting all ready to quit rafting" (*HF,* 128).

Twain, too, was ready to give up rafting, and perhaps the novel with it. The book had become like the river: "You can't tell the shape of the river, and you can't see no distance" (*HF,* 130). The steamboat comes from nowhere, and smashes "straight through the raft" (*HF,* 130). Jim and Huck go overboard, and when Huck emerges from his dive under the paddlewheel, he is alone.

IV

"Now, back you go to 14!" Twain wrote to one of his Angel Fish in 1908, "—then there's no impropriety" (*God's Fool,* 127). Whatever prompted Twain to write those words was also operative when he was writing *Huckleberry Finn,* for his impasse at chapter sixteen reflects, more than anything else, his unwillingness to bring Huck face to face with an adult world of decisions and limitations. Twain was working with two contradictory thrusts in the novel, a conscious intention to take a boy and "run him on through life," and a less conscious impulse to save the same boy from the wolves of the real world. It is the conscious intention that leads Twain to bring Huck to a decision of conscience, a decision that involves him with the world and with others. But it is the other impulse that prevents him from pushing Huck through that crisis to meet the full implications on the other side of it. The repeated cycles of escape from the world and re-entry into it that characterize Huck's journey are a reflection both of Twain's indecision about what to do with Huck and of Huck's own contradictory nature—the empiricism that marks him as being *of* the world, and the solipsism that prompts him to create his own world without reference to his past or environment.

The possibilities of escape clearly fascinated Twain and in part seduced him from his original intentions. For all the elements in the novel that make Huck's world more realistic than Tom's St. Petersburg and that therefore promise to initiate Huck into adulthood, the novel has been most emotionally charged in those other elements that suggest that Huck might be able to avoid becoming an adult. But complicating the whole matter was the growing probability that to remain a child with a child's freedom necessitated a blindness to the humanity of others.[24] To build on the autonomous Self was to experience a heady freedom, but the moral implications of that freedom were increasingly suspect.

There was no real solution to the dilemma for Twain. Huck could not be both free and adult, nor could he be both child and compassionate. We know from Walter Blair's work with the manuscripts that Twain set aside the novel after chapter sixteen, unwilling or unable to go on (*MT&HF,* 151). The break in progress occurred late in the summer of 1876, and thematically it echoes the same disturbing principle Twain had encountered earlier in "Carnival of Crime." It must have been clear to Twain that Huck's commitment to Jim, born of human sympathy, threatened to enslave him and defeat his bid for freedom. It is no coincidence that "Carnival of Crime" explores a character who avoids enslavement by destroying his human sympathy, and who

[24]My reading of the novel contrasts with the more traditional interpretation, succinctly stated by E. Hudson Long: "In *Huckleberry Finn* circumstance and temperament in Huck produce a clash between sympathy and the will to freedom on the one hand, and custom and law, on the other . . ." See E. Hudson Long, *Mark Twain Handbook* (New York: Hendricks House, 1957), 384.

creates a new self in the process. But if "Carnival of Crime" probes the logical extensions of Huck's dream of ease and comfort, those extensions were not suitable for Huck. Twain set aside the unfinished novel and did not resume work on it until 1879. When he did begin to work with *Huckleberry Finn* again, it was after he had nearly completed *The Prince and the Pauper,* wherein a boy's dream leads to a test of his sympathy, and wherein the boy's compassion survives. Perhaps, too, it was Tom Canty's success in remaining benevolent that prompted Twain to resurrect Jim. Perhaps he felt that, in spite of the problem Jim posed for Huck, Huck could manage to have, like Tom Canty, both his dream and his friend.

The two chapters of 1879-1880 comprise the Grangerford-Shepherdson feud, and more than being a long-delayed continuation of the novel, they represent a fresh start. In these two chapters the action of the first seven chapters is compressed and repeated, from Huck's near absorption into society to his symbolic dying out of it. Huck no sooner meets the Grangerfords than he is ushered, at gun-point, into their house, and "As soon as I was in, the old gentleman he locked the door and barred it and bolted it" (*HF,* 133). Neil Schmitz points out some of the parallels between the constricting qualities of the Grangerford household, with its emphasis on filial duty, and the confinements Huck had experienced with Miss Watson and Pap.[25] He notes especially that Pap's drunken attack on Huck in chapter six is repeated symbolically with the elder Grangerford pushing his sons toward death in the feud: "I don't like that shooting from behind a bush," says Col. Grangerford to Buck. "Why didn't you step into the road, my boy?" (*HF,* 146). The training of the Grangerford children seems calculated to deny them any identity of their own by remaking them into images of their father.

There are other parallels between these chapters and the earlier ones. Huck is again "getting used to" the new ways, and he even tells us that he "liked all that family, dead ones and all, and warn't going to let anything come between us" (*HF,* 141). And as much as Huck finds Emmilene Grangerford's funereal pictures disquieting, there is still the old fascination with death and dying:

[25]Schmitz, 128.

> Poor thing, many's the time I made myself go up to the little room that used to be hers and get out her poor old scrapbook and read in it when her pictures had been aggravating me and I had soured on her a little. . . . Poor Emmelene made poetry about all the dead people when she was alive, and it didn't seem right that there warn't nobody to make some about her, now she was gone; so I tried to sweat out a verse or two myself, but I couldn't seem to make it go, somehow. (*HF,* 141)

If Huck fears physical death, still there is the attraction to a state in which death, and the aging process that leads to death, need not be faced. "Death bitter to the flesh," as Bunyan puts it, "but sweet to the soul."[26]

The Grangerfords' son, Buck, functions in these chapters as a reversed image of Huck and as a surrogate Huck whose death will once again release Huck from confinement. As a "civilized" Huck, he represents what Huck could become in society—the dutiful son who seeks to gain the approval of his father and family, and who in so doing pursues the death of his autonomous Self. What Buck wants most of all is not to be himself, but to be another Col. Grangerford, and the murder of a Shepherdson would be for him a baptismal rite confirming him in that identity and in a long-sought adulthood. Ironically but appropriately, it is his own death that performs that function. Buck and his father die in the same battle; the event that makes Buck most like his father, and makes him an adult, kills him as well.

As a surrogate Huck, Buck in his death signifies Huck's own death *out* of this family, and Huck uses it as a second counterfeit suicide. As Huck prepares to leave the shore and strike out again on the river, he thinks of Buck's body and tells Jim, "All right—that's mighty good; they won't find me, and they'll think I've been killed, and floated down the river—there's something up there that'll help them to think so . . ." (*HF*, 155).

Confinement, adoption, the death of the father, a symbolic suicide, and a break for the river. The major events of the first part of the novel had been repeated, and Twain was ready to start again Huck's journey down the river.

[26]*Pilgrim's Progress,* 364.

But this time the direction Twain takes seems more positively weighted toward an escape *from* the world rather than an initiation *into* it. For one thing, Twain had apparently decided, with chapter sixteen, that the raft journey was to end. It was only in the middle of the feud chapters that he decided to continue with the journey, and he made a note to himself to make the necessary adjustment: "Back a little, CHANGE—raft only crippled by steamer" (*MT&HF,* 253). And, when the raft is reconstituted and Jim reappears, a few changes are apparent. With the reunion of Huck and Jim, Huck tells us that

> We said there warn't no home like a raft, after all. Other places do seem so cramped up and smothery, but a raft don't. You feel mighty free and easy and comfortable on a raft. (*HF,* 156)

The words seem to reflect Twain's decision more than they do the truth of the matter as it has been developed thus far in the novel. There is "no home like a raft, *after all,*" in spite of the fact that life on the raft has not really been "free and easy," as Huck claims. On the contrary, his growing awareness of Jim as a separate human being has pushed Huck into very uncomfortable positions, positions in which his whole being feels "pinched." Furthermore, his conversations with Jim on the raft have repeatedly shown the two of them at odds. And Jim has never, up to now, considered the raft a "home"; for him it has been a vehicle, not a destination. Yet here, rather suddenly, we find Jim and Huck both viewing the raft as a refuge and an end. Jim has apparently come around to Huck's view of things.

For the next several paragraphs we are given a picture of the raft as an idyllic refuge from the world. "Two or three days and nights went by," Huck tells us; "I reckon I might say they swum by, they slid along so quiet and smooth and lovely" (*HF,* 157). It is largely through these paragraphs that we see what the raft could be, what the raft is *meant* to be, at least after the Grangerford episode: a substitute for Jackson's Island, a celestial playground wherein the boy and the man might exist as friends, without the impingements of an imperfect world where real people have real differences, and where it becomes necessary to curtail one's own desires in order to get along. These paragraphs are in fact the only ones of length in which the raft is described as a perfect place. Our emotional attachment to the raft is produced here and by Huck's repeated attempts to return to the raft when he is pulled away from it.

The most important thing about these paragraphs, perhaps, is that there is in them very little dramatization. The relationship between Huck and Jim in this perfect place is suggested, strongly and effectively, but there is no extended dramatization of their interaction. There is Huck's account of their conversations, and of their mild disagreement over whether the stars "was made, or only just happened" (*HF,* 159). But we do not ourselves hear either of them speak. The lyricism of the passages is effective, but it is also a substitute for showing dramatic relationships between Huck and Jim that might undercut the raft's idyllic quality. It is the one technique that can keep Jim human without making his humanity interfere with Huck's dream of freedom. Richard Poirier, in *A World Elsewhere,* touches on the problem that Twain faced, though he does not attribute it to the relationship between Huck and Jim:

> . . . this novel discovers that the consciousness it values most cannot expand within the environment it provides, that the self cannot come to fuller life through social drama, upon which the vitality of this and of most other novels of the last century at some point depend.[27]

If Twain was baffled at how to proceed after Huck's apology to Jim and his first battle of conscience, the Grangerford episode represents another attempt at setting Huck free. And Twain found the answer to the problems that stopped him before. He could retain Jim as a human being rather than a sub-human darky; he could depict a warm relationship between Huck and Jim; and he could preserve Huck's idyllic freedom of ease and comfort—all by substituting telling for showing, and by revising Jim's attitude toward the raft so that it coincided with Huck's. He could do all of this, that is to say, by keeping real experience at a distance, by submerging Jim's will in Huck's, by offering

[27]Richard Poirier, *A World Elsewhere* (New York: Oxford Univ. Press, 1963), 195.

Huck the same protection from life that he had given Tom in *Tom Sawyer*. The fact that these idyllic passages are so convincing testifies to Twain's power as a writer; the fact that we are so consistently seduced into believing them real testifies to our own desire to believe that such an ideal place might be achievable. It is easy for us to forget that Huck and Jim on the perfect raft consists largely of generalities, but that living consists of particulars.

So, too, must novels consist of particulars, of dramatized, specific interactions between human beings. Twain could not simply continue writing lyrically; something had to *happen* in the novel, and anything that happened—any dramatized social interaction—threatened to destroy what the lyricism had finally made possible.

The introduction of the King and the Duke provided Twain, as Blair points out, with a plausible means of continuing the river journey (*MT&HF*, 253). But Henry Nash Smith is correct when he says that with the King and the Duke episodes Twain "postpones acknowledging that the quest for freedom has failed," and that Huck is largely only a passive observer of the action.[28] Huck in fact *had* to be passive, since any real action on his part would throw him into too close contact with the world again, raising the spectre of commitment and imprisonment.[29] He could be *with* the King and the Duke, recording their activities, but not *of* them, just as he could report on the villages and villagers of the shore, but could not be identified with them. He was of another world, safely sanctified only so long as he remained aloof and uncommitted to those around him.

In this regard, Jim presented special problems. We have already seen how a recognition of Jim's humanity threatened

[28]Smith, *Development of a Writer,* 117.

[29]Quentin Anderson notes that the Emerson hero must be passive rather than active:

> Emerson most often, but by no means always, plumped for the receptive mode, because if we act we become involved in a sequence of actions and the immediate significance of our feelings is threatened. . . . To persuade each hearer that in his uniqueness he incorporated the meaning of the whole is what the preacher tried to do. But any attempt to act on this newly won grandeur landed his hearers in the plural world again. (Anderson, 45)

Huck with adulthood, and how at the same time a refusal to see Jim's humanity threatened to undermine his benevolence. In the King and the Duke sections, one is struck with Huck's rather bland acceptance of the indignities inflicted upon Jim, and with the unconvincing nature of the excuses Huck makes for his tolerance of them. The Duke, for example, prints handbills advertising Jim as an escaped slave, and proposes a plan to satisfy anyone who questions Jim's presence:

> . . . we can tie Jim hand and foot with a rope, and lay him in the wigwam and show this handbill and say we captured him up the river. . . . Handcuffs and chains would look still better on Jim, but it wouldn't go well with the story of us being so poor. Too much like jewelry.

Huck responds only by saying that "We all said the duke was pretty smart, and there couldn't be no trouble about running daytimes" (*HF,* 176). Later Jim manages to hint that the ropes are a burden, and Huck finds it necessary to explain again why Jim is tied:

> Jim he spoke to the duke . . . because it got mighty heavy and tiresome to him when he had to lay all day in the wigwam tied with the rope. You see, when we left him all alone we had to tie him, because if anybody happened on him all by himself and not tied, it wouldn't look much like he was a runaway nigger, you know. (*HF,* 203)

This is simply not the same Huck who humbled himself to Jim and determined never to play another trick on him. And it is not satisfactory, after all, to say merely that Huck must accede to Jim's victimization because the King and the Duke are now in control of things. The real problem lies in the fact that Huck, though he talks privately throughout the book to the reader, never voices a complaint or indicates that he is upset with this treatment of his friend. The closest he comes to such an indication is his telling Jim that "we've got them on our hands, and we got to remember what they are, and make allowances." "What was the use to tell Jim these warn't real kings and dukes?" Huck continues. "It wouldn't a done no good; and besides, it was just as I said; you couldn't tell them from the real kind" (*HF,* 201).

If Huck seems to have changed, so too has Jim. He comes close, at times, to being the darky he was at the beginning of the novel, when Tom Sawyer wanted to tie him to a tree. His gullibility and long-sufferance render him less than human—certainly inconsistent with the character both Huck and the reader have come to know, and more fit as the butt of practical jokes. Twain seems bothered by the inconsistency, for he gives us passages in chapter twenty-three in which Jim's humanity is again affirmed:

> He was thinking about his wife and his children, away up yonder, and he was low and homesick; because he hadn't ever been away from home before in his life; and I do believe he cared just as much for his people as white folks does for their'n. It don't seem natural, but I reckon it's so. (*HF*, 201).

Huck's reaction is curious, for it is rather off-hand. He considers the matter only in the abstract, only as a white boy learning more about black people. No *personal* commitment arises out of his new knowledge, no determination to set Jim on the road to freedom again. And when Jim tells of his sorrow at having unjustly punished his deaf and dumb daughter, we are left only to imagine Huck's reaction. And it is entirely imaginable, by this time, that Huck has no reaction at all—or chooses to stifle whatever reaction he might have. Jim's tale, in fact, seems to be included more for the benefit of the reader than for Huck, as though Twain were assuring us that Jim *is* still human, *does* have feelings, even though Huck is not responding to Jim as he once did.

The emphasis on Jim's sorrow over his daughter immediately precedes yet another of his humiliations. The Duke allows, finally, that being tied up might be "kind of hard," and so dresses Jim in a King Lear costume. ". . . then he took his theatre-paint and painted Jim's face and hands and ears and neck all over a dead dull solid blue, like a man that's been drowned nine days," says Huck. "Blamed if he warn't the horriblest looking outrage I ever see. . . . Why, he didn't only look like he was dead, he looked considerable more than that" (*HF*, 203–4).

It is as though Twain were straddling the issue of Huck's

relationship with and commitment to Jim. For as much as he reminds the reader that Jim is still suffering, and suggests that the idyllic friendship between Huck and Jim continues, he keeps Huck at a distance from Jim, and will not allow Huck to respond as sincerely, as humanely as he did in the apology scene. If Jim's humanity tended to undercut Huck's freedom before, Twain is careful not to let it interfere again. We are meant to believe in Huck's sympathy and in his commitment to Jim, but from chapter twenty to chapter thirty-one, Twain gives us very little evidence of it.

If Twain was hesitant about dramatizing Huck's relationship with Jim—hesitant about putting Huck in too close a relationship with him again—still it was necessary to keep him belevolent, not only because natural goodness befitted the child, but also because that characteristic was necessary for the ironic vision of Southern society. Huck's natural sympathy for others is demonstrated, therefore, in situations that do not commit him to any action that would impair his essential isolation. In chapter twenty-one, as Kenneth Lynn points out, Huck's compassion for the "drunk" man in the circus contrasts with the callousness of the crowd.[30] In the Wilks episode, Huck's sympathy for Mary Jane and her sisters prompts him to stage a plan that will save them and get rid of the King and the Duke. "Miss Mary Jane," Huck tells the Wilks girl, "you can't abear to see people in trouble, and *I* can't—most always" (*HF,* 239). And later, Huck tells us that "It made my eyes water a little, to remember her crying there all by herself in the night, and them devils laying there right under her own roof, shaming her and robbing her . . ." (*HF,* 245). But in all of these expressions of his sympathetic nature, Huck is never subjected to a situation in which his benevolence commits him permanently to another person, or one in which he must be absorbed into and identified with any sort of society.

Not, at least, until chapter thirty-one, when the King and the Duke sell Jim back into slavery. The postponement of the issue ends here, and one can hardly avoid asking *why* Twain chose to have Jim sold, since such an act would precipitate the same

[30]Lynn, 237.

situation for Huck that had frustrated the novel four years earlier. The answer must be speculative, of course, but one can at least perceive that the alternatives were few, and all of them dreadful.

Twain could have had Huck and Jim escape successfully from the King and the Duke. But then what? If the journey were to continue, Huck and Jim would be alone again on the raft, and some sort of dramatization of their interaction would be necessary—and that would threaten again to undermine Huck's ideal freedom. And, if there were to be more adventures, with other rapscallions in other villages, there was no end to the novel in sight at all.

He could have had Huck and Jim drift off, lyrically, into the sunset, suggesting that Huck's ideal freedom had been achieved at last, *with* Jim. But that would have left unresolved the whole issue of slavery, and would not have fit plausibly with either their location in the South or the character of society that had been developed. And either alternative would have violated the narrative form of the novel, since Huck speaks to us always in the past tense, from some constantly implied point at which the journey has ended.

There may have been other considerations as well. Twain had opted for a picaresque narrative after the Grangerford episode—the classic means by which the innocent meets a harsh world, loses his illusions, and adjusts to the demands of reality. But Huck has not, by chapter thirty-one, lost his dream of a world of ease and comfort. For all of what he has seen, he has not really changed. He has been "run on through life," but he has emerged essentially untouched—captive, really, of a creator who could not bear to see him become limited and constricted like everybody else, whether the limitations stemmed from a corrupt conscience or a natural sympathy with others. In having Jim sold back into slavery, Twain may have been responding once more—finally—to his original intentions, determined this time to have Huck commit himself to Jim, take the consequences, and assume his adulthood.

But that is not what happens. Instead, the final chapters of the novel move into Tom Sawyer's elaborate escape plan. Huck's growth to responsibility is again cut short. Prepared to see a dramatization of Huck's commitment to Jim, we see instead

Huck's—and Twain's—refusal to take that commitment seriously.

Huck's decision to go to Hell for Jim is the moral high point of the novel, and both we and Twain admire him most at that moment. But in our admiration for him, and in our desire to see him act on his commitment, we become like the rest of the adults in the novel. Like the Widow Douglas, or like Pap, we hope to see Huck become an image of ourselves. We do not, finally, wish him to be *himself* so much as we wish him to conform to our own expectations. Twain's dilemma at this point is extreme. His choice is to make of Huck something we can admire and approve—and something Twain himself could admire and approve— or to keep Huck true to his deepest longings for ease and comfort and freedom. One of the problems with the last chapters of the novel is that Twain never squarely faced this choice. They display, instead, an uneasy amalgam of a Huck we want to admire and a Huck who, if he is not admirable, is nevertheless true to himself.

Huck sets out to the Phelps' farm to free Jim, to act on his regained human commitment. But as he approaches the farm he twice thinks of death:

> When I got there it was all still and Sunday-like, and hot and sunshiny—the hands was gone to the fields; and there was them kind of faint dronings of bugs and flies in the air that makes it seem so lonesome and like everybody's dead and gone; and if a breeze fans along and quivers the leaves, it makes you mournful, because you feel like it's spirits whispering—spirits that's been dead ever so many years—and you always think they're talking about *you.* As a general thing it makes a body wish *he* was dead, too, and done with it all. (*HF,* 277)

And a few moments later,

> I heard the dim hum of a spinning-wheel wailing up and sinking along down again; and then I knowed for certain I wished I was dead—for that *is* the lonesomest sound in the whole world. (*HF,* 278)

The Huck who comes to save Jim, the adult who would accept

human commitment and its obligations, dies painlessly and with little fuss when Aunt Sally christens him with a new name. In that re-christening, Huck begins a new life with a new destiny. "It's Tom Sawyer!" Aunt Sally fairly shouts, and Huck assumes the new identity with relief: "If they was joyful, it warn't nothing to what I was; for it was like being born again, I was so glad to find out who I was" (*HF*, 282).

Huck's assumption of Tom's name is a practical and fortuitous way out of his immediate problem with the Phelps family. It enables him to explain plausibly his presence at their farm. But more important, it makes explicit something that has all along been implicit in the novel: the fact that Huck and Tom are not nearly so different in character as Twain had originally thought, that in important respects they are interchangeable twins. Both boys desire above all else an exemption from the limitations of the real world. Both wish to defy time and natural law in order to remain children—even if it means that the dignity and humanity of others must be ignored or denied in the process. Huck approaches the Phelps' farm thinking of and wishing for death, and death is precisely what he gets: not in terms of an initiation into adulthood, but in terms of a regression to childhood. "Being Tom Sawyer was easy and comfortable," Huck can say, because above all else it lets him off the universal hook of growing up (*HF*, 283).

One interpretation of Huck's new identity is that it precludes any real possibility of Huck's reaching freedom, that it absorbs him finally into a social identity and a social role. For Tom, it is argued, is the exponent of civilization, and with Tom's name Huck becomes "civilization's fair-haired boy."[31] James Cox argues that Huck, "In the very act of choosing to go to hell . . . has succumbed to the notion of a *principle* of right and wrong. He has forsaken the world of pleasure to make a moral choice. Precisely here is where Huck is about to negate himself . . ." (*Fate of Humor*, 180).

This approach parallels my own reading of the novel, but Cox argues further that Huck "with an act of positive virtue . . . commits himself to play the role of Tom Sawyer. . . . To commit

[31]Stone, 158.

oneself to the idea, to the *morality* of freeing Jim, is to become Tom Sawyer" (*Fate of Humor,* 180). Cox believes that to have a conscience of any sort (in Cox's terms, either "Northern" *or* "Southern") is to be Tom Sawyer, so that the end of the novel, "far from evading the consequences of Huck's [decision to free Jim], realizes those consequences" (*Fate of Humor,* 180). I would argue, on the contrary, that Huck's new identity is the very thing that enables him to free himself from conscience. With Tom's name, Huck can *be* Tom—can be, that is, an asocial child who knows no restraints in the pursuit of self-gratification.

Cox argues further, and rightly, that in the novel "there is no fire-and-brimstone hell but only civilization—which is precisely where Huck finds himself as a consequence of his own determination" to free Jim (*Fate of Humor,* 182). Huck does find himself in the midst of society at the Phelps', but he does not become a part of that society. For there is another hell, as well: that condition that arises from a refusal to join civilization, from a refusal to enter the prison of adulthood. Tom's elaborate escape plans arise from a child's desire to play, not from an adult's desire to work. He has no abiding commitment to Jim or to anybody else. His only commitment is to his imagination, and his efforts are all aimed at making the world conform to his ideas of how it should be.

Huck's acquiescence to Tom and his games clearly makes him a party to the cruelties and indignities inflicted upon Jim in the last chapters. Still, there is something to be said for the fact that Huck does not himself initiate those cruelties. Huck cannot be excused, but he does exist somewhere on the moral sidelines, a half-reluctant, half-willing participant whom we are hesitant to condemn. It is a strategy by which Twain seeks to avoid an outright condemnation of Huck, while still pursuing a truth he was reluctant to admit: that to remain a child in the real world was not to maintain a spontaneous benevolence, but to treat others as tools and fools, as playthings to be manipulated and sacrificed on the altar of Self.

The Phelps' farm becomes a carnival ground complete with freak shows and con artists, where the dignity of others is set aside in order to indulge a gluttonous imagination. Twain puts the burden of this truth on Tom, *uses* Tom to pursue its grotesque implications, but he knows, even if he is unwilling to admit it fully, that it applies to Huck as well. And so Twain preserves for Huck some semblance of innocence—a thin patina that does not stand close inspection, but a semblance nevertheless. He has Huck object to Tom's procedures (for they are not practical), but not to the pains inflicted upon Jim. And, as if to disguise this moral defect in Huck, he has Jim not only suffer without serious complaint, but willingly participate in his own betrayal, as though to give his blessing to the sin.

To turn the whole escape into a farce might relieve it of its serious implications, or at least obscure them. Leo Marx is probably correct when he says that "Clemens did not intend us to read the ending so solemnly."[32] But the elements of farce and burlesque seem contrived to evade thematic implications with which Twain could not effectively deal emotionally, and the result is that the ending of the novel becomes a patchwork of elements in which the serious and painful implications are first hinted at and then diluted with laughter. Huck's treatment of Jim is shabby—but then it doesn't really matter, because Jim agrees to it, after all. Jim is locked away and given a dog's diet—but then of course he is really free, after all. Jim suffers from spiders and rats, but presumably he enjoys the game, for he's only a nigger, and niggers don't feel pain like white folks do. And finally, Huck can play at Jim's expense, but that doesn't really matter either because the object is still the same: to free Jim.

None of it works, of course. Twain tries to keep Huck innocent and benevolent, when every page increases his guilt in our eyes. He tries to keep Huck committed to Jim, when clearly Huck no longer perceives Jim as a human being. He tries to have Tom take the burden of guilt, when it is clear that Huck's share is equally as great—perhaps greater, since we expect more of him.

What emerges from the final pages of *Huckleberry Finn* is the unwelcome recognition that Huck's quest for an ideal freedom is as dangerous and destructive as Tom's quest for a life of romantic

[32]Leo Marx, "Mr. Eliot, Mr. Trilling, and *Huckleberry Finn*," *The American Scholar*, 22, No. 4 (Autumn 1953); rpt. in *Adventures of Huckleberry Finn*, ed. Scully Bradley, et al. (New York: Norton, 1962), 331.

play. Both dreams can be realized in a carefully controlled St. Petersburg, or in a generalized, lyrical world where the particulars of social interaction can be glossed. But to realize them in a world where living is serious work rather than shallow play is to destroy the dignity not only of others, but of the Self as well. Tom's play turns the serious issue of Jim's bid for freedom into an easily ignored farce and undercuts the dignity Jim had earlier displayed. And Huck's own freedom can be realized only by his acquiescence in the destruction of Jim's humanity. The dark partner to that freedom is the destruction of his own humanity as well.

James Cox, in his "Remarks of the Sad Initiation of Huckleberry Finn," writes that "There is bitter irony in Huck's assumption of Tom's name because the values of Tom Sawyer are so antithetical to the values of Huck Finn; in the final analysis, the two boys cannot exist in the same world."[33] The antithesis of values is precisely what the reader wishes to believe, and it is precisely what Twain wanted to believe. Tom's aggressive manipulation of others for his own pleasure seems too callous and bestial to have much in common with the compassion we have seen in Huck. But in pushing his saintly Huck to the extreme, in confronting him with the choice of a confining adulthood or a self-determining childhood, Twain came to see that the values of Huck and Tom were fundamentally the same. To create a Self without reference to one's past or environment is possible in the real world only through a total devotion to the Self, through an expansion of ego that pushes aside the weaknesses of conscience and of compassion for father, mother, brother, sister. Both Huck and Tom seek to act in the world without reference to time and without reference to others; both seek a life of total freedom, uncluttered with the hard choices and maturing experiences that daily confirm the limitations of human beings and their necessary submission to the world of fact. Both seek to fulfill themselves in fantasy, and outside the charmed circles of St. Petersburg and the raft, the result is cheap, sordid, and destructive. Tom "had a dream," Huck tells the doctor who comes to tend Tom's wound,

[33]James Cox, "Remarks on the Sad Initiation of Huckleberry Finn," *Sewanee Review*, 62 (July 1954), 331.

"and it shot him." The doctor's reply: "Singular dream" (*HF*, 347).

Huck's symbolic killing of his father, which cut his ties with the past and with the world of ordinary circumstances, was in the beginning a configuration of high promise. It thrust him into an environment where all the best seemed possible. He was to avoid the constricting influences of a corrupt and hide-bound culture; he was to escape the constraints of a culture which enslaved its white sons in tradition and its black sons in chains; he was to fulfill his essential Self by transcending the limitations of fact and by building his own world, a world that allowed the free and simultaneous enjoyment of Self and Other without conflict. He was to become something better, too, than a mere boy with prepubescent dreams of piracy and treasure; he was to realize in fact a visionary world worthy of the saints, a world that sprang unbidden and uncorrupted from his own unfettered mind and personality.

Both Twain and the reader are in the beginning willing to urge him on, confident that Bunyan's "Life, life, eternal life" could be purchased without the payment Evangelist demands: the sacrifice of others. Confident, too, that the heaven of eternal infancy would be preferable to the hell of a shackled adulthood. But the final act is a humorless revelation that heaven and hell are married, that the Desired Country is morally indistinguishable from the City of Destruction, and that the heroic refusal to accept adulthood and death only means a death of another sort: a moral annihilation that results in a tranquil but terrible refuge beyond good and evil, where freedom gives one the right to say, with Napoleon, "What have crimes . . . to do with me?"

For the most horrible thing about Tom and Huck is that in the midst of their betrayal of Jim they do maintain a grotesque innocence. There is in them no malice, no desire to harm Jim or to make fools of those around them. They are simply unconscious of any moral implications that might be attached to their play. Thus, while we may object on moral grounds to the game, our objections mean nothing. Tom and Huck have nothing to do with the moral imagination we hold in so high regard. Emerson had defined heroism as "an obedience to a secret impulse of an individual's character," and warned that it "works in contradiction to the voice of mankind and in contradiction, for a time, to the voice of the great and good" (*CWE* II 251). Having urged Huck to go out and fulfill his essential Self, we can hardly condemn him now for doing so.

The novel plays itself out in a moral vacuum, in which Tom's rules replace the dictates of right and wrong. It is difficult, therefore, to determine who might be winners and who losers in the game. Perhaps Huck is a winner. Having been threatened with a moral imagination that would preclude ease and comfort and saddle him with obligations, he saves his freedom by a brave trust in a secret impulse. His reward comes on the final page of the novel, when he discovers from Jim that Pap is dead not just symbolically but in fact. Thus released from prison again, Huck can light out for the unregulated Territory, where he and Tom and Injun Joe can live in ease and comfort, and where others are routinely sacrificed to the demands of an insatiable imagination.

Jim, on the other hand, may be the loser. Unlike Huck, he remains faithful to a wounded friend, and his reward is re-enslavement and a near-lynching. Of course he gains his "freedom" in the end—"as free as any cretur that walks this earth," as Tom says (*HF,* 360). Jim is free to work and buy his family, free to think himself rich for selling his dignity to the boys for forty dollars; free to be the darky in a white society. He is not nearly so free as Tom and Huck, but then neither of them walks *this* earth so much as he walks some other land—a territory terrifying to us and to Twain, but one shaped and contoured to their own specifications.

If we ultimately come to question the wisdom of Huck's journey to freedom, perhaps our confusion is only a replica of Emerson's puzzlement over Napoleon. Our immediate response is to call Huck, as Emerson called Napoleon, "an impostor." The Huck we get is not the Huck we were promised, and so we content ourselves, perhaps, with Leo Marx's judgment that the ending of the novel shows a "lack of moral imagination" in the author, just as Emerson saw in Napoleon "no moral centre." But we should do well to consider that if Twain had a lapse of moral imagination, he had something to put in its place: the courage to explore the final implications of Huck's dream, even if it threatened to destroy the ideal of childhood that anchored him in a sea of adult treacheries.

In the beginning of the novel, Huck resigned from Tom's robber gang; Tom's dreams were not for him. But the alternative to dreaming was to wake up, and to grow up. At the end of the novel Huck does not resign. Growing up is against his constitution, and the life of a dreaming boy is after it. It is a minor figure in the novel, old Mrs. Hotchkiss, who characterizes the life of dreaming. She talks of Jim, of course, but she describes the dream:

> Well, Sister Phelps, I've ransacked that-air cabin over an' I b'lieve the nigger was crazy. I says so to Sister Damrell—didn't I, Sister Damrell?—s'I, he's crazy, s'I—them's the very words I said. You all hearn me: he's crazy, s'I; everything shows it, s'I. Look at that-air grindstone, s'I; want to tell *me*'t any cretur 'ts in his right mind's agoin' to scrabble all them crazy things onto a grindstone, s'I? . . . He's plumb crazy, s'I; it's what I says in the fust place, it's what I says in the middle, 'n it's what I says last 'n' all the time—the nigger's crazy—crazy's Nebokoodneezer, s'I. (*HF,* 349–50).

In his notebook entries for February 1891, Twain envisioned a peculiar sequel for the story of Huck and Tom:

> Huck comes back sixty years old, from nobody knows where—and crazy. Thinks he is a boy again and scans always every face for Tom, Becky, etc.
>
> Tom comes at last from sixty years' wandering in the world, and attends Huck and together they talk of old times; both are desolate, life has been a failure, all that was lovable, all that was beautiful is under the mold. They die together. (*Notebook,* 212).

It is not difficult to determine why life would be a failure for these two: either because the real world blocked the fulfillment of their dreams, or because it did not.

IV

A Connecticut Yankee in King Arthur's Court

Dream delivers us to dream, and there is no end to illusion.
—Emerson, "Experience"

Between narrow walls we walk:—insanity on one side, & fat dulness on the other.
—Emerson, *JMN* VII 399

I

About a year after the publication of *Huckleberry Finn,* Twain began working on his next major novel, *A Connecticut Yankee in King Arthur's Court.* Of all his fiction, *A Connecticut Yankee* is Twain's most topical work. Louis Budd and Howard Baetzhold have shown how closely related are the details of the work to many social issues being discussed in England and the United States in the 1880s.[1] In many ways the novel may be read as a social tract—a villification of ideas and institutions that Twain found objectionable and a hymn of praise for those he favored. But the novel holds our interest today not for its topical satire or for its revelations of Twain's own socio-political beliefs and preoccupations, but rather for its disturbing quality of desperation. Even more evidently than in *Huckleberry Finn,* the novel's forward movement is accompanied by eddies and undercurrents that occasionally form "breaks" on the surface and that

[1]Louis J. Budd, *Mark Twain: Social Philosopher* (Bloomington: Univ. of Indiana Press, 1962); Howard G. Baetzhold, *Mark Twain and John Bull: The British Connection* (Bloomington: Univ. of Indiana Press, 1970).

finally threaten to rise up and turn the novel back on itself. It is this movement and countermovement that causes critics to conclude, as does Henry Nash Smith, that Twain harbored a fundamental distrust of the American technology he goes to such lengths to praise in the novel.[2]

But the causes of the novel's ambivalence lie deeper than in Twain's divided notions about American technology. *A Connecticut Yankee* remains a "confused and confusing novel" [3] because more than any of his other works it reflects the irresolvable conflicts within Twain himself.[4]

The Adventures of Tom Sawyer led Twain to uneasy glimpses of malevolent possibilities for a protagonist who could treat the globe as his toy. With *Huckleberry Finn,* those possibilities rose to the surface, and it became clear that one who would persist in fashioning the world to the demands of his own imagination could do so only at the expense of others, and of his own moral character. The sort of empowered Self that attracted Twain so strongly ended by repelling him as well. Its powers were superhuman and constituted, ultimately, an encroachment on divine prerogatives—a situation perfectly acceptable in fantasy, in a play world where the stakes were unimportant, but one more and more questionable in any real world, where the consequences of one's actions rippled into the lives of others.

If Twain had dismissed his pursuit of such characters after *Huckleberry Finn,* certainly the difficulty he encountered with that novel would have made such a dismissal understandable. But his interest in the possibilities of transcending the limitations of experience was not the product of mere choice; it constituted a given of his character, and as such it could not *be* dismissed. And in the 1880s and 1890s, as Cox points out, Twain

[2]Smith, *Development of a Writer,* 157, 161.

[3]Baetzhold, 131.

[4]This observation is by now widely accepted. Henry Nash Smith notes that "the composition of *A Connecticut Yankee* brought into play basic contradictions in Mark Twain's attitudes." See his *Mark Twain's Fable of Progress: Political and Economic Ideas in "A Connecticut Yankee"* (New Brunswick: Rutgers Univ. Press, 1964), 60–61. Roger Salomon remarks, too, that Hank is a projection of "unresolved psychic and intellectual problems" (*Twain and the Image of History, 114*).

"could not confine the creative forces behind [his dreaming characters] to literature alone":

> By the time he wrote *Huckleberry Finn,* they were not only operating inside the novel . . . they were encroaching from the outside as well, having led Twain from investments in a steam generator, a steam pulley, a new method of marine telegraphy, a watch company, an insurance house, a new process of engraving (the Kaolatype) into two huge projects: the Webster Publishing Company . . . and the Paige typesetting machine.[5]

Much of Twain's involvement in business affairs stemmed from his desire to increase his fortune. But there was another motive as well that led him to invest in a myriad of new inventions. For if it was difficult for him to believe that Czar Alexander was made of mere flesh and blood, and if Napoleon seemed somehow able to dream himself to a throne, so too did inventors seem a higher order of men. In response to news that his brother Orion had been developing a new invention, Twain wrote in 1870 that

> An inventor is a poet—a true poet—and nothing in any degree less than a high order of poet—therefore his noblest pleasure dies with the stroke that completes the creature of his genius, just as the painter's & the sculptor's & other poets' highest pleasure ceases with the touch that finishes their work—& so only he can understand or appreciate the *legitimate* "success" of his achievement, littler minds being able to get no higher than a comprehension of a vulgar moneyed success. . . . To be Governor of Nevada is to be a poor little creeping thing that a *man* may create . . . but to invent even this modest little drilling machine shows the presence of the patrician blood of intellect—that "round & top of sovereignty" which separates its possessors from the common multitude & marks him as one not beholden to

[5]James M. Cox, "*A Connecticut Yankee in King Arthur's Court:* The Machinery of Self-Preservation," *Yale Review* 50 (Autumn 1960), 96.

> the caprices of politics but endowed with greatness in his own right.[6]

Twain's suggestion that the inventor/poet stands outside the common rule of favor and disfavor—that he exists not to please the "littler minds" around him but the demands of his own genius—echoes Emerson's description of the poet, who stands "isolated among his contemporaies by truth and by his art" (*CWE* III 5). On the poet, says Emerson,

> a new nobility is conferred . . . and not in castles or by the swordblade any longer. The conditions are hard, but equal. Thou shalt leave the world, and know the muse only. Thou shalt not know any longer the times, customs, graces, politics, or opinions of men, but shalt take all from the muse. (*CWE* III 41)

The poet for Emerson was one for whom "small and mean things serve as well as great symbols" (*CWE* III 17), and whose new forms have "a certain power of emancipation and exhilaration for all men. We seem to be touched by a wand which makes us dance and run about happily, like children. We are like persons who come out of a cave or cellar into the open air. . . . Poets are thus liberating gods" (*CWE* III 30).

For Twain too the inventor/poet was a "liberating god." Twain's enthusiastic response to and extensive involvement in inventions of all sorts was motivated not just by the profits he hoped to realize, but by the new perspectives they symbolized. They represented for Twain new historical milestones, not just in technological progress but in human stature. They were concrete expressions of an inherent but seldom realized power of creativity. In *A Connecticut Yankee* he lists the great inventors of history, calling them "the creators of this world—after God" (*WMT* IX 369), and as such they were, like Hank Morgan, Promethean characters whose business it was to lead us out of darkness.

It is just such a liberating effect Twain must have felt when he contemplated the productions of inventors, and the prime exam-

[6]*Mark Twain, Business Man,* ed. Samuel Charles Webster (Boston: Little, Brown, 1946), 114–15.

ple of that liberation is to be found in his involvement with the typesetter invented by James W. Paige, whom Twain met in the Colt Arms factory in 1880. "He is a poet," wrote Twain, "a most great and genuine poet, whose sublime creations are written in steel. He is the Shakespeare of mechanical invention" (Kaplan, 284).

Paige's verse was an extraordinarily complicated machine of some eighteen thousand separate parts, and between 1881 and 1894 Twain poured some $300,000 into its development. Twain "wrote that he loved to sit by the machine by the hour and merely contemplate it." In seeing it in operation for the first time, he noted that "All the witnesses made written record of the immense historical birth."[7] Much of Twain's fascination for the typesetter lay in its dramatic ability to outstrip mere human performance. Unlike men, who were slow and who occasionally erred, the machine was quick and nearly, if not totally, infallible. In the margins of one galley proof set by the machine Twain noted, "This is just as it came from the machine—proof not corrected. The cleanest proof that ever was; the *man* has made 2 mistakes, but the *machine* has made *not a single error*."[8] In 1889 Twain envisioned a competition between six hand compositors and one man operating the typesetter. The state Governor and Lieutenant Governor were to referree the match, and issue hourly bulletins on the progress of the race.[9]

Kaplan, in his description of Twain's emotional attachment to the typesetter, suggests, but does not make explicit, the roots of Twain's fascination:

> A mechanical typesetter would have to *think* in order to work, Clemens persisted in believing, and the machine he saw at Colt's appeared to be able to think. The inventor of such a machine must be a divine magician, he also believed, and the machine itself a living, intelligent organism which, as it was improved and articulated, paralleled human ontogeny. (Kaplan, 283)

[7]Cox, "The Machinery of Self-Preservation," 97.
[8]*Mark Twain, Business Man,* 311.
[9]*Selected Mark Twain-Howells Letters, 1872–1910,* 289.

Both the inventor and his invention—the artist and his art—were for Twain concrete examples of transcendence. The machine, in a kind of alchemical transmutation, had been lifted to human stature, and the artist approached the divine. Something of the same notion occurs in Emerson's essay on the poet, who perceives that "within the form of every creature is a force impelling it to ascend into a higher form" (*CWE* III 20).

In a later work, "No. 44, The Mysterious Stranger," Twain describes a scene in which an entire printing shop is efficiently operated without benefit of human intervention. The work is done through the magical prowess of the transcendent figure Satan, whose earthly name (No. 44, New Series 864, 962) resembles nothing so much as a machine's patent identification:

> At other cases you would see "sticks" hovering in the air just above the space-box; see a line set, spaced, justified and the rule slipped over in the time it takes a person to snap his fingers; next minute the stick is full! next moment it is emptied into the galley! and in ten minutes the *galley's* full and the case empty! It made you dizzy to see these incredible things, these impossible things. ("No. 44," 282)

Paige and his typesetter, then, seemed to Twain to parallel the same principle of transcendence that he saw in the empowered Self of his fiction. And just as Twain found that benevolent Self difficult to portray in a world of real experience, so too did the promised "liberation" of the inventor/poet prove to be more illusion than fact. Repeated delays, breakdowns, and failures of the typesetter bedeviled Twain's faith in it. And just as Twain was unable to release himself from his commitment to the empowered Self, he was equally unable to release himself from his hopes for the typesetter's completion. Just as the empowered Self seemed destined to turn Good Boy into Bad Boy, so did Paige fluctuate in Twain's mind from a "most great and genuine poet" to a con-man and charlatan, a "daring and majestic liar":

> Paige and I always meet on effusively affectionate terms, and yet he knows, perfectly well, that if I had him in a steel trap I would shut out all human succor and watch that trap, until he died. (*Notebook,* 233)

The inventor/poet, a variation on the creative empowered Self, was a figure of both hope and disappointment. The machine itself Twain described variously as a "cunning devil," a "sublime magician," and a "sick child"—all epithets that apply equally well to the duplicitous empowered Self of his fiction. In 1893, with his finances in such disarray as to offer him only two months' living expenses, Twain wrote that

> The bloody machine offered but a doubtful outlook—and will still offer nothing much better for a long time to come; for when Davis's "three weeks" are up there will be three months' tinkering to follow I guess. That is unquestionably the boss machine of this world, but it is the toughest one on prophets, when it is in an incomplete state, that has ever seen the light. Neither Davis nor any other man can foretell with any considerable approach to certainty when it will be ready to get right down to actual work. . . .[10]

Finally, the ultimate collapse of the machine in 1894 left Twain dazed:

> It hit me like a thunder-clap. I went flying here and there and yonder, not knowing what I was doing, and only one clearly defined thought standing up visible and substantial out of the crazy storm-drift—that my dream of ten years was in desperate peril. . . . Have you ever been like that? . . . There was another clearly defined idea—I must be there and see it die. That is, if it must die.[11]

Twain's expectations regarding technology were not caused by his faith in the Paige typesetter. Rather, his faith in that machine and his long-standing interest in other technological inventions was an outgrowth of his pre-existent hope that man might break through the confinements of the dull and ordinary round of life. Twain's vocabulary in describing Paige and his typesetter repeatedly invokes images of the miraculous and the magical. It reflects what Leo Marx has called "the rhetoric of the technological sublime" which "Emerson . . . adopted to his own purposes."

[10]*Mark Twain's Letters to His Publishers, 1867–1894,* ed. Hamlin Hill (Berkeley: Univ. of California Press, 1967), 357.

[11]*Mark Twain, Business Man,* 396.

In *Nature,* Marx notes, Emerson suggests that new inventions, though they may be products of the Understanding, are nevertheless "evidence of man's power to impose his will upon the world." Man

> no longer waits for favoring gales, but by means of steam, he realizes the fable of Aeolus' bag, and carries the two and thirty winds in the boiler of his boat. To diminish friction, he paves the road with iron bars, and, mounting a coach with him, he darts through the countryside, from town to town, like an eagle or a swallow through the air. By the aggregate of these aides, how is the face of the world changed, from the era of Noah to that of Napoleon![12]

In his journal of 1843, Emerson again finds technology a harbinger, if not an expression, of man's working Reason: "Machinery & Transcendentalism agree well. Stage Coach & Rail Road are bursting the old legislation like greet withes" (*JMN* VIII 397).

Twain, too, felt that the "old legislation," which keeps man trapped in time, in history, and in a dull compromise with reality, might be approaching a long-delayed end. Whitman's lines in "Passage to India" also suggest something of Twain's feelings when Paige and his machine captured his imagination:

> A worship new I sing,
> You captains, voyagers, explorers, yours,
> You engineers, you architects, machinists, yours,
> You, not for trade or transportation only,
> But in God's name, and for thy sake O soul.[13]

For Whitman and Emerson, machine power seemed harbingers of man's latent energies—energies enough to sail beyond the continent's limits and to strike out for, and reach, an as yet unrealized India of the soul. Twain, too, could see in his mind's eye an immanent convergence of extravagant dream and tangible reality. Only a fixed predisposition to believe that romance could become reality could lead him, after all, to credit Paige's claims for so many years. Twain's preoccupations with technology was

[12]Quoted in Leo Marx, *The Machine in the Garden: Technology and the Pastoral Ideal in America* (London: Oxford Univ. Press, 1964), 230.

[13]*Leaves of Grass,* 412.

rooted in his hope that the world might be redesigned, that reality might be radically changed, through an act of will. If the airy visions of the poet could be realized in iron and steel, then surely the dreams of a better, more satisfying world could be made flesh. The burgeoning machine culture was an example of man becoming, as Emerson termed him, the creator in the finite.

Emerson had a philosophic base for his vision of man. The epiphanic moments in which he experienced a felt connection between his consciousness and the empirical world led him to articulate carefully the premises which led logically to his idea of the empowered Self. If, upon examination, that vision seems extravagant, we can at least understand how he arrived at it, and, within the confines of Emerson's framework, we can more readily accept his belief in it. Twain had no such philosophical base. He had only his dissatisfaction with a violent and disappointing world, a growing rage that the world should be as he found it, and an inchoate belief that it should be and could be more accommodating.

He also had an interest in dreams and the dream experience, which often seemed to him as real or even more real than his waking life. In *Life on the Mississippi* he could for a moment find refuge from a troubled world by calling it a dream, and by entering a fantasy world of boyhood which he could for a moment call "real." In *Tom Sawyer* he could broach the topic of dreams and reality by having Aunt Polly claim that a body does in a dream what he would do awake, and run off to conquer Mrs. Harper's realism with Tom's dream. If in *Huckleberry Finn* Twain could question the morality of confusing dream and reality—as he does when Huck insists that Jim only dreamed of their separation in the fog—he nevertheless found himself committed to Huck's dream of freedom, and he struggled laboriously to make it replace the Pokevilles and Bricksvilles of his own life.

In the early 1880s Twain had not decided what he thought about dreams. He apparently felt dreams intensely, and he was willing to entertain the notion that they had some connection with his waking life. Certainly the act of dreaming was closely related to the act of writing fiction—both were expressions of an imagination released from the confines of reality. (*A Connecticut*

Yankee, of course, had its inception in Twain's "Dream of being a knight errant in armor in the middle ages" [*Notebook,* 171]). But the interchange of dream and reality, while it held some sort of relief from a cold world and was perhaps fundamental to his life as an artist, was also dangerous, for it smacked of madness. To believe reality a dream and the dream reality was to strike hard at the very organization of the world, and to move too far in that direction was to call existence itself into question. It was also to flirt more and more openly with the solipsism that had long been implicit in his writing, in works like *Tom Sawyer, The Prince and the Pauper,* and *Huckleberry Finn.* Without the benefits of a philosophical regimen or vocabulary, Twain was moving, almost blundering, into conceptions of an intimate relationship between the mind and what it perceived. He was more and more seriously drawing together, as Emerson had, the Me and the Not Me in a way that would fuse them and make them divinely, or perhaps diabolically, interdependent.

In a few years Twain would expound at some length on his "dream theory," and insist that dreams contained an "actuality" that was every bit as real as anything in the waking world (*Notebook,* 352). In the mid-1880s, as he began work on *A Connecticut Yankee,* he had already considered the nature of his dream experiences and had used the topic as material in his works. Suffice it to say that dreams, like the idea of the empowered Self, were double-dealing. In one respect they offered a softer, more amenable world, and insofar as artistic production was related to the act of dreaming, they were a profitable endeavor that secured Twain both riches and fame. On the other hand, Twain was aware that to follow dreams too far, to entertain too seriously the notion that they might become real, was to flirt with lunacy. Huck, after all, had been pulled into Tom's dream, and Twain conceived of him later to be "crazy." Jim, too, had accommodated himself to Tom's dream, and he was called by Mrs. Hotchkiss "crazy." And Hank Morgan, slammed on the head by a man called Hercules (who in mythology released Prometheus from the chains that bound him to the rock), is released from a very real arms factory in Hartford and propelled into a world of extraordinary possibility—a world he at first suggests is an "asylum" for "lunatics" (*WMT* IX 52, 63), of whom Hank might well be one. Hercules' crowbar, Hank tells us, "seemed to spring every joint in my skull and make it overlap its neighbor" (*WMT* IX 51).

The result is a tale in which the neighboring worlds of dream and reality do indeed overlap. We are confronted with a world apparently created entirely by Hank, a dream world with its inception in Hank's own startled imagination, but a dream world which leaves tangible (if questionable) evidence of its independent existence. Whether Hank's world is real or not is never satisfactorily explained in the novel. But it is important that it remains a question, for it is one that Twain had begun to entertain more and more seriously, and one which he would explore more directly in "The Great Dark" and other pieces. For the moment, it is enough to note that the whole issue of whether a dream world might be real, or might become real, is intrinsically related to the theme of the empowered Self—the Self that might be released from a too confining world of experience in order to refashion its environment to accommodate the demands of its imagination. The hope that wishes might come true, that fantasy might be realized, was still working. What was different was that Twain had a stronger sense of the dangers involved in pursuing such a hope, and a steadily rising suspicion that human beings might not after all be capable of dreaming of better things or, worse still, might find a sadly deficient reality entirely to their liking.

II

Even before Hank Morgan is pushed into sixth-century England, he has about him the smell of power. As he introduces himself, we hear in his tone Twain's own pride in his protagonist's ability to control and even create the world around him. There is in Hank the promise of something extraordinary:

> I am a Yankee of the Yankees. . . . Why, I could make anything a body wanted—anything in the world, it didn't make any difference what; and if there wasn't any quick new-fangled way to make a thing, I could invent one—and do it as easy as rolling off a log. (*WMT* IX 50)

It is not difficult to imagine Twain thinking of James W. Paige as he wrote these lines. The extravagance of Hank's claim, even the boasting tone, must have seemed justified to a Twain impressed beyond all bounds by a mechanic who had turned vision to matter, matter to miracle. If Hank Morgan is a tall-tale hero, a Paul Bunyan of the mechanics, still the picture must have seemed realistic to Twain. With his brash irreverence, his self-confident pushiness, and his drive to have things his own way, Hank was for Twain the antithesis of all the hapless creatures who knew, or thought they knew, "their place." Socially and ideologically, Hank Morgan was for Twain the self-made man personified, the incarnation of that plucky individual who knew his own mind and had places to go and the wherewithal to get there. He has a degree of personal force matched only by the machines he creates. He is the American type and symbol—a man bursting with energy and know-how, a man not to be slowed or derailed with ease.[14]

The blow Hank receives from Hercules does not derail him, or even slow him down. It does, however, cause the world to go out in darkness for a time, and it is the means by which Hank comes to a new "awakening." The tale that follows is of course implausible, and we are left free to call it fantasy or dream. But the world Hank awakens to (at least outside the confines of Camelot) is not different in kind from the one he left. With its brutality and its inhumanity, it resembles the nineteenth century in too many respects, and Twain makes full capital of these resemblances as the novel progresses. Yet if the world is not really different in its essentials, Hank's perspective is, and this makes all the difference. The primitive, violent, and superstitious world Hank enters is viewed from a point at which Hank's powers have been fully realized. To appreciate his position, we must try for a moment to imagine how our own world might appear to a man who had entirely succeeded in the reformation that Emerson so heartily called for.

"At present," said Emerson, "man applies to nature but half his force. He works on the world with his understanding alone.

[14]Henry Nash Smith (*Development of a Writer,* 151) sees Twain's initial description of Hank as a "generic image of the American Adam that had been current in the United States for more than a century."

. . . His relation to nature, his power over it, is through the understanding, as by manure. . . ." But the man whose axis of vision is coincident with the axis of things—the man, that is, who peers at the world through the eyes of Reason—might well be contemptuous of the pettiness of man's exercises. "Meantime, in the thick darkness, there are not wanting gleams of a better light—occasional examples of the action of man upon nature with his entire force." Emerson goes on to list items such as the history of Christ, the miracles of enthusiasm, self-healing, hypnotism, and the "achievements of a principle, as in religious and political revolutions" (*CWE* I 72–73).

There are implicit parallels between the consciousness that Hank *loses* and the Understanding that Emerson felt so impeded man's attainment of his rightful stature. Similarly, the "dream" in which Hank sees the world anew is a strange state of wakefulness, akin to Emerson's Reason. Emerson could call the impediments of a solid-seeming world "phantoms" and "illusions" and "appearances" which should not be mistaken for ultimates. When once the eyes of Reason open, these appearances vanish, to show man with "the gods still sitting around him on their thrones" (*CWE* VI 325). "Men who make themselves felt in the world avail themselves of a certain fate in their constitutions which they know how to use. But they never deeply interest us unless they lift a corner of the curtain, or betray, never so slightly, their penetration of what is behind it" (*CWE* VI 317).

Hank's dream suggests such a lifting of the curtain. The mechanical prowess he exhibits in Arthur's world may be seen as a metaphor for the sorts of power Emerson had longed to see in action. Both Twain and Hank may have reservations about its actuality, yet Emerson anticipates even this: "There is illusion that shall deceive even the elect. There is illusion that shall deceive even the performer of the miracle. Though he make his body, he denies that he makes it. Though the world exist from thought, thought is daunted in presence of the world" (*CWE* VI 319–20).

To see Hank's dream as a reflection of the Emersonian "vision" is of course to attach labels to it that Twain never would have considered. Still, Hank does perform miracles (not wholly explicable) and he does approach, for a time, the stature of a

Christ. He does precipitate a religious and political revolution. He enacts the entire role of Emersonian Man, prompted by his own constitution rather than by tradition.

> What if you shall come to discern that the play and playground of all this pompous history are radiations from yourself, and that the sun borrows its beams? What terrible questions we are learning to ask! The former men believed in magic, by which temples, cities, and men were swallowed up, and all trace of them gone. We are coming on the secret of a magic which sweeps out of men's minds all vestige of theism and beliefs which they and their fathers held and were framed upon. (*CWE* VI 318–19)

Hank, in the course of the story, will set himself in opposition to all creeds, all history and time. He will become determined that the cultural progress of England should be the lengthened shadow not of tradition but of himself. He would swallow up the men and temples of Arthurian England and refashion them to mirror his own lineaments—efficient, mechanical, and democratic.[15]

The dream motif that Twain uses in *A Connecticut Yankee* adds considerable ambiguity to the novel, especially when the dream-world of Arthurian England comes to resemble, in its cultural premises and institutions, the actual world of the nineteenth century. The ambiguity is heightened again when, at the end of the tale, Hank believes the nineteenth century to be a dream and the Arthurian world to be real. Twain never resolves the ambiguity; it remains a tantalizing method of underscoring his own growing concern with the nature of reality. What can be said about it, however, is that it leads thematically in the

[15]The solipsism implied in such an endeavor suggests an interesting parallel with Shelley's *Prometheus Unbound,* especially since Twain was so obviously working with the Promethean myth. In Shelley's play, Prometheus, representing the mind of man, is released from his chains by Hercules (the mind's own strength) so that the world might come at last to an age of harmony and fulfillment. Thematically, the world's reformation depends upon that of the mind; all that exists comes to be only as an overflowing from the mind.

direction of pure solipsism, an idea more systematically developed in *The Mysterious Stranger.*

A Connecticut Yankee incorporates in its movement characteristics of both *Tom Sawyer* and *Huckleberry Finn.* Twain probably did not set out to "solve" the dilemmas he had encountered in those earlier works, but certainly he meets them again, and the ambivalences in Hank's character are in part the result of Twain's efforts to walk gingerly among the shards of problems he had never successfully resolved.

In *Tom Sawyer,* Tom was able to control his world because the people of St. Petersburg bowed easily to his yoke. They were as child-like as Tom himself, and they followed eagerly his every adventure for the entertainment it might bring to their lives. He was successful, too, because Twain himself actively exorcised from the tale those exponents of an adult, or realistic, environment that might seriously threaten Tom's success. The same is true in the opening chapters of *A Connecticut Yankee.* In its pastoral simplicity, Camelot is another version of Cardiff Hill. St. Petersburg had been characterized as a "tranquil world" and a "peaceful village" upon which the sun shone down "like a benediction" (*WMT* IV 57). Camelot, as Hank discovers upon his awakening, lies in a "soft, reposeful, summer landscape, as lovely as a dream. . . . The air was full of the smell of flowers, and the buzzing of insects, and the twittering of birds" (*WMT* IX 56). If St. Petersburg was a village of children, so too is Camelot. The Arthurians are repeatedly described as children, a "childlike and innocent lot" (*WMT* IX 66) characterized by a willingness to believe in outlandish fantasies:

> Sir Kay spoke of me all the time, in the blandest way, as "this prodigious giant," and "this horrible sky-towering monster," and "this tushed [sic] and taloned man-devouring ogre;" and everybody took all this bosh in the naivest way, and never smiled or seemed to notice that there was any discrepancy between these watered statistics and me. (*WMT* IX 77)

Like the people of St. Petersburg, who were willing to believe Muff Potter "the bloodiest looking villain in this country," the Arthurians habitually dismiss the evidence of their eyes; the story world of fantasy, no matter how bizarre, is to them more credible than empirical data. It is precisely this characteristic of Camelot that enables Hank to achieve power so quickly and so easily.

But Hank, unlike Tom, does not participate in self-delusion. He is perfectly capable of seeing the world as it is, and his decriptions of the nastier aspects of life in Camelot serve to secure his position as an authoritative spokesman for the reader. His common sense is more trustworthy and admirable than the childlike hyperbole of the Knights, and by cutting through the delusion to the truth, he assumes a cognitive superiority over the unreasoning "animals" among whom he has fallen. Twain here establishes the relative values of nineteenth-century common sense and sixth-century superstition.

Still, there is more of Tom Sawyer in Hank than his hard-headed empiricism would suggest. He has, as he himself admits, a "circus-side" that delights in spectacle and attention. In this sense, he is himself a relative of the Arthurians he condemns. In planning his first "effect," the eclipse that is to save his life and establish him as a power in the kingdom, Hank feels himself "as happy a man as there was in the world. I was even impatient for to-morrow to come, I so wanted to gather-in that great triumph and be the centre of all the nation's wonder and reverence. Besides, in a business way it would be the making of me; I knew that" (*WMT* IX 91).

Hank also carries the egotism Twain had found in Tom Sawyer, and Tom's disturbing tendency to have his way at the expense of others. The threat that Hank levels at Arthur reflects through its vocabulary of violence the grim capabilities of an Injun Joe:

> I will smother the whole world in the dead blackness of midnight; I will blot out the sun, and he shall never shine again; the fruits of the earth shall rot for lack of light and warmth, and the peoples of the earth shall famish and die, to the last man. (*WMT* IX 88)

Hank's situation is desperate, but in view of what eventually comes to pass in the novel, Hank's mind already has a violent turn. He has previously told us, after all, that he is "a man that is full of fight" (*WMT* IX 50).

The ambiguous division between creativeness and destructiveness that Twain had found in Tom Sawyer is transferred whole to Hank Morgan. The eclipse itself is of two parts, one a destructive blotting out of the light, the other a restoration of light and health. From the beginning, Hank's power is double-edged, and this characteristic reflects not just Twain's uncertainty about technology, but his uncertainty about the empowered Self, and about the sanity of acquiring and exercising such power.

Nevertheless, the immediate effect of Hank's eclipse is that it secures him his freedom, and more: "Set him free!" Arthur orders, "and do him homage . . . for he is . . . clothed in power and authority, and his seat is upon the highest step of the throne" (*WMT* IX 96). And Hank has been set free indeed. In Camelot he is invested with powers that never would have been possible in Hartford. As he himself admits, "what would I amount to in the twentieth century? I should be foreman of a factory, that is about all." But in Camelot he is "Boss": "I was no shadow of a king; I was the substance, the king himself was the shadow. My power was colossal; and it was not a mere name, as such things have generally been, it was the genuine article" (*WMT* IX 109).

Just how "genuine" the article is is perhaps debatable. Hank uses his technological know-how to impress the Arthurians, and he passes it off as magic and miracle. But then, the authenticity of almost everything in the novel is finally questionable; all that happens, all that Hank describes hovers on a strange and wavering borderland between the genuine and the counterfeit, the real and the imagined. Hank himself is inclined to see himself as a charlatan, particularly in the early chapters, where his bluff and bravado over the eclipse is a tactic to impress a superstitious crowd. "*I* couldn't stop an eclipse," he says; "the thing was out of the question" (*WMT* IX 94).

Yet Hank's first two "miracles" are extraordinarily providential. In the first, the confusion over dates leads to confusion about where reality ends and fantasy begins: "Something was wrong about that eclipse," says Hank, "and the fact was very unsettling. If this wasn't the one I was after, how was I to tell whether this was the sixth century, or nothing but a dream?" (*WMT* IX 94). The second "miracle," the destruction of Merlin's tower, is equally fotuitous, for in his eagerness to discredit Merlin's powers Hank takes a considerable chance. Having packed the tower with gunpowder and installed his lightning rod trigger, he announces the miracle beforehand and trusts that a storm will rise on the predicted day. But the day dawns sunny and bright, "almost the first one without a cloud for three weeks" (*WMT* IX 103). At last, however, the weather changes, and a cloud appears, its position perfect. Hank allows Merlin his chance to "break my enchantments" (*WMT* IX 104), and Merlin "worked himself up slowly and gradually into a sort of frenzy, and got to thrashing around with his arms like the sails of a windmill." Nothing happens, and then Hank takes his turn:

> I made about three passes in the air, and then there was an awful crash and that old tower leaped into the sky in chunks, along with a vast volcanic fountain of fire that turned night to noonday. (*WMT* IX 104–5)

We are free to put Hank's success down to "luck," or even to admit that the odds are in his favor. But surely the world accommodates itself to him in a surprising manner. The cloud could have appeared, if at all, in another portion of the sky; the tower could have exploded during Merlin's gyrations; or Hank could have been left making passes in the air for hours, and looking as foolish as Merlin. But Hank's success in these episodes testifies to a power that does seem magical in the novel. As Henry Nash Smith observes, "When the Yankee refers to his 'miracles,' he is perhaps only half-joking. . . . He claims a quasi-mythical status that Mark Twain seems inclined to grant him."[16]

With his success Hank begins to consider his position in a new light, as though he no longer considers himself a charlatan:

> I saw that I was just another Robinson Crusoe cast away on an uninhabited island, with no society but some more or less tame animals, and if I wanted to make life bearable I must do as he did—invent, contrive, create, reorganize things; set brain and hand to work, and keep them busy. Well, that was in my line. (*WMT* IX 100)

[16]Smith, *Mark Twain's Fable of Progress,* 88.

Like Tom Sawyer, Hank revels in both his position and the acclaim that attends it: "To be vested with enormous authority is a fine thing; but to have the onlooking world consent to it is a finer" (*WMT* IX 108). But if his ego is largely satisfied, still his content is not whole. He discovers that, his power notwithstanding, he is not respected:

> Here I was, a giant among pygmies, a man among children, a master intelligence among intellectual moles: by all rational measurement the one and only actually great man in that whole British world; and yet . . . the sheep-witted earl who could claim long descent from a king's leman, acquired at second-hand from the slums of London, was a better man than I was. Such a personage was fawned upon in Arthur's realm and reverently looked up to by everybody. . . . There were times when *he* could sit down in the king's presence; but I couldn't. (*WMT* IX 113–14)

The Arthurians' reverence for aristocratic lineage offends not only Hank's democratic principles, but his pride as well. His petulant reaction is similar to what Tom Sawyer might have felt, had he suddenly been demoted to third in command of his pirate gang. Hank searches for, and finds, the source of such offensive beliefs. For one thing, tradition has solidified the idea of noble prerogatives to the point that it is no longer questioned; for another, the Church, with its doctrine of the divine right of kings, has lifted the concept to the status of a sacrament.

Hank's musing over the problems of tradition and belief sets him apart from Tom Sawyer. He is Tom Sawyer with a mind, an "interior problematic," as Lukács calls it, and while Hank here becomes a clear spokesman for Twain's own social and political beliefs, the fact that Hank *does* have a mind considerably complicates his—and Twain's—position. It is not enough for Hank as a character to sail through Arthur's kingdom with the singlemindedness with which Tom took over St. Petersburg or the Phelps' farm. His eyes cannot be totally focused on himself; he must look around him and begin to estimate his position *vis-à-vis* his environment. As soon as he begins to find fault with a status quo in which he has already assumed power, he begins to commit himself to a larger world. He becomes entangled, that is, in the same problems that plagued Huck in his desperate journey with Jim.[17]

III

Leo Marx observes that Huck Finn's warning to Jim ("Hump yourself, Jim, they're after us!") is a spontaneous commitment to another human being.[18] The warning comes from a naturally sympathetic heart, and that heart becomes a foundation for Huck's later moral dilemmas. The case, as I have shown, is not quite so simple, and neither is it with Hank Morgan. Clearly, Hank wavers between an elaborate sympathy with the downtrodden, and a dismaying callousness that enables him to hang a group of musicians without a flutter of emotion. Nevertheless, as Hank ponders the social customs and moral assumptions of Arthur's England, he comes to be more and more Twain's spokesman for sufferers. Hank's journey with Sandy takes him outside the confines of Camelot itself and into a world filled with poverty, disease, and cruelty, and, as Clark Griffith notes, he eventually "openly avows the existence of his conscience, speaking of it as a 'trouble and bother' to be sure, yet conceding how it can nonetheless stir him to anger in the midst of what he calls scenes of the 'grisly' and 'terrible.'"[19] The journey with Sandy and the later journey with Arthur produce in Hank a growing compassion for others and a desire to reform the institutions that keep them under heel. The man who so delights in satisfying himself is prodded to satisfy others as well.

In "The Once and Future Boss: Mark Twain's Yankee" Chadwick Hansen suggests that Hank's humanitarianism is a veneer, and that his real personality, portrayed with conscious consistency by Twain, is that of a dictator for whom the ends justify the means. Hank, says Hansen, is "a prefiguration of the central political personality of the twentieth century," and that "it was Mark Twain who saw him first":

[17]My argument here parallels that of Clark Griffith in his article, "Merlin's Grin: From 'Tom' to 'Huck' in *A Connecticut Yankee,*" *NEQ* 48 (March 1975), 35ff.

[18]Marx, "Mr. Eliot, Mr. Trilling, and *Huckleberry Finn,*" 330.

[19]Griffith, "Merlin's Grin," 36.

> The Yankee is continually inviting us to weep over the victims of medieval brutality. . . . Yet he is not a person of genuine feeling. . . . what passes for feeling in him is not sentiment but sentimentality.[20]

Hansen calls our attention to the fact that Hank's demonstrations of sympathy really smack of "an emotional bath for himself," and certainly there is truth to the accusation. Yet the belief that Twain intended us to see through the sentimentality and judge Hank adversely is difficult to credit. More probably, Twain is torn between his desire to make Hank humane and his knowledge, gained painfully in *Tom Sawyer* and *Huckleberry Finn,* that a person like Hank is far more likely to be tyrannical than kind.

One cannot help noting also the discrepancies in Twain's own personality between his shows of affection and his more spontaneous and unpredictable outbursts of cruelty. In 1902 Twain was forbidden access to his wife, Livy, who was suffering from nervous collapse and "heart trouble." Hamlin Hill speculates that he was banished from her room "for fear he might tell his wife about a steady series of epileptic 'faints' [his daughter] Jean had begun having. Then when a severe chill Jean suffered in late December developed into pneumonia, he was further forbidden, again for fear of his making revelatory comments which would cause Mrs. Clemens to have a relapse." As Livy recovered, her husband was allowed to see her for short periods, yet was himself aware of his impulsive potential for harming her: "For the first time in months I heard her break into one of her girlish old-time laughs. With a word I could freeze the blood in her veins!" (*God's Fool,* 55–56).

There are similar events recorded which suggest that an imp of the perverse worked restlessly within Twain. In 1891 his daughter Susy begged him not to use the Golden Arm ghost story in his address to her Bryn Mawr graduating class. Having first assured her he would delete the story from the program, he then used it anyway. As Kaplan records the incident, Susy "ran up the aisle and out of the room, weeping." Twain apologized to her later:

[20]Chadwick Hansen, "The Once and Future Boss: Mark Twain's Yankee," *NCF* 28 (June 1973), 71, 73.

> All I could hear was your voice saying, "Please don't tell the ghost story, Father—promise not to tell the ghost story," and I could think of *nothing* else. Oh, my dear, my dear, how could I! (Kaplan, 310)

Finally, a third incident. Twain's daughter Clara

> remembered disturbing inadvertencies, seeming moments of demonic possession. She was in a rest home recovering from a nervous breakdown brought on by Livy's death when Jean was hurt in a riding accident and, according to the newspapers, crushed. Clemens telephoned to Clara's doctors to keep the papers away from her—he himself would come and gently tell her about the accident. When he arrived he showed her the headlines nonetheless, and then he gave her his own highly colored and needlessly suspenseful account (Jean's injuries, it turned out, were minor). "The dear man certainly intended to spare me a shock," Clara said years later about the display of mingled concern and cruelty, "and some strange spirit led him into contrary behavior." (Kaplan, 308)

Such incidents suggest that Hank Morgan, like Tom Sawyer and Huck Finn before him, is to a great degree of projection of Twain's own personality. Hank's ambivalent character, his contrary bursts of sympathy and cruelty, are not simply the result of Twain's failure in artistic control, or of a carefully considered plan to "mask" a monster with a transparent veneer of fraudulent humanity which we are expected to penetrate. His is rather a vent for Twain's own contradictory impulses and attitudes. In his compassion for humanity, in his often sickly sweet sentimentality, and in his terrifyingly casual violence and cruelty, Hank Morgan is the picture of his creator. The disturbing thing is that all of the contradictory facets of Hank's personality are genuine and sincere. We should prefer that they cancel each other out, or that one should become defining, but understandably neither finally happens.

Twain does exert a measure of control over his protagonist. The cruelty and callousness that so cause critics to question Hank's motives as he moves to reform England seem secondary to

Twain's overall intention. They suggest, as I have implied, either spontaneous eruptions of Twain's own darker side, or a measure of his uncertainty over the purity of the empowered Self's heart. On the whole, however, Twain was intent on showing the empowered Self operating for the good of others in a world much like our own. This time he very much wanted to show Huck really freeing Jim.

The civilization that Hank describes in chapter ten includes most of the major technological devices of the nineteenth century. He lists schools, churches (presumably Protestant, and of various denominations), factories, electricity, the telephone and telegraph, a military academy—there is presumably much more. "I had the civilization of the nineteenth century booming. . . . It was fenced away from public view, but there it was, a gigantic and unassailable fact—and to be heard from, yet, if I lived and had luck" (*WMT* IX 128).

But for as much emphasis as his technology receives in the novel, it is not the crux of Hank's reform. The crucial element in his reform of the Arthurian world is his attempt to change the attitudes of the people, and it is precisely here that Hank encounters difficulty. For a long while, he has a democrat's faith in the ability of the common man to supervise himself and act in his own interests and those of his fellows. In speaking of one established law, *le droit du seigneur,* Hank touches on the point:

> Men write many fine and plausible arguments in support of monarchy, but the fact remains that where every man in a state has a vote, brutal laws are impossible. Arthur's people were of course poor material for a republic, because they had been debased so long by monarchy; and yet even they would have been intelligent enough to make short work of that law which the king had just been administering if it had been submitted to their full and free vote. (*WMT* IX 288)

Hank is at times encouraged in his faith by men who admit to their resentment of the aristocracy. In chapter thirty, "The Tragedy of the Manor House," Hank nearly despairs as he discovers that the "oppressed community had turned their cruel hands against their own class in the interest of the common oppressor" (*WMT* IX 343). But moments later, one of the oppressed confesses that he helped to hang his neighbors "for that it were peril to my own life to show lack of zeal in the master's cause":

> There it was, you see. A man *is* a man, at bottom. Whole ages of abuse and oppression cannot crush the manhood out of him. Whoever thinks it is a mistake, is himself mistaken. Yes, there is plenty good enough material for a republic in the most degraded people that ever existed—even in the Germans—if one could but force it out of its timid and suspicious privacy. . . . Yes, there was no occasion to give up my dream yet awhile. (*WMT* IX 345–46)

Hank would turn "children" into "men," "more or less tame animals" into human beings with reason. He would set them free by giving them power over their own lives and by making them actors rather than reactors. But the implications of such a change are far-reaching, not just in the benefits that might be accrued, but in the elements required to effect such a change. In his desire to give the people a republic, he would set the Arthurians free from history, tradition, culture, time itself. He would place them in another world altogether—do for them, in fact, what Hercules had done for him: "awaken" them to a world of staggering possibility where all previous boundaries have been swept away.

The material benefits of such a transformation cannot be gainsaid. Certainly what Hank envisions for England is better than what it has. But behind the introduction of electricity, telephones, and telegraphs is the transfiguration of the people themselves. They too would learn to be mechanics and inventors, "creators of this world—after God." This would be Hank's grandest "effect." With the magic of his machines and his ideas Hank would do what Emerson tried to do with the magic of his eloquence: show men their better selves, and reveal to them both the debilitating effects of outworn tradition, and the rewards of overthrowing their fathers. To act not from inherited belief, Hank would say to them, is to gather a rich harvest. Twain insisted that Hank was possessed of "the good heart & the high intent."[21] What intent could be higher?

Implicit in Hank's program is his belief that, behind their slave personae, the people of England are at bottom replicas of himself. With his schools and his man-factories, Hank would crack the molds of tradition and lead others to discover themselves—Hank Morgans all, creatures in his own image. He would have them do no less than what he has apparently done for himself: dream themselves and their world into a better existence.

In *Huckleberry Finn* the *sine qua non* of a better world was Huck's escape from his father. In that novel, Pap "dies" several times over. He is believed to have drowned at the beginning of the book (though Huck is unconvinced); in the wilderness cabin Huck falls asleep with his rifle pointed at Pap's chest; Jim discovers Pap's body in the floating house; "Pap" dies again in the person of Colonel Grangerford; and at the end, before Huck "lights out," Jim reveals Pap's death to Huck. Finally, if one subscribes to the idea that Jim becomes Huck's substitute father, then "Pap" may again be killed—by the boys—in their refusal in the final chapters to recognize Jim as a human being. Pap, in his role of reality principle (time, history, tradition, generation—whatever confines and limits man), had to be exterminated repeatedly in order that the boys might live comfortably in wishes and dreams.

This family antagonism is an important element in Freud, who saw in the primal crime of patricide the embryo of a neurotic but civilized society. Norman O. Brown, in *Love's Body,* explicates the political parallels of patricide:

> Freud seems to project into prehistoric times the constitutional crisis of seventeenth-century England. The primal father is *absolute monarch* of the horde; the females are his *property.* The sons form a *conspiracy* to *overthrow* the despot, and in the end substitute a *social contract* with *equal rights* for all.[22]

[21]Dixon Wecter, ed., *The Love Letters of Mark Twain* (New York: Harper, 1949), 257.

[22]Norman O. Brown, *Love's Body* (New York: Random House, 1966), 3.

That social organization which substitutes for monarchy, Brown goes on, is one based on Fraternity:

> The energy which builds fraternal organization is in rebellion against the family and the father; it is youthful energy. Ortega Y Gasset can see that the primeval political association is the secret society, not the grey-bearded senate, because he is willing to acknowledge the youthful, or sportive, or playful origin of the state. . . . The ideology of utilitarianism which in the origin of the state and everywhere in life sees only obedience to necessity and the satisfaction of elementary vital needs, is senile, and in politics sees only senatorial activity. Youthful energy has that exuberance which overflows the confines of elementary necessity, and rises above labor into the higher—or is it lower—sphere of play.[23]

"Youthful energy," "secret society," "sphere of play"—we are not far from Tom Sawyer's robber gangs, formed in secret caves and sealed with blood oaths directed against the families of its members. (Huck, of course, has no family. "Well," Tom asks, "ain't he got a father?") We are not far either from Hank's secret civilization, staffed largely by boys, that stands "as sure a fact, and as substantial a fact as any serene volcano, standing innocent with its smokeless summit in the blue sky and giving no sign of the rising hell in its bowels" (*WMT* IX 128). The civilization that Hank would create requires the overthrow of the fathers, of monarchy, of reality. He would have the sons of Arthur catch up into themselves the prerogatives and powers of the fathers—become their own fathers, with the powers of generation amplified to such an extent that they can create themselves.

Twain had long been interested in the French Revolution, and had for years despised the revolutionary mobs of the Reign of Terror. He even amended the revolutionary motto: "Liberty (to rob . . . burn and butcher)—Equality (in bestiality)—Fraternity (of Devils)."[24] Yet by the time he came to write *A Connecticut Yankee* his views on the French Revolution had modified:

[23]Ibid., 13, 14.
[24]Baetzhold, 42.

> Next to the 4th of July & its results, it was the noblest & holiest thing & the most precious that ever happened in this earth. And its gracious work is not done yet. . . .[25]

Baetzhold makes a convincing case that Twain drew on Carlyle's *The French Revolution* for specific scenes in the novel. The scene in which Hank destroys Merlin's tower holds strong resemblances to Carlyle's description of the Feast of Pikes:

> . . . the chief physical details of the Yankee's exhibition—the torch baskets; the wind, rain, and lightning; the lightning rod; and even a "miracleworker"—are present in Carlyle's description of the French ceremonies. . . . The lightning-rod appears, though only symbolically, as Carlyle wonders how the blessing of heaven is to be invoked upon the oath-taking and, in his question, all but enunciates the spirit of what the Yankee would ultimately attempt to accomplish in England: "By what thrice-divine Franklin thunder-rod shall miraculous fire be drawn out of Heaven, and descend gently, life-giving, with health to the souls of men?"
>
> . . . .
>
> It is almost, in fact, as if he [Twain] had in mind Carlyle's remark near the beginning of his discussion of the symbolic impact of the Feast of Pikes that in "decisive circumstances" man frequently turns to "Symbolic Representation" in an effort to make visible "the Celestial invisible Force that is in him."[26]

It is perhaps a critical cliché to suggest that Hank's assault on Merlin's tower is an assault on fathers—on the phallic powers through which they rule and subdue their sons. But it is after all Merlin who stands guard over the age of tradition, superstition, and faith. And the description of his tower is graphically phallic:

> This old stone tower was very massive—and rather ruinous, too, for it was Roman, and four hundred years old. Yes, and

[25]*Selected Mark Twain-Howells Letters, 1872–1910,* 286.
[26]Baetzhold, 147, 148.

> handsome, after a rude fashion, and clothed in ivy from base to summit, as with a shirt of scale mail. It stood on a lonely eminence, in good view from the castle, and about half a mile away. (*WMT* IX 102)

Hank Morgan is Emerson's god in action. He prefers a peaceful revolution, a gradual dismantlement of the trappings of history and time. He would, he says, avoid the terror and bloodshed of an immediate revolution: "What this folk needed, then, was a Reign of Terror and a guillotine, and I was the wrong man for them" (*WMT* IX 229). But in fact the direction in which he would lead England conducts inevitably to violence. Something must go down, for Hank moves toward fraternity and away from monarchy, toward play and away from work, toward youth and away from age, toward dream and away from reality.

At this point we can begin to recognize the full dimensions of Hank's "reform." While we can agree with Twain that a "fraternal" society—a republic—might be a freer and happier society than that provided by monarchy, we must hedge a bit, as Twain seems to do, when we consider the direction in which Hank moves. For Hank is very much like Huck. *No* society—monarchical *or* fraternal—can be his resting place for long. *Any* social organization will blunt his youthful energy and place barriers in the way of his fulfillment. Hank is not so much the remaker of civilization as he is its nemesis. To change the terms a bit, he is not so much the refashioner of reality as he is its destroyer. In place of civilization and reality, Hank would institute the total sufficiency of the Self.

It is here that Twain hesitates. To destroy even an unpleasant reality—subject it to the powers of imagination—is to court either perfect sanity or a wild lunacy, either Paradise or annihilation. At the ogre's castle, Hank and Sandy peer at what to her are ladies in a castle, and to him are pigs in a pigsty. Hank, in humoring Sandy, agrees that his own vision must be in error:

> If these ladies were hogs to everybody and to themselves, it would be necessary to break the enchantment, and that might be impossible if one failed to find out the particular process of enchantment. And hazardous, too; for in attempting a disenchantment without the true key, you are

> liable to err, and turn your hogs into dogs, and the dogs into cats, the cats into rats, and so-on, and end by reducing your materials to nothing, finally, or to an odorless gas which you can't follow—which of course amounts to the same thing. (*WMT* IX 230)

"Thanks, oh sweet my lord," Sandy answers, "thou talkest like an angel" (*WMT* IX 230).

Hank's progress in the "reform" of England is not so much interrupted when he leaves for France as it is fulfilled. For in his absence the sons begin to turn against the father. Launcelot takes up arms against the king, his symbolic father, and in the civil war that follows, Mordred slays Arthur, his biological father. It is no accident that the Church names both Mordred and Hank in the Interdict, for both are perpetrators of patricide. Hank's crime is far greater than Mordred's, however, for when he offers his challenge to all the nobles of England, and to the Church, he is challenging the supremacy of the reality principle itself. It is time at last to break through the enchantment that makes people "hogs to everybody and to themselves," and to risk turning all into an odorless gas.

The crisis is the more extreme because the people of England have refused to dream along with Hank. Clarence chooses a group of boys to make war on the aristocracy; their elders have turned to support the nobles. ". . . the Interdict woke them up like a thunderclap!" Clarence tells Hank; "it revealed them to themselves. . . . With boys it was different" (*WMT* IX 466).

> I began to get this large and disenchanting fact through my head: that the mass of the nation had swung their caps and shouted for the Republic for about one day, and there an end! The Church, the nobles and the gentry then turned one grand all-disapproving frown upon them and shriveled them into sheep! From that moment the sheep had begun to gather to the fold—that is to say, the camps—and offer their valueless lives and their valuable wool to the "righteous cause." Why, even the very men who had lately been slaves were in the "righteous cause," and glorifying it, praying for it, sentimentality slobbering over it. . . .

> Imagine such human muck as this; conceive of this folly! (*WMT* IX 473)

The nation of Hank Morgans that Hank was sure lay in embryo beneath layers of tradition does not appear. The world, it would seem, no longer bends to Hank's will—is not an extension of Hank himself; Self and Other are separate entities. But Hank will try one final time to exert his dominance over the world and test who is boss.

Hank watches with Clarence as the massed fathers of England approach his cave fortress, and the outer line of defense, the sand-belt, which has been seeded with torpedoes:

> Suddenly we heard the blare of trumpets; the slow walk burst into a gallop, and then—well, it was wonderful to see! Down swept that vast horse-shoe wave—it approached the sand-belt—my breath stood still. . . . Great Scott! Why, the whole front of that host shot into the sky with a thunder crash, and became a whirling tempest of rags and fragments; and along the ground lay a thick wall of smoke that hid what was left of the multitude from our sight.

Simultaneously with this first blow against the aristocracy, Hank destroys the potential for any alternative civilization:

> I touched a button, and shook the bones of England loose from her spine!
>
> In that explosion all our noble civilization-factories went up in the air, and disappeared from the earth. (*WMT* IX 476)

Hank can call this destruction "a pity" and "a military necessity," but clearly it is the culmination of what he has wanted all along, without his having been quite aware of it.

The slaughter that follows is nightmarish, and for a moment Hank falters, or seems to:

> The thing disturbed me so, that I couldn't get any peace of mind for thinking of it and worrying over it. So, at last, to quiet my conscience, I framed [a] message to the knights.

But the strength of Hank's conscience—the final barrier to his dominance—is not great. The message is worded in such a way that, even if delivered, it could only have provoked the knights' pride and led them to a hopeless attack: "We know your strength—if one may call it by that name." Even in the note Hank asserts the primacy of "mind" over "mere animal might," dream over substance:

> Reflect: . . . we number 54. Fifty-four what? Men? No, *minds*—the capablest in the world; a force against which mere animal might may no more hope to prevail than may the idle waves of the sea hope to prevail against the granite barriers of England. (*WMT* IX 480)

In any case, Clarence easily persuades Hank not to deliver the note and to plunge ahead with the battle. Hank gives his conscience another name and shoves it aside: "I tore up the paper and granted my mistimed sentimentalities a permanent rest" (*WMT* IX 481).

It would be gratifying to say with certainty that Twain parts company with Hank in the Battle of the Sand Belt. But the end of Hank's career—and the end of the novel itself—both retain insoluble ambiguities. The battle itself is a conflict between the dreamer who would deny that the world is of ultimate substance, and the great world, which continually offers itself as a solid and insuperable fact. "Ye were conquerors; ye are conquered!" Merlin's final testimony would support Clarence's estimation of the outcome:

> We were in a trap, you see—a trap of our own making. If we stayed where we were, our dead would kill us; if we moved out of our defences, we should no longer be invincible. (*WMT* IX 489)

To give oneself up to dream, and to assert that the world is a projection of the self and is therefore subject to the self, seems to lead to calamity and death. And we certainly have cause to question the sanity of those who would behave as Hank.

Yet what are we to say of him? His punishment at Merlin's hands is not death, but sleep. "Ye shall all die in this place," he tells Clarence, "—every one—except *him*. He sleepeth now—

and shall sleep thirteen centuries" (*WMT* IX 489). Is sleep a punishment? Or a reward?

Certainly we cannot view with pleasure the restoration of a brutal monarchical system in England. The triumph of history is not to be cheered, for it spells the defeat of man. Hank was a hope, not just for a better system, but for a radical freedom that might release man from all limitations and make him a god.[27] If the destruction of the Arthurian world and all it represents was necessary, surely that world was not worth having, not when one so much better lay just over the horizon, just on the other side of a great crime.

The anarchic implications of Hank's dream must have disturbed Twain. The frenetic violence that Hank calls down on the world is a bloody and unconscionable business, and Twain was not ready to sanction it. Still, what Hank destroyed deserved destruction, and what he offered was a prize not easily declined. The Battle of the Sand-Belt, the battle between reality and dream, ends in a stalemate. The possibilities that Hank personifies might be insane to normal lights; they might be a madness that threatens both dream and dreamer. They might involve the risk of annihilation, a reduction of everything, including oneself, to an "odorless gas which you can't follow." But Hank is not destroyed in the cave, any more than he was destroyed by Hercules in the opening pages of his story. He is condemned to a sleep, and in that is the promise of an eventual awakening.

"Our life is but an apprenticeship," says Emerson, "to the truth that around every circle another can be drawn; that there is no end in nature, but every end is a beginning; that there is always another dawn rise on mid-noon, and under every deep a lower deep opens."

> There is no outside, no inclosing wall, no circumference to us. The man finishes his story,—how good! how final! how

[27]John S. Dinan opposes my reading of Twain's allegiances almost diametrically. Observing that Hank echoes Emerson's artist, Dinan believes the echo to be "ironic," and that Twain "thinks all this is ridiculous, of course." See his "Hank Morgan: Artist Run Amuck," *Massachusetts Studies in English* 3 (Spring 1972), 72–77.

> it puts a new face on all things! He fills the sky. Lo! on the other side rises also a man and draws a circle around the circle we had just pronounced the outline of the sphere. Then already is our first speaker not a man, but only a first speaker. His only redress is to forthwith draw a circle outside of his antagonist. . . . The result of today, which haunts the mind and cannot be escaped, will presently be abridged into a word, and the principle that seemed to explain nature will itself be included as one example of a bolder generalization. In the thought of tomorrow there is a power to upheave all thy creed, all the creeds, all the literatures of the nation, and marshall thee to a heaven which no epic dream has yet depicted. . . . Men walk as prophecies of the next age. (*CWE* II 301, 304–5)

In "Illusions" Emerson speaks of the world that is created out of thought, and of the hesitations it causes in the thinker:

> Though the world exist from thought, thought is daunted in presence of the world. One after the other we accept the mental laws, still resisting those which follow, which however must be accepted. (*CWE* VI 320)

If sixth-century England is a creature of Hank's fantasy, still it is real enough to daunt his dream of a grander world. What is necessary is another "lighting out," another sleep and awakening so that another circle might be drawn. It is a matter of infinite expansion: Hank dreams a world into substance; that substance constitutes limitations and boundaries which in turn must be overcome. From revelation, to revolution, to revelation. "Wisdom consists in keeping the soul liquid, or, in resisting the tendency to too rapid petrifaction" (*JMN* IX 322). Norman O. Brown repeats the idea:

> Instead of reification, perishable form. Truth will not stand or stay or keep; it is nothing to be had or hoarded or passed from hand to hand; it is no commodity or store of past labor; it is either new or not at all.[28]

Hank's cyclic movement from sleep to wake to sleep again

[28]Brown, *Love's Body,* 234.

suggests Emerson's steadily expanding concentric circles, and the whole movement suggests Twain's sure but somewhat reluctant drift into pure solipsism. Twain may be wary of the results, but increasingly his fiction suggests that Self and Other are not separate, not finally disparate entities, but reflections of each other. To reach beyond appearances, man need only conquer himself. Hank does not win in this game, but neither does he clearly lose.

In his discussion of psychoanalysis, dreams, and madness, Norman O. Brown speaks of the identification of Self and Other, and of its implications:

> Fusion: the distinction between inner self and outside world, between subject and object, overcome. To the enlightened man, the universe becomes his body.
>
> . . . .
>
> Fusion, mystical participation. Primitive animism is suffused with the unconscious identification of subject and object: *participation mystique.* Civilized objectivity is nonparticipating consciousness, consciousness as separation, as dualism, distance, definition; as property and prison: consciousness ruled by negation, which is from the death instinct. Symbolical consciousness, the erotic sense of reality, is a return to the principle of ancient mystical science, mystical participation, but now for the first time freely; instead of religion, poetry.
>
> . . . .
>
> Psychoanalysis began as a further advance of civilized (scientific) objectivity; to expose remnants of primitive participation, to eliminate them; studying the world of dreams, of primitive magic, of madness, but not participating in dreams or magic, or madness. But the outcome of psychoanalysis is the discovery that magic and madness are everywhere, and dreams are what we are made of. The goal cannot be elimination of magical thinking, or madness; the goal can only be conscious magic, or conscious madness; conscious mastery of these fires. And dreaming while awake.[29]

[29]Ibid., 253–54.

Twain takes Hank Morgan to the verge of destroying civilized objectivity, and even civilization itself. He leads him to the brink of creative madness, but then draws back, appalled at but mesmerized by what he sees there. Finally, he brings Hank Morgan back, to meet—who else?—"Mark Twain," a tourist in history and time, and a man strongly susceptible to the spell of Hank's narrative. As Hank falls asleep, Twain takes up the manuscript and drifts into Hank's recorded dream. It takes him a full night to read it through, substituting Hank's dream for his own:

> The dawn had come when I laid the Manuscript aside. The rain had almost ceased, the world was gray and sad, the exhausted storm was sighing and sobbing itself to rest. (*WMT* IX 491)

He finds Hank ("my stranger") in delirium, adrift in time, and convinced that his starting point, the nineteenth century, was a dream, and that the sixth, where he is "Boss," is the site of "all that could make life worth the living" (*WMT* IX 493). Nor does Mark Twain give him the lie. Rather, he bends over his stranger and speaks "merely a word, to call his attention." The effect is immediate: "His glassy eyes and his ashy face were alight in an instant with pleasure, gratitude, gladness, welcome" (*WMT* IX 492). We are not told what word it is that Mark Twain whispers. But if it is "Sir Boss," as likely it is, then Twain was confirming not only Hank's belief in the reality of his dream, but his own belief as well—and this in spite of the dark and apocalyptic vision to which his hero had conducted him.

V

The Mysterious Stranger

I am most of the time a very young child who does not pretend to oversee nature & dictate its law. I play with it like other infants as my toy. I see sun & moon & river without asking their causes. I am pleased by the mysterious music of falling water or the rippling & washing against the shores without knowing why. Yet child as I am I know that I may in any moment wake up to the sense of authority & deity herein. A seer, a prophet passing by will bring me to it . . . nay I shall think it in the austere woods & they will tremble & turn to dreams.

—Emerson, *JMN* VIII 217

Yesterday I saw pencil sketches done by Stewart Newton whilst confined in the Insane Asylum a little before his death. They seem to betray the richest invention, so rich as almost to say, "Why draw any line since you can draw all? Genius has given you the freedom of the universe, why then come within any walls"?

—Emerson, *JMN* VII 166

I

"I want to show you my typesetting machine," Twain wrote to Howells just before the publication of *A Connecticut Yankee:*

> —& it will be taken to pieces before long, for a final & permanent revising & perfecting. After patiently & contentedly spending more than $3,000 a month on it for 44 consecutive months, I've got it done at last, & it's a daisy.

> . . . Come & see this sublime magician of iron & steel work his enchantments. . . .[1]

The "contentment" with which Twain poured his fortunes into the Paige typesetter was not to last—was exaggerated even at the time this letter was written. The typesetter was even then a source of exasperation, and after 1889 the constant delays that attended Paige's "perfecting" became for Twain an oft-repeated lament. By early 1891 Twain was threatening to pull out of the investment altogether, but, as Paine notes, he "had got to a point where he did not own the machine—the machine owned him" (*Notebook,* 211). He would continue to finance the machine for another few years, always hoping that his money—and his faith—would be handsomely rewarded in the end.

There were other problems for Twain in the first half of the nineties. The typesetter, his own enormous living expenses, and the stock market crash of 1893 all combined to leave him teetering on the edge of financial disaster. His publishing firm was on the verge of collapse, and his debts mounted steadily. In the summer of 1893, he was saved from disaster by Henry Huddleston Rogers, who took over all of Twain's business affairs, including the typesetter. Within two years Rogers convinced Twain to declare bankruptcy on his publishing house and to dissolve all contracts with Paige.

While the business failure struck hard, the collapse of the typesetter dream probably struck harder. "With the death of the machine," Kaplan notes, "Clemens began to comprehend the bankruptcy as more than a financial reverse. With it came a loss of faith and a sense of betrayal, a kind of symbolic failure of manhood, failure as a husband and father" (Kaplan, 332). But the release from troubling business transactions freed Twain to work more expeditiously on his current novel, *Personal Recollections of Joan of Arc.*

It is worth noting that Twain tended to bury himself in this particular work at the very time his own life seemed to be taking a turn for the worse, and at the time when the machine dream seemed finally unrealizable. For *Joan of Arc* is yet another of Twain's attempts to portray an empowered Self at large in the

[1]*Selected Mark Twain-Howells Letters, 1872–1910,* 288-89.

world. It is Joan's fortune to subdue a recalcitrant world, to rise above the limitations that lay so heavily on the rest of us. In this sense, the writing of the novel seems Twain's opportunity to do in fancy what he could not seem to do in fact. Most of the writing came easily, apparently. He told Rogers that the book seemed to write itself: "I merely hold the pen" (Kaplan, 331).

At the same time, Joan was an impossible girl—her career like a dream—yet there was (or seemed to be) plenty of evidence that hers was a *factual* story. Her history was proof, once again, that romance could somehow break into a fact- and time-ridden world, and that limiting experience need not always have the last word.[2]

In 1904 Twain published an essay on Joan of Arc in which he calls attention to some details of her history that particularly intrigued him. In some of what he says, it is difficult not to play with contexts and to wonder whether Twain did not see himself in Joan. "In Joan of Arc at the age of sixteen," he writes, "there is no promise of a romance. She lived in a dull little village on the frontiers of civilization; she had been nowhere and had seen nothing. . . ."[3] The "dull little village" could as well be Hannibal, and Joan, who had seen so little, could as well be Twain, whose own beginnings promised so little, but whose life became in many ways a rags-to-riches romance of travel and fame.

> She had no pleasure in the cruelties of war, and the sight of blood and suffering wrung her heart. Sometimes in battle she did not draw her sword, lest in the splendid madness of the onset she might forget herself and take an enemy's life with it.[4]

There is here the suggestion of Tom Sawyer, the child whose good heart somehow became the agent for others' pain, and of

[2]"Joan of Arc," says Roger Salomon, "can be most fruitfully examined as a final, desperate attempt to establish values apart from the futile treadmill of sin and suffering which constituted the life of man on earth." "To study Joan was, at least in part, to renounce the rule of reason, to admit exceptions to the laws of strict causality" (*Twain and the Image of History,* 168, 169).

[3]Charles Neider, ed., *The Complete Essays of Mark Twain* (Garden City, N.Y.: Doubleday, 1963), 313.

[4]Ibid., 315.

Twain, whose concern and love for humanity could somehow become mingled with bitterness at human failings.

> She was summoned before the University of Poitiers to prove that she *was* commissioned of God and not of Satan, and daily during three weeks she sat before that learned congress unafraid, and capably answered their deep questions out of her ignorant but able head and her simple and honest heart; and again she won her case, and with it the wondering admiration of all that august company.[5]

Tom Sawyer again, and Huck and Hank Morgan as well: protagonists whose origins oddly smacked of both heaven and hell, and whose conquest of adults and adult worlds stemmed, like Joan's, from "the marvelous intuitions of [an] alert and penetrating mind."[6]

Most pointedly, Twain is fascinated in the essay by Joan's success in overcoming her environment. "Broadly speaking," he says, "genius is not born with sight, but blind; and it is not itself that opens its eyes, but the subtle influence of a myriad stimulating exterior circumstances." Yet

> Joan of Arc stands alone, and must continue to stand alone, by reason of the unfellowed fact that in the things wherein she was great she was so without a shade or suggestion of help from preparatory teaching, practice, environment, or experience.[7]

For this, Twain says, she is "the Riddle of the Ages."

Twain's motives in writing *Joan of Arc* are not completely ascertainable. He himself claimed the book was a labor of love, and that it was twelve years in the making (ten in preparation, two in writing). James Cox calls that motive into question, noting that Twain's work on the book was not nearly so rigorous as he later claimed, and citing letters in which he expresses concern about the profits he might glean from the novel's sale

[5]Ibid., 314.

[6]Ibid., 318. The narrator of *Joan of Arc* is one of Joan's childhood friends, the Sieur Louis de Conte, whose initials identify him as being, at least in part, the author's spokesman. See Albert Stone's *The Innocent Eye,* 213.

[7]Neider, *Complete Essays,* 320–21.

(*Fate of Humor,* 250–51). Still, the subject caught Twain's energies to a considerable degree, and at the very time when his faith in the typesetter had taken on the "aspect of a dissolved dream" (Kaplan, 331). If the machine was proving a disappointment, perhaps Joan could take its place. In any case, the story of the maiden-saint could not fail to capture Twain's imagination, since the child-titan had been a theme close to the core of his dreams for most of his career. One early reviewer of the novel noticed the degree of Twain's fascination when he described the book as "devotion running into idolatry."[8]

Joan of Arc was published in 1896, and has since fallen into a deserved obscurity. Melodrama and sentimentality are tendencies Twain had long had in his writing; in *Joan of Arc* these are given free rein, with the result that both Joan and her enemies become caricatures rather than characters. But this failing was perhaps inevitable. Twain wrote the novel from historical guidelines, from histories that provided not only a ready-made plot but a ready-made attitude as well, and one which he was quite ready to accept uncritically. Roger Salomon has noted that the nineteenth-century conception of Joan was a "creation of Armagnac tradition," and he cites a description of that tradition: "'clerical, conservative or monarchist, nationalist or romantic.'"[9] More realistic histories, he goes on, give evidence of Joan's having been trained from an early age in horsemanship and arms. But the histories that Twain read, and which to him were "fact," enabled him to do for the first time what had so long eluded him: disengage angel from devil, and so see the empowered Self in all the glory of its heavenly possibilities.

This disengagement, however, oversimplified character and plot, and while it relieved him of the strangling complexities he had labored over before, it ruined his art. His imagination was far too unencumbered by any earthly matters concerning Joan; he did not have to conjure her up as a human being like others, for she was *not* like others, and "history" was testimony to that "fact." In his copy of Michelet's *Jeanne d'Arc* (1853), Twain read the testimony of women from Joan's village to the effect that Joan had never menstruated. In the margin Clemens noted, "The

[8]Quoted in Salomon, 168.
[9]Ibid., 170.

higher life absorbed her and suppressed her physical (sexual) development" (Kaplan, 315). That the author of the debunking *Innocents Abroad* could believe such a thing testifies to the degree of his involvement with Joan and with the enpowered Self.

The Joan that came to Twain in his reading, and the Joan he so wanted to believe in, was a ready-made saint. She was what Tom should have been, what Huck should have been, and what Hank Morgan should have been. She was a heroine both in history and outside of history, and of her benevolence there was no question.

Howells, in his criticism of the novel, shows himself to be nearly as fascinated with the child Joan as Twain. The questions he asks in his essay must have been those Twain asked himself:

> What can we say, in this age of science, that will explain away the miracle of that age of faith? For these things really happened. There was actually this peasant maid who believed she heard voices from heaven bidding her take command of the French armies and drive the English out of her country; who took command of them without other authority than such as the belief of her prince and his people gave her; who prophesied of the victories she should win, and won them; who broke the power of the invaders. . . . It reads like a wild and foolish invention, but it is every word most serious truth. It is preposterous, it is impossible, but it is all undeniable.
>
> . . . What was it all? Was Joan's power the force dormant in the people which her claims of inspiration awoke to mighty deeds? If it was merely that, how came this poor, ignorant girl by the skill to lead armies, to take towns, to advise councils, and to change the fate of a whole nation? It was she who recreated France. . . . Could a dream, an illusion, a superstition do this? What, then, are dreams and illusions and superstitions, that our wishes should be so eager to get rid of them?[10]

Twain's narrator in the novel, the Sieur Louis de Conte, believes that Joan's "vast powers and capacities were born in her, and that she applied them by an intuition which could not err"

[10]Howells, *My Mark Twain,* 133–34.

(*JA*, 235). Albert Stone in *The Innocent Eye* suggests that her power derives not from the people and not from the Holy Voices, but from "some mysterious source anterior to reason and to human institutions."[11] The major symbol of this source he finds in the Fairy Tree, which gives Joan "'the seeing eye'" and "'the creating mouth.'"[12] The "Song of the Children," a hymn sung in honor of the Fairy Tree, suggests its magical powers to keep its devotees eternally young, eternally children:

> Bide alway green in our young hearts,
> Arbre Fee de Bourlemont!
> And we shall alway youthful be,
> Not heeding Time his flight;
> And when in exile wand'ring we
> Shall fainting yearn for glimpse of thee,
> O rise upon our sight!
> (*JA*, 13)

The tapping of that pre-civilized power gives Joan near godlike powers. With them she can bring the dead to life:

> She was the sun that melted the frozen torrents and set them boiling; with that sun removed, they froze again, and the army and all France became what they had been before, mere dead corpses—that and nothing more; incapable of thought, hope, ambition, or motion. (*JA*, 322)

The eruption of a miraculous child into the miserably limited world of the Middle Ages was for Twain a fact. In a bad time, he could turn to "history" and find confirmed there the old dream. But he also found there a record of defeat. Joan ended at the stake, after all—betrayed by the King and by the Church, by that adult world she had tried to save. And so history was not so clear-cut. It was at once proof that experience could be dominated, and proof that it could not. The end of Joan's story was, logically, a trap, and one which could not be got round easily. For a time apparently Twain considered ending the novel with Joan's victory at Orleans.[13] Such a tactic might have avoided the victory of

[11] Stone, 221.
[12] Ibid., 223.
[13] Budd, 166.

experience, but it would have been an obvious undercutting of history—the very thing that justified faith in the dream in the first place. There is some evidence, too, that the original manuscript ended with Joan at the stake, and that the present "Conclusion" chapter, in which Joan becomes a symbol of patriotism, was added later.[14] At the end of the novel, therefore, Twain was facing the old problem—how to place an empowered Self in experience and yet save him from it. In the case of Joan, history itself first offered the answer—and then snatched it away.

Yet in his dramatization of Joan's end, Twain at least suggests a solution. As Joan lingers in prison, and as all hope fades for her rescue, she has "The Vision of the Tree," and her demeanor is described by a messenger, Manchon:

> And for a little time she was lost in dreams and thinkings, and her lips moved, and I caught in her mutterings these lines, which she said over two or three times, and they seemed to bring peace and contentment to her. I set them down. . . .

The lines from Joan's "dreams and thinkings" are those from the "Song of the Children":

> "And when in exile wand'ring we
> Shall fainting yearn for glimpse of thee,
> O rise upon our sight!"
>
> (*JA,* 446)

Joan's death is not so much a defeat by experience as it is the "release from prison" her friends had long been awaiting. Through her execution she returns home to the Fairy Tree, to vision and dream. That return confirms her heroism and her power.

II

Personal Recollections of Joan of Arc was published in May 1896, and Howells' essay on the book appeared in *Harper's Weekly* the same year. Howells' questions in that essay concerning dreams,

[14]Salomon, 172.

illusion, and superstitions seem somewhat rhetorical—intended to make his audience pause perhaps, and even shiver a bit at Joan's uncanny powers. But Twain himself could take them much more seriously. In January 1897 he entered a long passage in his notebook on his "dream theory." There he asserts the existence within every person of another "self" who "is in command during somnambulic sleep":

> We have a spiritualized self which can detach itself and go wandering off upon affairs of its own. . . . I *am* acquainted (dimly) with my spiritualized self and I know that it and I are one, because we have a common memory; when I wake mornings, I remember that [sic] it (that is, *I*) have been doing, and whither it (that is, *I*) have been wandering in the course of what I took to be unreality and called Dreams, for want of a truthfuller name.
>
> Now, as I take it, my other self, my dream self, is merely my ordinary body and mind freed from clogging flesh and become a spiritualized body and mind with the ordinary powers of both enlarged in all particulars a little, and in some particulars prodigiously. . . .
>
> . . . .
>
> . . . I go to unnameable places, I do unprincipled things; and every vision is vivid, every sensation—physical as well as moral—is real.
>
> When my physical body dies my dream body will doubtless continue its excursions and activities without change, forever. (*Notebook*, 349–51)

He goes on to recount his most recent dream, the meeting of his dream self and a "negro wench who was sitting in grassy open country." "It was not a dream," he insists, "—it all *happened*." The details of the dream had "*actualities*" that "were at that moment in existence somewhere in the world" (*Notebook*, 351–52).

Eight months after this entry Twain began work on a story which in all of its reworkings was heavily reliant upon a "dream self" character. The story was eventually heavily edited and published after Twain's death as *The Mysterious Stranger.*[15] All the versions concern a character of supernatural powers who appears in a small village and who affects the lives of its inhabitants. Moreover, all the versions deal to a greater or lesser degree with the theme of dream and reality—a theme which clearly preoccupied Twain from 1897 to at least 1904.[16] *The Mysterious Stranger* may also be viewed as a sort of last attempt on Twain's part to come to terms with two of the ideas that had plagued him for almost thirty years: the notion of a circumscribed world which limits man, and the notion of a radical freedom from circumstance and experience. It is a "last" attempt not only because the story was written towards the end of his life, but also because the two ideas are pushed to their logical—and terrifying—extremes. This quality of extremity suggests a kind of urgency on Twain's part, as though he felt some necessity to come to terms with what Tuckey calls his opposing "psychologies" at last, and to put a vexing problem behind him once and for all.[17]

Bernard De Voto offered in 1942 a provocative explanation for Twain's apparent mood of despair in his last years. It was largely a

[15]The textual problems *The Mysterious Stranger* presents for the critic are by now familiar. They include questions about which of three versions of the story is to be considered authoritative, and questions concerning the legitimacy of the "all is a dream" conclusion of the "No. 44" version, which Paine and Frederick Duneka attached to the unfinished "The Chronicle of Young Satan" version and published as Twain's completed tale. My own approach is to accept the "all is a dream" chapter as an appropriate ending to "The Chronicle of Young Satan," and I have used this form—*without* the editorial additions of Paine and Duneka—as *The Mysterious Stranger.* For an argument that opposes my decision, see Shalom J. Kahn's *Mark Twain's Mysterious Stranger: A Study of the Manuscript Texts* (Columbia: Univ. of Missouri Press, 1978), 8 and *passim.* For comments supportive of my approach, see James Cox, *Fate of Humor,* 271; Edmund Reiss, "Forword" to Mark Twain, *"The Mysterious Stranger" and Other Stories* (New York: New American Library, 1962), xiii; and John S. Tuckey, *"The Mysterious Stranger:* Mark Twain's Texts and the Paine-Duneka Edition," in *Mark Twain's* The Mysterious Stranger *and the Critics,* ed. John S. Tuckey (Belmont, Calif.: Wadsworth, 1968), 90.

[16]For a summary of Twain's interest in this theme, see William Gibson's introduction to *Mark Twain's Mysterious Stranger Manuscripts,* 29–33. Twain pursued the theme in letters, notebook entries, and uncompleted stories like "Which Was the Dream?" (1897) and "The Great Dark" (circa 1898).

[17]Tuckey, "Mark Twain's Later Dialogue," 533.

psychological explanation, and one based on the personal disappointments Twain experienced in the nineties. The bankruptcy, the death of his daughter, Susy, the failing health of his wife, the waning of his literary powers—all of these, De Voto suggests, built up intolerable burdens of guilt in Twain which he sought to exorcise. The first path to renewed innocence was his assertion of having been betrayed—to see himself as a virtuous man brought low by someone else. The second was an assertion that man and his universe were mechanistic: a man acts out of his nature, and so is not responsible for the consequences. Finally, there was the conclusion of *The Mysterious Stranger*—that all experience in a hideous world was after all only a dream. "The accusation [of guilt] begotten by his experience could be stilled," says De Voto, "by destroying all experience."[18]

The theory has much in its favor. Certainly it faces squarely the problem of a limiting world, to which Twain could never quite reconcile himself. And the biographical basis is strong, for in the nineties Twain's situation *was* that of a great man brought low. He had risen high—fantastically high—from those years in Hannibal. His was a record of having overcome an environment that seemed debilitating to others—his brother, Orion, for one, and, say, his childhood friend Sam Bowen, he of the baker's daughter, yellow fever, and whiskey. In many ways Twain had been magically exempt from the disasters that befell others. Instead of remaining a small town printer in Missouri, he rose to worldwide acclaim. He was friends with the literati; he even dined with kings and noblemen.

Yet he could always see that others were not so fortunate, that many were victimized by experience from first breath to last. And in the nineties his charmed circle wavered, its edges disintegrated, and the rough world came pouring in. It had never been far off, in spite of his success and his apparent insulation. But now it was burdensome in the extreme; the weight of it was hard, and perhaps more real than he remembered it. In one letter to Howells he opens by referring to his own superscription, "Vienna, Jan. 22/98":

> Look at those ghastly figures. I used to write it "Hartford,

[18]De Voto, 130.

> 1871." There was no Susy then—there is no Susy now. And how much lies between—one long lovely stretch of scented fields, & meadows, & shady woodlands; & suddenly Sahara! You speak of the glorious days of that old time—& they were. It is my quarrel—that traps like that are set.[19]

The "shady woodlands" were never all that ideal, of course. Yet it is characteristic of Twain to look upon a better past and heighten its joys and long to return to it. If one regards the "shady woodlands" as Twain did—as a kind of pastoral mecca from which a harsh world had been thoroughly excluded—then the nineties were for him a reacquaintance with an actual world, all the more dry and threatening for its contrast with an idyllic life once enjoyed. The more disasters of that "Sahara" that pressed him, the more he was forced somehow to come to terms with it. The closer it came, in other words, the harder he looked at it—and always in the back of his mind was the long-held and ever-insistent dream that the Sahara was not invincible.

Now, in the waning years of his life, Twain was faced a final time with the same desperate disparity that so plagued Emerson. Even one of the precipitous occasions was the same: the death of a child. For Twain, Susy's death transformed the green world to a wasteland, and it was never more terrifyingly real. For Emerson, the death of his son brought about a similar revelation: "This ineffable life which is at my heart will not . . . enter into the details of my biography," he wrote in 1842, "and say to me . . . why my son dies in the sixth year of his joy."[20] "If . . . the world is not a dualism, is not a bipolar Unity, but is *two,* is Me and It, then there is the Alien, the Unknown, and all we have believed & chanted out of our deep instinctive hope is a pretty dream" (*JMN* VII 9).

For Emerson, the necessary thing was to maintain faith in a vital connection between the Me and the It. Experience—harsh, uncompromising, sharp—had to bend, had to give way to his overwhelming investment in idealism. Whicher points out that

[19]*Selected Mark Twain-Howells Letters, 1872–1910,* 317.

[20]Quoted in Sacvan Bercovitch, *The Puritan Origins of the American Self* (New Haven: Yale Univ. Press, 1975), 179.

as Emerson became more "aware" of experience—of the limitations of human nature—he fell into a provisional skepticism. "He substitutes an ethics of balance," Whicher says, "an Aristotelian quest of the mean, for the suicidal greatness-or-nothing ethics of transcendentalism: 'I know that human strength is not in extremes. . . . What is the use of pretending to powers we have not? . . . Why exaggerate the power of virtue? Why be an angel before your time?'" (Whicher, 118).

Yet Emerson could not rest with skepticism. If skepticism "speaks for his deepening respect for experience, his sharpened awareness of the actual frailty and insignificance of man," Emerson nevertheless "springs back to his idealism. If the old confidence in the Deity within was contradicted by the facts, it became that much more intransigent—moved, in short, that much closer to a plain solipsism" (Whicher, 120). In "Experience" Emerson switches quickly from humility to egoism. "Nature, art, persons, letters, religion, objects, successively tumble in, and God is but one of [our] ideas. Nature and literature are subjective phenomena; every evil and every good thing is a shadow which we cast" (*CWE* III 76). Emerson's movement is one from a faith that insulates him from an alien experience, through an uneasy encounter with a monstrous "It," and back to the refuge of a yet more extreme faith.

That Emerson's proud assertion of victory over experience, his claim that "the individual is the world," should be echoed some five decades later by a character named "Satan" is one of the ironies of American literature. Yet that it should be so is not wholly unexpected. Beneath the patina of virtue with which Emerson cloaked his hero there had always stirred something unholy. The fact, as we have seen, was not entirely lost on Emerson. His troubled perusal of Napoleon I was enough to suggest that his ideal Man in action might end as less than virtuous. And it was not lost on Twain either, for repeatedly his characters became all too willing to surrender virtue and benevolence in the pursuit of an unparalleled domination over experience. In some ways the direction taken by a Tom Sawyer or a Huck Finn, a direction which produced an astonishing callousness toward others, was similar to that which Emerson found himself taking at times.

Emerson faced his inability to find power at work in the practical world by shifting at times to an idealism that left him as no more than a detached spectator of earthly goings-on. Side by side with his unfulfilled dreams of heroism in action there was a heroism through thought, which involved "a detachment from the seeming reality of appearances through a union with the Cause" (Whicher, 133). "In the security thus granted," Whicher observes, "he could turn back and overlook the world, contemplating the queer tangle of mortal life, and even his own shortcomings, with the equanimity of a spectator" (Whicher, 134). Yet this stance troubled Emerson, for it led to an emotional disengagement from the world and from the self. The stance of pure observer allowed a kind of freedom from experience, a victory over the rude world, but it could be won only at the expense of one's humanity.

The genesis of Emerson's move toward a "plain solipsism" and of his cultivation of a cold spectatorship lay in an increasing familiarity with a circumscribed world, one that forbade the realization of vision. The same increasing familiarity may be said to have victimized Twain, and in many ways his reaction was similar to Emerson's. In its extreme presentation of both a harsh and uncompromising world on the one hand, and an assertion of solipsistic "victory" on the other, *The Mysterious Stranger* goes to the crux of the problem that confronted both Emerson and Twain.

Given Twain's growing pessimism about the world and about human beings, it is not surprising that in his last major literary effort he would use a technique almost diametrically opposed to the one he used long before in *Tom Sawyer.* In that novel he had gone to some lengths to save his protagonist from any real encounter with a world that would limit him in his pursuit of satisfaction. In *The Mysterious Stranger,* however, Twain spends most of his time making certain that his protagonist, Theodor Fischer, experiences the world in all its brutality.

Most of *The Mysterious Stranger,* of course, is polemic. Satan is used as a mouthpiece for Twain's misanthropy, and the dramatic frame for the polemic is relatively slight. But in its general contours, the dramatic movement of the tale is one of initiation, for Satan's revelations have the effect of moving the narrator,

Theodor, out of innocence and into experience. "Eseldorf was a paradise for us boys," says Theodor in the beginning ("YS," 36), but under Satan's tutelage he discovers that the paradise is really a hell. Eseldorf itself, Theodor is made to see, is a village of hypocrites and thieves, betrayers and murderous mobs. Always the weak and the good are victimized by the strong and the wicked, and even those who would be kind often end by being vicious. Theodor himself, whose gentle tone bespeaks a gentle nature, casts his stone with the rest at a dying woman. Eseldorf, it is clear, is merely representative of the world.

Systematically Satan undermines Theodor's ignorance and innocence. In the beginning Theodor can look with eager anticipation to the visits of the region's prince and his family, for "When they came it was as if the lord of the world had arrived, and had brought all the glories of its kingdoms along" ("YS," 36). The image smacks of a boy's delight in fairyland—kings, princes, and magic lamps. But later the "lord of the world" is redefined with the rest of his kind:

> Nobody but a parcel of usurping little monarchs and nobilities who despise you; would feel defiled if you touched them; would shut the door in your face if you proposed to call; whom you slave for, fight for, die for, and are not ashamed of it. . . . ("YS," 138)

Similar deflations occur with Theodor's boyish idea of adventure. In their visits to Felix Brandt, Theodor and his friends are entertained with stories of "ghosts and horrors of every kind, and of battles and murders and mutilations, and such things, [which] made it pleasant and cosy inside" ("YS," 44). Yet later, introduced to *real* murder and mutilation, Theodor recoils. At Theodor's wish, Satan conducts him to a torture chamber where they watch the interrogation of a prisoner on the rack:

> . . . they drove splinter after splinter under his nails, and he shrieked with the pain. . . . I could not endure it, and had to be whisked out of there. ("YS," 72).

Theodor's initiation from innocence to experience expands from the merely personal to the philosophic. Satan tutors him in history, both present and future, to convince him that man is most productive in blood and misery. ". . . before our eyes nation after nation drifted by, during two centuries, a mighty procession, an endless procession, raging, struggling, wallowing through seas of blood . . . and always we heard the thunder of the guns and the cries of the dying" ("YS," 137).

The most disillusioning of Satan's lessons, however, concerns the Moral Sense and determinism. Father Peter considers the Moral Sense ("the faculty which enables man to distinguish between good and evil") as "the one thing that lifts man above the beasts that perish and makes him heir to immortality" ("YS," 60). But like most of man's ideas about the world and about himself, this is shown to be in error. The Moral Sense, says Satan, is the very faculty which enables man to be and to do evil. It is also a near synonym for his being "made of dirt," and for his being "a museum of disgusting disease; a home of impurities" ("YS," 55), and thus subject to death. "There shouldn't *be* any wrong," Satan claims,

> and without the Moral Sense there *couldn't* be any. And yet [man] is such an unreasoning creature that he is not able to perceive that the Moral Sense degrades him to the bottom layer of animated beings and is a shameful possession. ("YS," 73)

One need not press Twain too hard in the tale on philosophic consistency. The Moral Sense, Satan says at one point, gives man the "liberty to choose" between good and evil actions, though "in nine cases out of ten he prefers the wrong" ("YS," 72–73). Yet in his illustration of determinism Satan argues that man has no free will at all, and that all of his actions are rigidly ordained in an unbreakable chain of cause and effect. The first action of a man "determines the second and all that follow after." The result, naturally, is that all men's fates are equal in value—that is, equally valueless. "He is a prisoner for life," says Theodor as the lesson sinks in, "and cannot get free" ("YS," 115–16).

Satan, of course, has the power to break the chain. But as he does so, another bleak lesson is brought home to Theodor: that man can be really happy only in an early death, or in insanity. Nickolaus' future is changed so that he might drown, and so avoid forty-six years of paralysis; Father Peter is made happy by being shocked into lunacy. "Are you so unobservant," Satan chides Theodor when Theodor objects to Father Peter's fate,

> as not to have found out that sanity and happiness are an impossible combination? No sane man can be happy, for to him life is real, and he sees what a fearful thing it is. Only the mad can be happy, and not many of those. The few that imagine themselves kings or gods are happy. . . . I have taken from this man that trumpery thing which the race regards as a Mind; I have replaced his tin life with a silver-gilt fiction. . . . I said I would make him permanently happy, and I have done it. ("YS," 163–64)

Theodor's is a hard lesson. Satan's visits continue for something over a year, and in that time Theodor moves from a sleepy paradise in a sleepy world into a glaringly bright awareness of his—and man's—limitations. The world he comes to see under Satan's guidance is a trap, and man is little more than a "suffering machine" caught in its toils.

Yet there is another side, an opposite side, to Theodor's lesson. For even as he is being pushed *into* experience, both he and the reader are also being given quite a different vision in the person of Satan himself. Satan stands above it all. As an angel, he is not subject to the world. He embodies, in fact, all of those powers that Twain had tried to give to his earlier protagonists. "I am not limited, like you," he tells Theodor. "I am not subject to human conditions" ("YS," 53). He is Tom Sawyer to extremes, a Hank Morgan with no thought of reforming the world he observes. Time is no obstacle to him, for he is eight thousand years old and still a child. Space is an artificiality for him; he can wish himself into any century and any corner of the universe. He is much given, like Tom Sawyer, to entertainment, for his pictures of history and civilization are "theatre" ("YS," 137), and he spends his first visits in entertaining Theodor and his friends with magic tricks. He need only wish a thing to have it become real, and, again like Tom, he has the ability to enlist the approval and fascination of others:

> He *made* us forget everything; we could only listen to him, and love him and be his slaves, to do with as he would. He

> made us drunk with the joy of being with him. ("YS," 50)

Theodor stands squarely between two opposing visions, and in this he is a surrogate for Twain himself. On his left is the heart of experiential darkness; on his right is a vision of total freedom from and total power over circumstance. Increasingly aware of his forsaken position in the first, he nevertheless can look over to the other, and feel its irresistible pull and attraction—the more so as he is increasingly repelled by the imprisoning world. For Satan "was a fresh breeze to the weak and the sick, wherever he came" ("YS," 65). He imparts an enlivening energy to all those he touches. His presence is signaled by "a most cheery and tingling freshening-up sensation" ("YS," 64). With Satan, Theodor gains brief but tantalizing glimpses of heaven. When he plays music, Theodor can say only that

> there is no music like that, unless perhaps in heaven, and that was where he brought it from, he said. It made one mad, for pleasure; and we could not take our eyes from him, and the looks that went out of our eyes came from our hearts, and their dumb speech was worship. He brought the dance from heaven, too, and the bliss of paradise was in it. ("YS," 52)

Satan carries about him a "witching ecstasy," an intoxicating appeal that seduces Theodor almost completely. At the same time that Theodor is being initiated into experience, he is being tempted, even drawn, out of experience. "Away in the night," says Theodor at one point, "Satan came and roused me and said—'Come with me. Where shall we go?'" And Theodor's answer is given without hesitation: "Anywhere—so it is with you" ("YS," 111).

But going "anywhere" with Satan is not so cheering a journey, not only because of the disillusioning pictures of the world he brings to Theodor, but also because of what Satan is. Theodor/Twain is apparently unwilling to endorse fully the vision of freedom that Satan represents. One suspects that Twain knew all along where the Satan character was leading; he had already seen him in the angel Tom and in the magician Hank. But here all pretense at benevolence and concern for others is stripped away, and the moral shortcomings of the empowered Self are faced squarely.

Satan exhibits a power that is purely solipsistic; for him there is no separation between Self and Other. Reality comes into being at his will, as an overflowing of his mind.

> My mind *creates*! Do you get the force of that? Creates anything it desires—and in a moment. Creates without materials; creates fluids, solids, colors—anything, everything —out of the airy nothing which is called Thought. ("YS," 114)

In one of his first demonstrations of such power, Satan creates a microcosm of the world—hundreds of miniature people who busily construct a miniature castle. When two of the workmen he has created begin to quarrel, Satan

> reached out his hand and crushed the life out of them with his fingers, threw them away, wiped the red from his fingers on his handkerchief and went on talking where he had left off: "We cannot do wrong; neither have we any disposition to do it, for we do not know what it is." ("YS," 49)

The scene is Satan's first demonstration of moral incapacity— an inability to feel an emotional involvement with others. But far from being a limitation, his emotional disengagement is what frees him to act in any way he chooses. Theodor and his friends are "shocked and grieved at the wanton murder," and later, when the entire castle and all its inhabitants are destroyed, Theodor remarks that "Our hearts were broken, we could not keep from crying" ("YS," 52).

Theodor's emotional reactions—his good-hearted concern over the pain of others—is an index to his fallen nature and to his subjection to circumstance. For him, others have an assumed objective existence which makes their pain meaningful and real. But Satan, free from such an assumption and from the emotional constraints that attend it, can look on pain and suffering with a spectator's detachment, and find it either boring, amusing, or simply unworthy of attention and comment. Satan's primary message to Theodor is that others are really not worth one's concern. His extreme detachment is another instance of Tom Sawyer's indifference to Jim at the Phelps' farm. Others are simply the material with which one may play. Satan's comment on laughter at the end of the tale perfectly describes the emotional detachment he advocates:

> You have a bastard perception of humor, nothing more; a multitude of you possess that. This multitude see the comic side of a thousand low-grade and trivial things—broad incongruities, mainly; grotesqueries, absurdities, evokers of the horse-laugh. The ten thousand high-grade comicalities which exist in the world are sealed from their dull vision.
>
> . . . .
>
> Will a day come when the race will detect the funniness of these juvenilities and laugh at them—and by laughing at them destroy them? For your race, in its poverty, has unquestionably one really effective weapon—laughter. . . . Against the assault of Laughter nothing can stand. You are always fussing and fighting with your other weapons: do you ever use that one? No, you leave it lying rusting. As a race, do you ever use it at all? No—you lack sense and the courage. ("YS," 164–66)

Man's "dull vision" prevents him from laughing at *both* the victim and the victimizer. Twain is advocating here a satirical stance as a social force, of course, but behind it stands the power—and innocence—of the practical joker for whom *all* targets are fair game. Laughter, the joke, is a destructive force because it divests the target of seriousness and meaning. But with every such assault, the detachment and power of the joker are increased, for with his laughter he stands apart, superior and untouched. Eventually, all the world is resolved into a source of amusement.

Satan's callousness, like Tom's, is at once admired and condemned by Twain. Satan is relieved from responsibility by virtue of his lack of Moral Sense. Yet Theodor's misgivings are also Twain's. Theodor's summation of his feelings toward Satan describes Twain's attitude toward all the empowered protagonists he had created to date, with the exception of Joan:

> It made us miserable; for we loved him, and had thought him so noble and beautiful and gracious, and had honestly *believed* he was an angel; and to have him do this cruel thing—ah, it lowered him so, and we had had such pride in him. ("YS," 49)

But like Emerson's hero, Satan is not to be held to the moral standards of those who labor under the Fall; his mastery of experience "bears no obvious or necessary relation to virtue" (Whicher, 68). Theodor's comment late in the tale is one that Emerson might have made about Napoleon: "We fully believed in [his] desire to do us kindnesses, but we were losing confidence in his judgment" ("YS," 132). The empowered Satan, removed as he is from concerns of morality, can say with Napoleon that "men of my stamp do not commit crimes" (*CWE* IV 231). Like Napoleon, Satan is an empowered Self without a moral core.

Through Theodor, then, Twain explores more searchingly than ever before the alternative visions of life with which he had invested most of his major novels. Experience—brutalizing, fallen, and intolerably limiting—is paired with an ideal freedom and power which, while it offers an alternative to experience, is never fully acceptable. Radical freedom *is* a relief from experience; it is even filled with joy. When Theodor dances to Satan's heavenly tune—the music that made him "mad, for pleasure," —it is on the grave of those miniature human beings that Satan so easily destroyed:

> He was full of bubbling spirits, and as gay as if this were a wedding instead of a fiendish massacre. And he was bent on making us feel as he did, and of course his magic accomplished his desire. . . . In a little while we were dancing on that grave. . . . ("YS," 52)

Satan's moral stance recalls that of "Mark Twain" in "Carnival of Crime," who in his release from Conscience turns on his pious aunt: "In my joy I spare you, though I could throttle you and never feel a pang!" (*Writings* XX 325).

III

The last chapter of *The Mysterious Stranger* was appended to the "Eseldorf" version by Albert Bigelow Paine after Twain's death. Its appropriateness will always be questionable, but as Edmund Fussell points out, the solipsism advanced there by Satan is "a theme imbedded in the whole story," and is not wholly unprepared for.[21] Satan's assertion that "all is a dream" and that he himself is a product of Theodor's own mind finds some support in the foregoing chapters. The name Satan adopts as an earthling, "Traum," means "dream," and his first appearance occurs after the boys have been prepared to meet supernatural beings through the stories of the old servingman Felix Brandt. Furthermore, Satan at times makes his appearances at suspiciously fortuitous moments—that is, when troublesome events press in on Theodor and lead him to wish that Satan would come and put things right. Thus when Marget and Ursula are beginning to go hungry, Theodor walks in despondency, and Satan appears to grant Ursula the magic cat. At Father Peter's trial Theodor's "constant thought" is that Satan would come to save a worsening situation—as he does.

Yet we are not wholly free to regard Satan as insubstantial, as just a fantasy of Theodor's. He is not simply a boy's imaginary friend, for he does affect the world, and he does bring Theodor a knowledge of the world that could not have been in Theodor's experience. Satan may be Theodor's "dream self," but we must accept that self as having an "actuality" of its own—in spite of Satan's disclaimer of actuality in the last chapter. Fussell meets this problem by observing that Twain is "compelled to accept certain phenomenal levels as real in order to get on with the story, though eventually he will destroy the whole fabric."[22]

Fussell's point is well taken, but whether Twain in fact "destroys the whole fabric" in the last chapter is debatable. In a sense of course he does. For when Satan reveals to Theodor that "God—man—the world,—the sun, the moon, the wilderness of stars—[are] a dream, all a dream, they have no existence" ("No.

[21]E. S. Fussell, "The Structural Problem of *The Mysterious Stranger*," *Studies in Philology* 49 (1952), 97.
[22]Ibid., 98.

44," 404), it is a clear denial that "It" exists apart from "Me." Still, one is inclined to wonder whether that assertion destroys reality, or merely defines its origins. If the world is a projection of the self, that does not make it the less existent; it only makes its character subject to the self that projects it. It also makes one's own worldly identity and character subject to the "ultimate self"—the "Thought" that fashions it. Theodor, in other words, is offered a choice in Satan's revelation—has become "free" indeed. For the world that he imagines and projects, his "dream," can theoretically be controlled simply by fashioning a "Theodor" that refuses to be dominated by it. "Dream other dreams, and better!" Satan tells Theodor ("No. 44," 404), and implicit in that admonition is another: "Dream another self—and a better."

The story already contains an example. At his trial Father Peter wins acquittal (thanks to Satan/Traum); he is declared innocent and is released from prison. "The shock unseated the old man's reason," and he goes happily insane, convinced now that he is an Emperor surrounded by heroic nobles. On the first reading, of course, we must react as Theodor reacts—with frustration and disappointment. But as soon as we accept the solipsistic premise in the concluding chapter, we must redefine "insanity" and grant Father Peter his own reality:

> . . . he marched in imposing state, and when the crowds along the way saw how it gratified him to be hurrah'd at, they humored him to the top of his desire, and he responded with condescending bows and gracious smiles, and often stretched out a hand and said, "Bless you, my people." ("YS," 163)

The example of Father Peter is quickly followed by the parable of the fruitful tree. Satan takes Theodor to India, and with his magic he produces a tree with an "insane and uncanny variety of fruits" ("YS," 170). The tree is life-giving and enormous in its productivity. But when a "foreigner" tries to appropriate the tree, it withers to sterility. The foreigner is condemned: "Take good care of the tree," Satan tells him,

> for its health and yours are bound up together. It will never bear again, but if you tend it well it will live long. Water

> its roots once in each hour every night. . . . If you fail only once in any night, the tree will die, and you likewise. ("YS," 169)

Both the tree and the foreigner lapse into sterility.

The choice, for both Father Peter and the foreigner, is whether to trust Satan, whom James Cox calls "the embodiment of the creative imagination" (*Fate of Humor,* 276). Yet it is ultimately unclear whether Satan can or should be trusted. In his revelation in the last chapter, Satan engenders in Theodor "a vague, dim, but blessed and hopeful feeling" that life *is* a dream, a vision. As Satan assures him that it is true, "a gush of thankfulness rose in my breast, but a doubt checked it before it could issue in words" ("No. 44," 403–4). Theodor doubts because of the life he has experienced. But the thought that it might all be only a vision is a "great hope." And as Satan clarifies further, saying that *"Life itself is only a vision, a dream,"* Theodor remembers that he "had had that very thought a thousand times in my musings" ("No. 44," 404). What Theodor discovers is his "ultimate self"—not Theodor Fischer, but an "inextinguishable, indestructible" thought that is antecedent to Theodor Fischer and that gives substance to the name. He discovers that in fact *he* is Satan—that he creates out of nothingness, that he is "of the aristocracy of the Imperishables" ("YS," 55). The final truth of his existence is that he is Cause, not Effect, and that all reality is the shadow which he casts. Had he but realized it before, all his sufferings would have been unnecessary.

It is a great hope, for he need only "dream other dreams, and better" to create a self and a world more in harmony with each other. And yet there is distrust, for to become Satan is not only to attain the godlike powers that Satan has exhibited (a grand freedom from consequences, a power to create and alter circumstance at wish and will); it is also to attain the grace (if grace it is) to regard all that is created as finally trivial and worthless—the stuff of a joke. To take it seriously, after all—to invest it with worth and meaning—is to be fooled by one's own dream, to be captured and imprisoned, weighted down with the world's care and feeding. But to treat it as a toy, as expendable, is to retain control and freedom.

Yet to regard as worthless the grand Effect is to regard the

Cause as equally worthless. If Satan/Theodor cannot dream a dream worth taking seriously, then he is himself the stuff of a joke. And so it is that Theodor is merely "a vagrant Thought, a useless Thought, a homeless Thought," wandering like some worthless, down-at-the-heels tramp through the empty eternities. Theodor gains at last the freedom and powers of a god—a mastery over an otherwise intolerable reality. But that victory, shifted quickly in the juggler's hands, becomes at the same time a grand and crushing defeat, for the power finally attained is ultimately unmasked as unparalleled impotence. Both creator and created, both Cause and Effect, become only theater—fancy shows devoid of any seriousness.

It is no wonder, then, that Theodor's "great hope" and "gush of thankfulness" are suddenly undercut as the whole truth breaks in upon him. He ends as a tramp abroad on "shoreless space," free to create whatever new self and whatever new trivia he will, but the word that finally describes him is something less than honorific: "He vanished," Theodor says of Satan, "and left me appalled" ("No. 44," 405).

Theodor Fischer is the natural descendant of all of Twain's empowered protagonists. Repeatedly in his career, Twain had tried to dramatize a hero with the power to dominate experience in such a way that it could be refashioned into something more acceptable than it was. "There shouldn't *be* any wrong," Satan tells Theodor ("YS," 73), and the words are meant to bring home to Theodor man's limits. They echo Emerson's own complaint: ". . . there ought to be no such thing as Fate. As long as we use this word, it is a sign of our impotence & that we are not yet ourselves" (*JMN* VIII 228).

But the ability to rise above fate, Twain found, repeatedly led to a destructive egoism. Good Boy Tom evidenced a disturbing callousness; Huck Finn endangered his own humanity by pursuing his dream of ease and comfort; Hank Morgan sealed himself off in a magician's cave and gloated, "We will kill them all." And Satan, alias Theodor, embodies in his innocence a moral detachment from the world that renders everything he creates worthless, and which, while it saves him from an imprisoning experience, nevertheless calls into question the value of the power and freedom he at last achieves.

If Theodor, in his position as a kind of fulcrum from which two modes of existence are seem simultaneously, is a surrogate for Twain, then perhaps in his position as a valueless creator he also reflects some of Twain's own fears. Theodor, at the end, lives a kind of triplicate existence. He is the "Thought" which produces the "Theodor" which dreams the world, in much the same way as Samuel Clemens is the ultimate self which produces the "Mark Twain" which dreams the worlds of Hannibal, Camelot, Eseldorf. And if Theodor at last comes to question the value of his creations and of himself, then *The Mysterious Stranger* may be Twain's own way of calling into question his own worth as an artist.

As far back as 1877 one can see evidence in Twain of what Hamlin Hill calls "an indisputable and almost overwhelming sense of inferiority" (*God's Fool,* 269). The Whittier Birthday Speech may not have been the social disaster Twain believed it to be, but its content may suggest why he reacted with such shame, and why he felt compelled to write an abject apology to Emerson. The speech concerned three rather seedy gamblers in a miner's cabin, impersonating Emerson, Oliver Wendell Holmes, and Henry Wadsworth Longfellow. Twain, traveling under his *nom de guerre,* arrives at the cabin in time to witness the travesty. When the miner declares that the arrival of "Mark Twain" makes *four* literary men in his cabin, and that "I'm a-going to move," "Twain" assures him that the three are not really Emerson, Holmes, and Longfellow:

> "Why, my dear sir, *these* were not the gracious singers to whom we and the world pay loving reverence and homage; these were impostors."
>
> The miner investigated me with a calm eye for a while; then said he, "Ah! impostors, were they? are you?"[23]

The joke, of course, concerns Clemens' pen name. But the miner (again a character with biographical ties to Clemens) digs deep, posing a question that for Twain had serious overtones. Perhaps Twain *was* an impostor—a seedy gambler impersonating a respected and genteel literary light, and perhaps even his very

[23]*Selected Shorter Writings of Mark Twain,* ed. Walter Blair (Boston: Houghton Mifflin, 1962), 154.

presence at the Whittier celebration, honor that it was, was some sort of fantastic mistake. Perhaps one day the world would find him out, revile him—or even laugh at him.

Hamlin Hill sums up the doubts that plagued him:

> Was he a journalist or a writer of books? Was he a comedian or a moralist, or were the two roles identical? Was his proper vein the raucous Western tall tale or the genteel historical romance? These were questions he debated from the 1860's until the end of his life. . . . He could "demean" himself and reach what he called his submerged clientele, or he could write books like *The Prince and the Pauper* or *Joan of Arc* and receive the approval of the literary establishment instead of prodigious royalties. (*God's Fool,* 271)

Theodor's end in *The Mysterious Stranger,* then, may not be unlike Twain's worst imaginings about himself. The tremendous creative energies he had expended for forty years or more— what did it come to? Might it all have been worthless, a joke at the last? And if it were true, what was to be done except stand apart from it, and laugh?

The emotional detachment from experience that Satan advocates and presumably issues to Theodor is foreshadowed in one of Twain's more unfortunate attempts at versifying. In "The Derelict," written in 1893, the following lines appear:

> The years they come and the years they go,
> As I drift on the lonely sea,
> Recking no more than the winds that blow,
> What is in store for me;
> For my shames are over, my soul at peace,
> At peace from the loathsome strife,
> And I wait in patience for my release
> From the insult of this world's life.[24]

If Twain saw man—and himself—as a derelict *in* experience, he could not find much of an alternative *outside* of experience. Theodor drifts in "shoreless space," blessedly indifferent to the

[24] Arthur L. Scott, ed., *On the Poetry of Mark Twain, With Selections from His Verse* (Urbana: Univ. of Illinois Press, 1966), 107.

creatures with which he peoples his worthless worlds. Life "there," in power, was derelict as well.

IV

"I think the last continuous talking he did," says Paine in his biography, "was to Dr. Halsey on the evening of April 17th. . . . A mild opiate had been administered, and he said he wished to talk himself to sleep." The subject of that talk was dual personality, "Jekyl and Hyde phases in literature and fact."[25] Vision and fact were still irreconcilable.

"Mark Twain lived curiously apart from the actualities of life," Paine observes:

> . . . he observed vaguely, or minutely, what went on about him; but in either case the fact took a place, not in the actual world, but in a world within his consciousness, or subconsciousness, a place where facts were likely to assume new and altogether different relations from those they had borne in the physical occurrence. . . .
>
> Insubstantial and deceptive as was this inner world of his, to him it must have been much more real than the world of flitting physical shapes about him. He would fix you keenly with his attention, but you realized, at last, that he was placing you not as a part of the material landscape, but as an item of his own inner world—a world in which philosophies and morals stood upright—a very good world indeed, but certainly a topsyturvey world when viewed with the eye of mere literal scrutiny. . . . Even members of his own household did not always stir his consciousness.
>
> He knew they were there; he could call them by name; he relied upon them; but his knowledge of them always suggested the knowledge that Mount Everest might have of the forests and caves and boulders upon its slopes, useful, perhaps, but hardly necessary to the giant's existence, and in no important matter a part of its greater life.[26]

[25]Paine, IV, 1575.
[26]Ibid., 1519–20.

What Paine here describes is something more than the artist's tendency to change externals to fit the practical demands of his art. With Twain the compulsion to subdue outer fact to inner vision carried with it the seeds of radical hope. Fact as fact for him tended to lose its rigidity—did not even become "real" until it had been refashioned to play its part in "a very good world indeed." Twain was not wholly given over to vision, but to the extent that he did give himself to it, he was always vulnerable to surprise. When the very good world he envisioned did not mesh with the outer landscape, his work took on irresolvable complexities. It lay strung in tension between the poles of what was and of what he hoped could be: a perception of duality which found its expression largely in the moral twinship of the empowered Self. The fact that Twain was *not* wholly a visionary, and that the empowered Self *was* morally duplicitous, is in part responsible for raising his work above the lesser genres of juvenile romance and topical satire. The constant interplay between Good Boy and Bad Boy, between limitation and compassion on the one hand, and unlimited power on the other, added immeasurably to the quality of his work.

Nor was that fact lost on Twain himself. In 1895 he described his troubles with one set of twins:

> Year before last there was an Italian freak on exhibition in Philadelphia who was an exaggeration of the Siamese Twins. This freak had one body, one pair of legs, two heads and four arms. I thought he would be useful in a book, so I put him in. And then the trouble began. I called these consolidated twins Angelo and Luigi, and I tried to make them nice and agreeable, but it was not possible. . . . They were wholly unmanageable, and not a day went by that they didn't develop some new kind of devilishness—particularly Luigi.

"Angelo was of a religious turn of mind," says Twain, "and was monotonously honest and honorable and upright." But Luigi "had no principles, no morals, no religion . . . an inextricable tangle, theologically—infidel, athiest, and agnostic, all mixed together."

The sharing of a common bloodstream involves the twins in a

comic tension: Angelo is a teetotaler, but is drunk most of the time because Luigi indulges to dissipation. Angelo prefers religions that baptize by immersion, but "every time Angelo got baptized Luigi got drowned and had to be pumped out and resuscitated." The inextricable joining of such opposite temperaments is the *sine qua non* of their literary possibilities. But as Twain worked with the pair,

> Luigi grew steadily more and more wicked, and I saw by and by that the way he was going on he was certain to land in the eternal tropics, and at bottom I was glad of it; but I knew he would necessarily take his righteous brother down there with him, and that would not be fair. . . . I was in such a hobble that there was only one way out. To save the righteous brother I had to pull the consolidated twins apart and make two separate and distinct twins of them. Well, as soon as I did that they lost all their energy and took no further interest in life. They were wholly futile and useless . . . they became mere shadows. . . .[27]

The sharp temperamental disparity between personalities fated to be linked provided great comic possibilities, and Twain made considerable capital of it. But the same disparity, translated into moral perspectives, became as troubling as the other was comic. And when it revealed itself as part and parcel of characters for whom Twain had the greatest of hopes, and of ideas to which he remained emotionally committed, the limitations of experience and the moral shortcomings of those who transcended them ceased to be comic. They became, instead, material for bitterness.

[27]*Mark Twain: Life As I Find It,* ed. Charles Neider (Garden City, N.Y.: Hanover House, 1961), 232–33.

VI

Conclusion

"Emerson's listeners and readers," says Quentin Anderson,

> wanted what he wanted; the freedom to imagine themselves possessed of a power literally realized by no man, and openly fantasied by most people only when they are infants: the power to dispose of the whole felt and imagined world as a woman arranges her skirt. (Anderson, 56)

The idea that such a power might be literally realized must strike us, as it does Anderson, as something more than incredible. But our astonishment may be no more than a comment—and perhaps a sad one—on how far we have drifted in a hundred and fifty years from what Lewis Mumford calls "The Golden Day," when "One breathed hope, as one might breathe the heady air of autumn."[1] Regardless of our own misgivings, Emerson's dream was one with which both his contemporaries and those who came after him had to come to terms. It constitutes "a continuing strand in the American imagination" (Anderson, 58), and one meets it again and again in our national literature: from Hawthorne and Melville who could not believe in it, to Whitman who praised it in song, to Fitzgerald, who, three-quarters of a century after Emerson, showed us how it could first make Gatsby great and then destroy him. But no American fiction writer of the nineteenth century seems to have had such a personal stake in Emerson's promise as did Mark Twain, and no

[1]Lewis Mumford, *The Golden Day: A Study in American Experience and Culture* (New York: Boni and Liverwright, 1926), 89.

American fiction writer pursued it with such intensity, and with such perseverance, as he did.

It must strike us as ironic that the man who first gained national fame as a debunker of facile illusions in *Innocents Abroad* should become so enamoured of an idea so insubstantial and hopeless. But Twain and Emerson were both artists at bottom, and each must have felt more alive in the exercise of his creative energies than he did in the pursuit of his daily rounds. Emerson turned nearly every day to his journal, putting his thoughts into words and so sharpening them and shaping them for inclusion in a public record. He could complain, meanwhile, of the gap between vision and experience that continually plagued him: "I am *Defeated* all the time; yet to Victory I am born" (*JMN* VIII 228). Similarly, Twain could lose himself completely in a manuscript. He came to think of his creativity as "the thing in me [that] forgets the presence of the mud image & goes its own way wholly unconscious of it & apparently of no kinship with it."[2] And when, in one of his "Mysterious Stranger" manuscripts, the "dream self" figure cries out to be released from "these bonds of flesh—this decaying vile matter" ("No. 44," 369), it is to a great degree Twain's own complaint against the "defeat" that would not make romance a reality.

Both men reacted to experience with a similar conviction: that it was not enough, that it left the creative part of man somehow out of account, and that it should be—could be—better and more fulfilling. Emerson's answer was to fashion a many-faceted philosophy that sought to guarantee man's renewal and deliverance from fleshly bonds. He did not deny the physical, or ignore it, but he did promise a conquest over it. He did promise that, when man's full creative potential came to life, the physical world would no longer enslave or demean him. With a powerful rhetoric he inspired faith and hope that the world existed not only *for* man, but *through* man, and that it would soon submit itself to his will.

The idea led logically to advocacy of a radical individualism and self-sufficiency. Yet even in his day this course was recognized as being implicitly dangerous, both in its tendency to reject

[2]*Selected Mark Twain-Howells Letters, 1872–1910,* 313.

tradition and history and in its undermining of social constructs. Emerson was aware that the hero he longed for was anarchic and selfish. But he held fast to the conviction that the universe was steeped in a benevolent and moral harmony, and that he who drank closest to its source would reflect that harmony in every deed. If heroism *seemed* contrary to the good in performance, nevertheless the *tendency* was always toward virtue, and Emerson was willing to risk, and at times delighted in, the unsettling interim.

Twain was not a philosopher: he built no systems to justify or explain what he felt emotionally. But early in his career one can see his dissatisfaction with experience. It led inexorably toward a shabby accommodation to limitations, and he reacted with a dream that bears many similarities to Emerson's own. He envisioned a character who might not have to make those accommodations, a hero who might break out of the prison of limitation into a brighter life.

Like Emerson, Twain pursued the dream through most of his career. Extravagant as it was, impossible as it was, he yet saw—or thought he saw—evidence of its realization: in Napoleon, who seemed literally to dream his throne into existence; in the Paige typesetter, which seemed a magical product of a magical mind; and in Joan of Arc, to whose miraculous exemption from ordinary circumstance history itself testified. In some ways he saw it in his own career, a classic example of pauper become prince. His extraordinary success seemed to testify to a Midas touch, and his faith in its potency led him continually into financial schemes that fell little short of Colonel Sellers' madcap plans in *The Gilded Age.* Always it seemed to Twain that his extravagant dreams were on the verge of becoming reality. In his later years he reveled in the title conferred upon him by his associates: "the King."

In his fiction Twain exaggerated the ability to master experience. But always in the exaggeration one senses his commitment to its truth, and one senses his frustration when mastery seems to falter or to lead in directions that were unacceptable. For always there was in his protagonists enough of himself, and of his dreams, to make their success or failure his own. Indeed, at times, one suspects that the working out of character and plot comes very close to a kind of self-examination, an introspective study, and that what Twain found there was not always to his liking.

Emerson's problem was one of reconciling the divinity of man he knew to be present with the comparatively tawdry experience of living. "They seem to lie—the actual life and the intellectual intervals—in parallel lines and never meet." His faith protested that man *was* a creator in the finite, and that he might exercise his powers fully when once he woke to Reason. In a way Emerson's problem was simpler than Twain's. Emerson need only speak theoretically. In a burst of rhetoric he might conjure the bright image of the empowered Self, but never was he required to draw a lengthy portrait of that Self acting in a busy and crowded world. He could assert that the huge world would come round to his hero, but never was he faced with describing the details of that enormous event. Always his hero existed in some ineffable and blurred Celestial City. But Twain tried to show that Self in the world. He tried to give it a name and a personality, a mind and a neighborhood. The result was that he found its brightness tarnished with something sinister.

In turning the empowered Self to flesh, Twain's first stumbling block was the problem of Self and Other. For Emerson, the separation of the Me and the Not Me was illusory; the empowered Self would show men their better selves and show them that his own deepest principles and theirs were identical. It was easy to say, but not easy to show in fiction. With *Tom Sawyer* Twain showed the empowered Self going its way within a community, and found that the huge world would come round only if it were not so huge—only if it were distorted or even excluded from the novel. When the world did rise up, and when Other showed itself to be separate from the empowered Self, Twain floundered. When it came to a choice between power and accommodation to the separate world, Twain chose power, and so found himself dealing with another problem that Emerson had anticipated: the problem of the Self's benevolence and virtue. Like Emerson, Twain found that the empowered Self had its destructive side, that mastery might involve callousness, and that real freedom from circumstance might mean a radical freedom from other people.

In short fiction and long, Twain explored both sides of what he had found in Tom Sawyer: a good heart with kindly intentions, and a selfishness that ignored the feelings of others. But *Tom Sawyer* established the pattern for much of his later fiction: an uncontrollable slide in his protagonists from good boy to monster. Good-hearted Tom shades off into Injun Joe; the kindly Huck Finn disappears into a mad freedom with Tom; the reformer Hank Morgan chooses at last to blot out a recalcitrant world. Repeatedly the intrinsic destructiveness of the empowered Self rose to eliminate, physically or symbolically, a world it could not control.

As Twain explored the empowered Self in action in the world, he became convinced that accommodation to the world was despicable, and that mastery over it and freedom from it was necessary. As experience became more sinister, the dream of freedom became more inviting, and even indispensable. Huck's dream of ease and comfort without restrictions seems brighter for its contrast with "sivilization," and the liberation Hank offers England seems the more necessary for the intolerable cruelty in Arthur's homeland.

Emerson too became increasingly aware of the intransigence of the world. As he looked harder at man's limitations, his assertion of man's intrinsic power over the world became more extreme. He moved closer to pure solipsism, as though the very assertion that the world was wholly a product of mind might render it the more malleable. In *A Connecticut Yankee* Twain begins to flirt seriously with such an idea. His continuing interest in the dream experience led him finally to believe that what one dreamed *did* have an "actuality" in the world. And in *The Mysterious Stranger* the solipsistic position is advanced in its boldest form.

But solipsism could not solve the problem of the empowered Self's moral and emotional incapacity. In his work Twain discovered that freedom from circumstance inevitably meant freedom from commitment, freedom from caring about the "otherness" of others. Whatever world was dreamed could theoretically be dominated, but it could not enlist the sympathies of its creator without irreparably injuring his freedom. And without commitment to it, the created world could never have much importance. It could only be trivial.

"I think we fly to Beauty as an asylum from the terrors of finite nature," says Emerson in his journal. "There we are safe. There we neither sicken nor die" (*JMN* VII 9). To be "safe" seems a prime motive in both Emerson and Twain in their pursuit of the empowered Self. Safety lay, in a sense, in a refusal to grow up—if by "growing up" one means seeking an accommodation with an external and imperfect world. Emerson's motif of youth and infancy as a metaphor for vision through Reason leads him to deny the necessity of aging, to assert that one can escape from history, time, and even death.

In Twain the same motif runs through his major works. Though his novels have often been approached as stories of initiation, he could never successfully dramatize a real initiation. His deepest imagination lay in loyalty to the character who could retain his infancy and not have to submit to things external to him. Tom, Huck, Hank, and Satan are all boys at heart, and each longs to retain an essentially infantile vision of the world, in which the ego is the center of existence. All that surrounds the ego may be seen as an extension of itself and as material for its enjoyment. In such a vision there is a radical innocence. It is prelapsarian; there is in it no knowledge of good or evil, and whatever actions flow from it avoid the neat labels of "satanic" or "angelic." From such a perspective, things are only what they are.

Both Emerson and Twain are often noted for their advocacy of experience. Twain delighted in puncturing a character's illusions to bring him face to face with a mundane reality.[3] And Emerson could urge his scholars to rush into life and grasp experience with both hands, to know facts as Thoreau would know beans. But this advocacy was coupled in both with a desire to hold experience at arm's length, to deny its immediacy and finality. In a journal entry in 1840, Emerson records that

[3]As James Cox points out (*Fate of Humor,* 54), the "Mark Twain" of *Innocents Abroad* never learns from experience. Repeatedly he expects the wonderful; repeatedly he is disappointed. If such mechanical repetition of inflation and deflation is humorous in *Innocents Abroad,* it was not so humorous in Twain's career. He, too, repeatedly expected the wonderful from his characters, and was repeatedly brought up short by their moral and emotional detachment.

> Now for near five years I have been indulged by the gracious Heaven in my long holiday in this goodly house of mine entertaining & entertained by so many worthy & gifted friends and all this time poor Nancy Barron the madwoman has been screaming herself hoarse at the Poorhouse across the brook & I still hear her whenever I open my window. (*JMN* VII 376)

Both *Nature* and "The American Scholar" must have been composed with the madwoman in the background, her visions and her screams constant counterpoints to the faith Emerson there recorded.

Shortly after the death of his first wife, Ellen Tucker, Emerson described her in terms that echo Twain's descriptions of Joan of Arc: "She moved ever in an atmosphere of her own, a crystal sphere, & nothing vulgar in neighboring persons & circumstances ever touched her." Emerson's biographer, Ralph Rusk, notes that Ellen's death was not quite real to Emerson:

> There were moments when he could hardly conceive of the reality of either physical or spiritual death. . . . in . . . verses he seemed half serious in his disappointment that she did not by sheer will power, as if she were some Ligeia, return to keep their secret pact to remain inseparable.[4]

And one evening in 1832, with Ellen Tucker two years dead, Emerson prized open her coffin. What, one wonders, did he expect to find?

Emerson's tendency was to place his faith between himself and experience, using it to soften the impact of a harsh world. Twain's work testifies to the same tendency, but he was never so successful in achieving a hard-won equanimity. "It would be natural," he told Howells in 1902,

> —so remorselessly historical—so like the traps set for men from the beginning of time—for Disaster to sneak along in my track for 7 years, disguised as Good Fortune; & then drop his handsome mask & grin at me out of his skinless skull. . . .[5]

[4]Rusk, 149–50.
[5]*Selected Mark Twain-Howells Letters, 1872–1910,* 359.

It is as good a summary as any of his long labors with the world. It is a good summary, too, of his long and compulsive fascination with the empowered Self. With Emerson, Twain was a partner in hope, always pulling to friendship with the Man-God, always believing him Beauty and Good Fortune. But when the mask dropped, as invariably it did, he was left confronting the leering grin. It was either Mark Twain's tragedy or his salvation—one cannot be sure which—that he could never bring himself to believe quite fully in what the grin told him.

Bibliography of Works Consulted

Books

Anderson, Frederick, William M. Gibson, and Henry Nash Smith, eds. *Selected Mark Twain-Howells Letters, 1872-1910.* Cambridge: Belknap Press of Harvard Univ. Press, 1967.

Anderson, Quentin. *The Imperial Self: An Essay in American Literary and Cultural History.* New York: Knopf, 1971.

Andrews, Kenneth R. *Nook Farm: Mark Twain's Hartford Circle.* Cambridge: Harvard Univ. Press, 1950.

Baender, Paul. "Mark Twain's Transcendent Figure." Diss. Univ. of California at Berkeley, 1956.

Baetzhold, Howard G. *Mark Twain and John Bull: The British Connection.* Bloomington: Indiana Univ. Press, 1970.

Bellamy, Gladys Carmen. *Mark Twain As a Literary Artist.* Norman: Univ. of Oklahoma Press, 1950.

Bercovitch, Sacvan. *The Puritan Origins of the American Self.* New Haven: Yale Univ. Press, 1975.

Blair, Walter. *Mark Twain and Huck Finn.* Berkeley: Univ. of California Press, 1960.

———, ed. *Selected Shorter Writings of Mark Twain.* Boston: Houghton Mifflin, 1962.

———, ed. *Mark Twain's Hannibal, Huck and Tom.* Berkeley: Univ. of California Press, 1969.

Bloom, Harold, ed. *Romanticism and Consciousness.* New York: Norton, 1970.

Blues, Thomas. *Mark Twain and the Community.* Lexington: Univ. Press of Kentucky, 1970.

Bradley, Sculley, Richmond Croom Beatty, and E. Hudson Long, eds. *Adventures of Huckleberry Finn.* New York: Norton, 1961.

Brashear, Minnie M. *Mark Twain, Son of Missouri.* Chapel Hill: Univ. of North Carolina Press, 1934.

Brooks, Van Wyck. *The Ordeal of Mark Twain.* New York: Dutton, 1920.

Brown, Norman O. *Life Against Death: The Psychoanalytical Meaning of History.* Middletown, Conn.: Wesleyan Univ. Press, 1959.

———. *Love's Body.* New York: Random House, 1966.

Budd, Louis J. *Mark Twain: Social Philosopher.* Bloomington: Indiana Univ. Press, 1962.

Bunyan, John. *The Pilgrim's Progress.* Ed. Roger Sharrock. Baltimore: Penguin Books, 1965.

Chase, Richard. *The American Novel and Its Tradition.* Garden City, N.Y.: Doubleday, 1957.

Cohen, Hennig, ed. *Landmarks of American Writing.* New York: Basic Books, 1969.

Cox, James M. *Mark Twain: The Fate of Humor.* Princeton: Princeton Univ. Press, 1966.

DeVoto, Bernard. *Mark Twain at Work.* Cambridge: Harvard Univ. Press, 1942.

Duncan, Jeffrey L. *The Power and Form of Emerson's Thought.* Charlottesville: Univ. Press of Virginia, 1973.

Emerson, Edward Waldo, and Waldo Emerson Forbes, eds. *Journals of Ralph Waldo Emerson.* Boston: Houghton Mifflin, 1911.

Emerson, Ralph Waldo. *The Complete Works of Ralph Waldo Emerson.* Ed. Edward Waldo Emerson. Boston: Houghton Mifflin, 1903.

Emerson, Ralph Waldo. *The Journals and Miscellaneous Notebooks of Ralph Waldo Emerson.* Ed. William H. Gilman et al. 14 vols. Cambridge: Harvard Univ. Press, 1960-.

Feidelson, Charles Jr. *Symbolism and American Literature.* Chicago: Univ. of Chicago Press, 1953.

Fiedler, Leslie A. *Love and Death in the American Novel.* New York: Dell, 1966.

Freud, Sigmund. *Civilization and Its Discontents.* Trans. and ed. James Strachey. New York: Norton, 1961.

Gibson, William M., ed. *Mark Twain's Mysterious Stranger Manuscripts.* Berkeley: Univ. of California Press, 1969.

Gohded, Clarence, ed. *Essays on American Literature in Honor of Jay B. Hubbell.* Durham: Duke Univ. Press, 1967.

Hauck, Richard Boyd. *A Cheerful Nihilism: Confidence and "The Absurd" in American Humorous Fiction.* Bloomington: Indiana Univ. Press, 1971.

Hill, Hamlin. *Mark Twain: God's Fool.* New York: Harper, 1973.

———, ed. *Mark Twain's Letters to His Publishers, 1867-1894.* Berkeley: Univ. of California Press, 1967.

Howells, William Dean. *My Mark Twain: Reminiscences and Criticism.* Ed. Marilyn Austin Baldwin. Baton Rouge: Louisiana State Univ. Press, 1967.

Kaplan, Justin. *Mr. Clemens and Mark Twain: A Biography.* New York: Simon & Schuster, 1966.

Kahn, Sholom J. *Mark Twain's Mysterious Stranger: A Study of the Manuscript Texts.* Columbia: Univ. of Missouri Press, 1978.

Kaul, A. N. *The American Vision: Actual and Ideal Society in Nineteenth-Century Fiction.* New Haven: Yale Univ. Press, 1963.

Leary, Lewis, ed. *A Casebook on Mark Twain's Wound.* New York: Crowell, 1962.

———, ed. *Mark Twain's Correspondence with Henry Huttleston Rogers, 1893-1909.* Berkeley: Univ. of California Press, 1969.

Lewis, R. W. B. *The American Adam: Innocence, Tragedy, and Tradition in the Nineteenth Century.* Chicago: Univ. of Chicago Press, 1955.

Long, E. Hudson. *Mark Twain Handbook.* New York: Hendricks House, 1957.

Lukács, Georg. *The Theory of the Novel.* Trans. Anna Bostock. Cambridge: MIT Press, 1971.

Lynn, Kenneth S. *Mark Twain and Southwestern Humor.* Westport, Conn.: Greenwood Press, 1959.

———, ed. *The Comic Tradition in America: An Anthology of*

American Humor. New York: Norton, 1958.

Marcuse, Herbert. *Eros and Civilization: A Philosophical Inquiry into Freud*. Boston: Beacon Press, 1966.

Marx, Leo. *The Machine in the Garden: Technology and the Pastoral Ideal in America*. New York: Oxford Univ. Press, 1964.

Matthiessen, F. O. *American Renaissance: Art and Expression in the Age of Emerson and Whitman*. New York: Oxford Univ. Press, 1941.

Miller, Perry. *The Transcendentalists*. Cambridge: Harvard Univ. Press, 1950.

Mumford, Lewis. *The Golden Day: A Study in American Experience and Culture*. New York: Boni and Liveright, 1926.

Neider, Charles, ed. *The Autobiography of Mark Twain*. New York: Harper, 1959.

———, ed. *The Complete Essays of Mark Twain*. Garden City, N.Y.: Doubleday, 1963.

———, ed. *Mark Twain: Life As I Find It*. Garden City, N.Y.: Hanover House, 1961.

Neufeldt, Leonard Nick, ed. *Ralph Waldo Emerson: New Appraisals*. Hartford: Transcendental Books, 1973.

Paine, Albert Bigelow. *Mark Twain: A Biography*. 4 vols. New York: Harper, 1912.

———, ed. *Mark Twain's Letters*. 2 vols. New York: Harper, 1917.

———, ed. *Mark Twain's Notebook*. New York: Harper, 1935.

Paul, Sherman. *Emerson's Angle of Vision*. Cambridge: Harvard Univ. Press, 1952.

Poirier, Richard. *A World Elsewhere: The Place of Style in American Literature*. New York: Oxford Univ. Press, 1966.

Robbins, J. Albert, ed. *American Literary Scholarship: An Annual* (1970). Durham: Duke Univ. Press, 1972.

Rogers, Franklin R., ed. *The Pattern for Mark Twain's* Roughing It: *Letters from Nevada by Samuel and Orion Clemens 1861-1862*. Berkeley: Univ. of California Press, 1961.

Rourke, Constance. *American Humor: A Study of the National Character*. New York: Harcourt, Brace, 1931.

Rusk, Ralph L. *The Life of Ralph Waldo Emerson*. New York: Scribner's, 1949.

Russell, Bertrand. *A History of Western Philosophy.* New York: Simon & Schuster, 1945.

Salomon, Roger B. *Twain and the Image of History.* New Haven: Yale Univ. Press, 1961.

Scott, Arthur L. *On the Poetry of Mark Twain, With Selections from His Verse.* Urbana: Univ. of Illinois Press, 1966.

Spengemann, William C. *Mark Twain and the Backwoods Angel: The Matter of Innocence in the Works of Samuel L. Clemens.* n.p.: Kent State Univ. Press, 1962.

Smith, Henry Nash. *Mark Twain: The Development of a Writer.* Cambridge: Harvard Univ. Press, 1962.

———. *Mark Twain's Fable of Progress: Political and Economic Ideas in "A Connecticut Yankee."* New Brunswick, N.J.: Rutgers Univ. Press, 1964.

———, ed. *Mark Twain: A Collection of Critical Essays.* Englewood Cliffs, N.J.: Prentice-Hall, 1963.

Stone, Albert E., Jr. *The Innocent Eye: Childhood in Mark Twain's Imagination.* New Haven: Yale Univ. Press, 1961.

Trilling, Lionel. *The Liberal Imagination: Essays on Literature and Society.* Garden City, N.Y.: Viking Press, 1960.

Tuckey, John S., ed. *Mark Twain's "The Mysterious Stranger" and the Critics.* Belmont, Calif.: Wadsworth, 1968.

———, ed. *Mark Twain's Fables of Man.* Berkeley: Univ. of California Press, 1972.

Twain, Mark. *Adventures of Huckleberry Finn (Tom Sawyer's Comrade).* New York: Charles L. Webster, 1885.

———. *The Works of Mark Twain.* Ed. John C. Gerber et al. 9 vols. Berkeley: Univ. of California Press, 1972-.

———. *The Writings of Mark Twain.* 25 vols. New York: Harper, 1907-18.

Wagenknecht, Edward. *Mark Twain: The Man and His Work.* Norman: Univ. of Oklahoma Press, 1961.

Watt, Ian. *The Rise of the Novel: Studies in Defoe, Richardson, and Fielding.* Berkeley: Univ. of California Press, 1957.

Webster, Charles W., ed. *Mark Twain, Business Man.* Boston: Little, Brown, 1946.

Whicher, Stephen E. *Freedom and Fate: An Inner Life of Ralph Waldo Emerson.* Philadelphia: Univ. of Pennsylvania Press, 1953.

———, Robert E. Spiller, and Wallace E. Williams, eds. *The Early Lectures of Ralph Waldo Emerson.* Vol. II. Cambridge: Belknap Press of Harvard Univ. Press, 1964.

Whitman, Walt. *Leaves of Grass.* Ed. Sculley Bradley and Harold W. Blodgett. New York: New York Univ. Press, 1965.

Wiggins, Robert. *Mark Twain, Jackleg Novelist.* Seattle: Univ. of Washington Press, 1964.

Williams, Oscar and Edwin Honig, eds. *The Mentor Book of Major American Poets.* New York: New American Library, 1962.

ARTICLES

Baetzhold, Howard G. "The Course of Composition of *A Connecticut Yankee:* A Reinterpretation." *AL 33* (May 1961), 195–214.

Banta, Martha. "Escape and Entry in *Huckleberry Finn.*" *MFS* 14 (Spring 1968), 79–91.

———. "Rebirth or Revenge: The Endings of *Huckleberry Finn* and *The American.*" *MFS* 15 (Summer 1969), 191–207.

Beaver, Harold. "Run, Nigger, Run: *Adventures of Huckleberry Finn* As a Fugitive Slave Narrative." *Journal of American Studies* 8, No. 3 (Dec. 1974), 339–61.

Benardete, Jane Johnson. "Huckleberry Finn and the Nature of Fiction." *Massachusetts Review* 9 (Spring 1968), 209–26.

Blair, Walter. "On the Structure of *Tom Sawyer.*" *Modern Philology* 37 (Aug. 1939), 75–88.

Branch, Edgar M. "The Two Providences: Thematic Form in *Huckleberry Finn.*" *College English* 9 (Jan. 1950), 188–95.

———. "Samuel Clemens: Learning to Venture a Miracle." *American Literary Realism* 8 (Spring 1975), 91–99.

Brodwin, Stanley. "Mark Twain's Masks of Satan: The Final Phase." *AL* 45 (May 1973), 206–27.

Browne, Ray B. "Huck's Final Triumph." *Ball State Teachers College Forum* 6 (Winter, 1965), 3–12.

Cox, James. "Remarks on the Sad Initiation of Huckleberry Finn." *Sewanee Review* 62 (July 1965), 389–405.

———. "*A Connecticut Yankee in King Arthur's Court:* The Machinery of Self-Preservation." *Yale Review* 50 (Autumn 1960), 89–102.

Dinan, John S. "Hank Morgan: Artist Run Amuck." *Massachusetts Studies in English* 3 (Spring 1972), 72–77.

Dyson, A. E. "Huckleberry Finn and the Whole Truth." *Critical Quarterly* 3 (Spring 1961), 29–40.

Eliot, T. S. "Introduction to *The Adventures of Huckleberry Finn.*" New York: Chanticleer Press, 1950; rpt. in *Adventures of Huckleberry Finn,* ed. Sculley Bradley, Richard Croom Beatty, and E. Hudson Long. New York: Norton, 1962, pp. 320–27.

Fetterly, Judith. "The Sanctioned Rebel." *Studies in the Novel* 3 (1971), 293–304.

———. "Disenchantment: Tom Sawyer in *Huckleberry Finn.*" *PMLA* 87 (Jan. 1972), 69–74.

———. "Yankee Showman and Reformer: The Character of Hank Morgan." *TSLL* 14 (Winter 1973), 667–79.

Fussell, E. S. "The Structural Problem of the Mysterious Stranger." *Studies in Philology* 49 (1952), 95–104.

Griffith, Clark. "Merlin's Grin: From 'Tom' to 'Huck' in *A Connecticut Yankee.*" *NEQ* 48 (March 1975), 28–46.

Hansen, Chadwick. "The Character of Jim and the Ending of *Huckleberry Finn.*" *Massachusetts Review* 5 (Autumn 1963), 45–66.

———. "The Once and Future Boss: Mark Twain's Yankee." *NCF* 28 (June 1973), 62–73.

Hill, Hamlin. "The Composition and the Structure of *Tom Sawyer.*" *AL* 32 (Jan. 1961), 379–92.

———. "Mark Twain." *American Literary Scholarship: An Annual* (1970). Durham, Duke Univ. Press, 1972, pp. 77–89.

Hoffman, Michael J. "Huck's Ironic Circle." *Georgia Review* 23 (Fall 1969), 307–22.

Holmes, Charles S. "*A Connecticut Yankee in King Arthur's Court:* Mark Twain's Fable of Uncertainty." *South Atlantic Quaterly* 61 (Autumn 1962) 462–72.

Johnson, Elwood. "Mark Twain's Dream Self in the Nightmare of History." *Mark Twain Journal* 15, No. 1 (Winter 1970), 6–12.

Keller, Karl. "Emerson and the Anti-Imperialist Self." In *Ralph Waldo Emerson: New Appraisals,* ed. Leonard Nick Neufeldt. Hartford: Transcendental Books, 1973, pp. 86–92.

Ketterer, David. "Epoch—Eclipse and Apocalpyse: Special 'Effects' in *A Connecticut Yankee.*" *PMLA* 88 (Oct. 1973), 1104–14.

Lane, Lauriat, Jr. "Why *Huckleberry Finn* Is a Great World Novel." *College English* 17 (Oct. 1955), 1–5.

Manierre, William R. "No Money for to Buy the Outfit: *Huckleberry Finn* Again." *MFS* 10 (Winter 1964-65), 341–48.

———. "Huck Finn, Empiricist Member of Society." *MFS* 14 (Spring 1968), 57–66.

Marx, Leo. "Mr. Eliot, Mr. Trilling, and *Huckleberry Finn.*" *American Scholar* 22, No. 4 (Autumn 1953), 423–40; rpt. in *Adventures of Huckleberry Finn,* ed. Sculley Bradley, Richard Croom Beatty, and E. Hudson Long. New York: Norton, 1962, pp. 328–41.

Miller, Perry. "Emersonian Genius and the American Democracy." *NEQ* 26, No. 1 (March 1953), 27–44; rpt. in *Emerson: A Collection of Critical Essays,* eds. Milton Konvitz and Stephen Whicher. Englewood Cliffs, N.J.: Prentice-Hall, 1962, pp. 72–84.

Monk, Samuel H. "The Sublime: Burke's *Inquiry.*" In *Romanticism and Consciousness.* ed. Harold Bloom. New York: Norton, 1970, pp. 24–41.

Parsons, Coleman O. "The Background of *The Mysterious Stranger.*" *AL* 32 (March 1960), 55–79.

Pearce, Roy Harvey. "Huck Finn in His History." *Etudes Anglaises* 24 (1971), 283–91.

Reiss, Edmund. Foreword. *"The Mysterious Stranger" and Other Stories.* New York: New American Library, 1962, pp. xiii–xv.

Rubin, Louis D., Jr. "Mark Twain: *The Adventures of Tom Sawyer.*" In *Landmarks of American Writing,* ed. Hennig Cohen. New York: Basic Books, 1969, pp. 157–71.

Santayana, George. "Tom Sawyer and Don Quixote." *Mark Twain Quarterly* 9 (Winter 1952), 1–3.

Schmitz, Neil. "The Paradox of Liberation in *Huckleberry Finn.*" *TSLL* 13 (Spring 1971), 125–36.

Smith, Henry Nash. "Emerson's Problem of Vocation—A Note on 'The American Scholar". *NEQ* 12 (March-Dec. 1939), 52–67; rpt. in *Emerson: A Collection of Critical Essays,* ed. Milton Konvitz and Stephen Whicher. Englewood Cliffs, N.J.: Prentice-Hall, 1962, pp. 60–71.

Tanner, Tony. "The Lost America—The Despair of Henry Adams and Mark Twain." *Modern Age* 5 (Summer 1961), 299–310; rpt. in *Mark Twain: A Collection of Critical Essays,* ed. Henry Nash Smith. Englewood Cliffs, N.J.: Prentice-Hall, 1963, pp. 159–74.

Tatham, Campbell. "Dismal and Lonesome: A New Look at *Huckleberry Finn.*" *MFS* 14 (Spring 1968), 47–55.

Tuckey, John S. "*The Mysterious Stranger:* Mark Twain's Texts and the Paine-Duneka Edition." In *Mark Twain's* The Mysterious Stranger *and the Critics,* ed. John S. Tuckey. Belmont, Calif.: Wadsworth Pub. Co., 1968, pp. 85–90.

———. "Mark Twain's Later Dialogue: The 'Me' and the Machine." *AL* 41 (Jan. 1970), 532–42.

Wecter, Dixon. "Mark Twain." In *Literary History of the United States,* ed. Robert E. Spiller, et al. New York: Macmillan 1963, Vol. 2, pp. 917–39.

Wexman, Virginia. "The Role of Structure in *Tom Sawyer* and *Huckleberry Finn.*" *American Literary Realism* 6 (Winter 1973), 1–11.

Wheelwright, Philip. "Poetry, Myth, and Reality." In *The Language of Poetry,* ed. Allen Tate. Princeton: Princeton Univ. Press, 1942, pp. 3–33.

Whicher, Stephen E. "Emerson's Tragic Sense." In *Interpretations of American Literature,* ed. Charles Feidelson, Jr., and Paul Brodtkorb, Jr. New York: Oxford Univ. Press, 1959, pp. 153–60.

Williams, James D. "Revision and Intention in Mark Twain's *A Connecticut Yankee.*" *AL* 36 (Nov. 1964), 288–97.

Index

Mark Twain and the Limits of Power was composed into type on the Mergenthaler Variable Input Phototypesetter in eleven-point Garamond with one-point line spacing. Garamond with italic was also used as display. The book was designed by Jim Billingsley, composed by Computer Composition, Inc., printed offset by Thomson-Shore, Inc., and bound by John H. Dekker & Sons. The paper on which the book is printed bears the watermark of S.D. Warren and is designed for an effective life of at least three hundred years.

THE UNIVERSITY OF TENNESSEE PRESS : KNOXVILLE